So You Want to Be a Screenwriter

HOW TO FACE THE FEARS AND TAKE THE RISKS

•

Sara C. Caldwell & Marie-Eve S. Kielson

ALLWORTH PRESS
NEW YORK

To the powerful stories that impact the lives of all who hear them;

To the inspiration of the storytellers who have had the courage to create them;

To all of the stories yet untold that will change our lives forever.

●

04 03 02 01 00   5 4 3 2 1

Published by Allworth Press
An imprint of Allworth Communications
10 East 23rd Street, New York, NY 10010

Cover design by Douglas Design Associates, New York, NY

Page composition/typography by Sharp Des!gns, Lansing, MI

ISBN: 1-58115-062-8

LIBRARY OF CONGRESS CATALOGING-IN-PUBLICATION DATA
Caldwell, Sara C.
So you want to be a screenwriter: how to face the fears and take
the risks / by Sara C. Caldwell and Marie-Eve S. Kielson.
    p.   cm.
Includes index.
ISBN 1-58115-026-8
1. Motion picture authorship. I. Kielson, Marie-Eve S. II. Title.
PN1996.C29 2000
808.2'3—dc21
00-032281

Printed in Canada

Table of Contents

Part III: Writer's Block and the Myths That Bind

Part IV: The Power of Collaboration

Acknowledgments

We wish to thank Tad Crawford, publisher, and Nicole Potter, editor, of Allworth Press for their belief in us and for their encouragement and acceptance of the mission of our book. To all at Allworth Press who have contributed their ideas, creativity, and energy to making this book a success.

Our gratitude to all who have shared their voices with us and who gave so generously of their time to our creative endeavor: Noah Baumbach, Ed Bernero, Carmen Brown, Tony Bui, Delle Chatman, Sharon Y. Cobb, Carla Hacken, Betty Hager, Josefina Lopez, Ken Mader, David Marconi, Harold Ramis, Anne Rapp, Adam Rifkin, and Paul Wei.

Our immense appreciation to Whitney Boole, Katherine Bulovic, Michael Faulkner, Michael Livingston, Sandy Mackey, Michelle Rifkin, Therese My Vuong, and Laurel Ward for their "behind the scenes" dedication, and for their patience and generosity of spirit in responding to all of our requests.

Thank you to Jessica Frank, who unselfishly and expertly used her wonderful editing skills to help refine our manuscript.

To photographers Stan Malinowski and Guy Viau for their creative genius, and to Agnieszka Kulon and Maria Arroy for making us feel special and "out of the ordinary."

We wish to thank Jean-Claude Bertet for his legal expertise and for the manner in which he has shared his time and spirit for this book.

Personal thanks from Sara Caldwell

Thanks to my family and friends for your constant and invaluable support throughout the writing of this book. Extra special thanks to my good friend, Joni Brander, for helping me through the rough spots; to Ben for your ongoing encouragement during difficult moments; to my wonderful children, Dylan and Chloe, for making sure that I spent time away from the computer; to Isaiah Brooms for staying true to your dream and to Dan Bassill for enabling so many other young Americans do so; and to my special friend, Vasile Stoica, for giving me the inspiration and courage to believe that anything is possible.

Personal thanks from Marie-Eve Kielson

To Daniel, my cherished partner, whose love and gentle heart has had the power to heal; to my precious daughters, Lisette and Claudine, whose talent and courage to claim their dreams is truly inspirational; to my dearest Maman who, throughout her life, presented me with an amazing model of great strength and dignity, as well as a creative spirit, which will live with me forever; to Dr. Leland Roloff, who took me gently by the hand and, with wit and wisdom, introduced me to my own voice; and to Eunice Brooks, who was always present to remind me to honor the "larger plan."

●

Foreword

At the end of the day, it all starts with the script.
Carla Hacken

W hen the authors asked me to write this foreword, I initially was not certain if I would be the perfect candidate. Although I spend most of my days reading, writing, and editing, I have never attempted to make a living as a writer, and I have never been in a position of having my written work evaluated and judged by others. Nevertheless, my fifteen years of experience as both an agent and a development/production executive has brought me in direct contact with almost every aspect of the business of making movies.

My own journey in this field began in high school, where I had two wonderful English teachers. They taught me to appreciate and evaluate great literature—not only to love it for its story content, but to understand the complexity of its structure. They had a great influence on me, which led me to pursue a creative writing and literature major at UCLA. I think more than anything else, studying literature is what has prepared me for the work that I do now.

As an executive at Twentieth Century Fox I read scripts every day for a variety of reasons. Mostly, I read scripts that are potential new projects for the studio, drafts of scripts already in development, and samples from writers we are thinking of hiring for specific projects. I have found that the only thing that really matters is the quality of the writing.

Throughout our lives, most of us read books, newspapers, and plays, but typically we do not read screenplays. Screenwriting is a unique craft that you have to spend time learning. A good screenplay has to be well-crafted. It has to have a basic three-act structure. It has to have a beginning, a middle, and an end. Some of the best screenplays will not necessarily follow this traditional structure and will be more idiosyncratic. The most impressive scripts that I have read of this kind tend to be the ones written by really experienced writers who know how to creatively play with the traditional structure. Here's an analogy: All buildings and houses are built on foundations, have four walls, and a roof. The average building is of average size, average height, and average appearance. However, we know that great architects have broken the traditional boundaries to create structures that are anything but average. These architects challenged the traditions, but did not do so until they had studied the necessary basics of their craft. The same applies to talented screenwriters who have taken the time to master the basic structure of a screenplay. They now have the skills that will enable them to move beyond the ordinary screenplay and write something special that stands out amongst the rest.

Although structure is important, what really separates a great screenplay from a good one is the script, in which the writer makes us care about the people, involves us in the story, and propels us to keep reading. A great screenplay transcends the written word and comes alive visually. It is comprised of great dialogue, interesting subject matter, and sympathetic characters. Most importantly, the writer must have some passion for the stories and characters he is depicting. There is an old adage that has some value: Write what you know. Whatever the genre, what makes a script so powerful for me is when I actually feel that I am being taken on a journey. For instance, I read many romantic comedies, and even though I know that the two main characters are going to get together in the end, the ones I love are those that surprise me and make me want to read every page to find out how this will happen.

This book addresses many myths about what it takes to succeed in Hollywood. Any myth has the potential of bearing some truth. One very common one is that you need to write for current trends in order to get attention. The truth is that we move at lightening speed in the film industry. Sometimes, by the time the movies hit the streets, that trend is already over.

Another myth raised in this book addresses the issue of whether or not it is beneficial for writers to live in Los Angeles. My recommendation is that people not move to Los Angeles until they have at least written a script and know that they are committed to screenwriting as their career. After you have seriously worked on your craft, I do believe that living in Los Angeles or New York is important, as it is imperative to become knowledgeable about how the business operates. One of the fundamental requirements of a writer selling material, or being a writer for hire, is being available to meet the people who will be in the position to employ you. There will always be the exception, but for the majority, who you know, what you know, will strongly impact where you go.

In the film industry, the issue of time is a difficult one for screenwriters to fully understand. Many believe that if they are able to sell a script, they will get a lot of money and the movie will immediately get made with only minor revisions. The truth is that there are typically many, many drafts of the script from its conception to the time it gets made. Often, rewrites are not even done by the original writer. Just as often, scripts are completely reconceptualized halfway through the development process due to various people's visions, i.e., the director versus the producer, the producer versus the studio, etc.

It is a myth that only well-known writers are the best at their craft. Some of the best writers I have hired for projects are people no one has heard of. There is a young New York playwright whom we hired fresh out of Juilliard and with whom we have been working consistently for two years. At the time we met him, he had never even written a screenplay and no one in Los Angeles had even heard of him. His fresh and unique voice inspired us to take a chance on him. It makes no difference to me how famous or successful a writer is. It is really about the quality of the work.

I am often asked about representation and how one goes about finding an agent. It is one of the more difficult tasks that a screenwriter must face, after the obvious challenge of the writing itself. Although I was an agent for many years, I do not have a single answer to this mystery. Writers acquire agents through a myriad of ways—who they know, being in the right place at the right time, their ability to promote themselves, or just pure luck. When I speak with writers who are concerned with this issue, I encourage them to concentrate on conquering the bigger picture—writing something wonderful.

Regardless of where you live or how you choose to pursue your career, the most important thing to consider is the writing itself. I cannot tell you how many people I meet who say that they want to be a writer, a director, or an actor, and they have never actually studied the craft or taken the necessary steps to make their living at it. Concentrating on writing quality scripts will give you the best chance for longevity as a writer. I have always believed that one way or another, good work will rise to the top, both metaphorically and literally.

—Carla Hacken, Executive Vice President, Fox 2000 Pictures

●

Preface

Marie-Eve Kielson

As I sat facing the outline for this book, I found myself going back to the beginning of its inception to remind myself of its original intent. About three years ago, I had the good fortune to meet Sara Caldwell, who at that time was living in Chicago and writing film scripts. It is amazing to me that in one brief moment we can meet someone who, years later, will reappear and change our life. Sara asked me to consult on a script that she had written. I was thrilled and fascinated by the story and characters she presented to me. This was the beginning of a relationship that has developed into a most meaningful and energizing one. I remember the long talks we have had about our respective professions. We have traveled very different paths, yet share a deep philosophical view of life that emerges in all of the work we have undertaken together. It was during one such discussion that Sara recommended that I write a book for screenwriters describing the work that I do in helping them uncover the hidden motivations of their characters.

I have been fortunate in being able to embrace my two professional loves— my role as a psychotherapist and that of psychological script consultant. I have learned a great deal about human behavior in my years of listening to the clients who have honored me with their remarkable stories, their courage, their struggles, and their histories, in which they would find new meaning. I believe that it is for this reason that Sara encouraged the writing of a book that would present this knowledge of the human condition to the writers who were searching for a deeper understanding of the characters they were creating. I look back at that moment and smile at what, at that time, seemed like a preposterous idea and one that was totally out of the realm of reality. What could Sara be thinking, and who would possibly be interested in such a book?

A seed had been planted, however, and it lay dormant, just at the recesses of my consciousness, until the moment was right for it to emerge. Two years later, Sara and I continued to discuss our dreams and aspirations, while sharing a wonderful relationship. It had become a long-distance one, for she had had the courage to follow her dream of becoming a screenwriter and had moved to Los Angeles. She was able to recognize that she would need to take the risks necessary to own her own interiority and claim what she must do as a writer. While we worked together on challenging projects, the idea that she had presented to me, of writing a book, kept its silent vigil.

One day, as I sat down in my husband's conference room, I began to fantasize about Sara's words and what it would actually mean to write this book. I realized immediately that I had no desire to travel this journey alone, for I have always benefitted from the energy derived from the collaborative process. In my role as a psychotherapist, the client and I are a team, working, sharing, and probing together to find answers and new understandings. As a psychological script consultant, the writer and I enter into a collaboration to find out who the characters are, what their reasons are for being in the story, and what they will eventually share with us, the audience, about why they act as they do. Again, it is the energy of the partnership that stimulates and brings life to my imagination. If writing this book meant creating it alone, I knew that it would simply not work for me. I, alone, could not represent the legitimacy that it deserves. If I were to write a book for screenwriters, then it must be done in a manner that honored the screenwriter's journey. What this book needed for its birth was the voices of both the writer and the psychotherapist, who could, together, share an intimate portrait of what it means to claim a dream and face the unknowns along the way.

The seed had been planted and the germination was underway. When I began to visualize the potential power of this combination, I felt a tremendous sense of excitement, and at the same time, a sense of calm knowingness. I became intrigued by the significance of such a partnership. The time was right. I phoned Sara and presented her with the idea that she had casually initiated three years earlier. Sara agreed to share in the book's journey and, to my great delight, offered me a new and wonderful opportunity in which to collaborate and to go forward on an amazing creative venture.

From the moment in which this idea was conceived to the moment of its completion, I have been made continuously aware of the power of collaboration. According to my Roget's Thesaurus, "collaboration" has as its synonyms "cooperation, teamwork, synergy," all extremely necessary elements in the creation of anything worthwhile. As Sara and I progressed with each chapter, with each idea that we felt would be necessary to fulfill the book's mission, this unique relationship has contributed the combined energy necessary to propel this book forward to its next destination.

I love going to the movies and, for a long time, took for granted all of the hundreds of names that appear on the screen at the end of each film. I no longer leave the theater the moment the film has ended. Now, I sit until the lights are turned on, and I marvel at all the human power and pure creative force it has taken to bring this film to me, the audience. Thousands of ideas and thousands of voices contribute new and often never-before-seen visions that make each story unique and everlasting. It is precisely the concept of collaboration that inspired, encouraged, and affirmed my belief that together, Sara and I could bring this book to fruition and, in so doing, commit all of our efforts to honoring its mission.

For some inexplicable reason, Sara and I had the good fortune to come together and travel the same creative path at this time in our lives. We both have a sense of responsibility to express our creativity for the purpose of empowering others. We both believe that a collaborative relationship can bring amazing results, whereas a solitary effort can often stifle the energy needed to bring about success. Our partnership continues to offer enlightenment to me, and I treasure the sharing, probing, and challenging moments that have already, in so many ways, propelled me to heights never before experienced.

It is my desire to bring to the screenwriter all the subtleties and inner workings of human beings as they create characters whose voices of truth will tell their stories. It is also my hope that this book will help to reiterate the importance of how we are all linked, and how crucial it is that we continue to have stories that help us to feel connected. As far as I am concerned, no matter what the genre, characters can be given a special way in which to communicate to the audience and, through their stories, enable us to gain a deeper understanding of ourselves. They offer us the opportunity to ponder, as well as providing the levity that we all need to experience from time to time.

My intent in coauthoring this book is to bring encouragement and inspiration to all who have chosen the path of storytelling. It is my great belief that dreams can be claimed if the dreamer will allow the dream. It is my respect for those who have stopped at nothing in order to listen to their inner voices that propelled me forward in sharing my ideas. It is my continued amazement and respect for the immense strength and creativity that lies inside of all of us that convinced me that this book would, indeed, find its rightful place and be received in the manner in which it was intended.

I thank Sara for her wisdom and wonderful skills as a storyteller and for the ongoing energy and determination she provided throughout the creation of this book. The collaboration has been invaluable and an experience I shall cherish, for without her, this book could not have been conceived. May its ideas and spirit provide all who read it with the courage to go forward on their own unique, creative journeys!

Sara Caldwell

When I first began screenwriting, I thought I would just write a script, get an agent, make a lot of money, and then rest on my laurels. As anyone who has been in the business for any length of time knows, that was a pretty naïve perspective. Yes, there are overnight successes, but they truly are the exceptions. For most people who attempt this type of career, there are many moments of intense trepidation, fear, self-doubt, and anxiety. Negativity rears its ugly head in many forms, from friends or family members who discourage us to the hundreds of rejection letters we will undoubtedly receive.

The screenwriting world is a strange place that morphs in shape from one day to the next, so that it seems impossible to find any logic within it. How do we find an agent? How do we sell our screenplays? How do we get staff writing jobs? There are no guides along the way, other than "experts" who claim to know how to charter these dark territories. For the right price, they will show us how to write a script that sells, how to get an agent, how to pitch a project, how to negotiate a deal. The truth is that although others can offer us their wisdom based on their own experiences, they can't tell us what is right for us. Every day, we encounter people and situations that veer our lives in new directions, opening doors to new opportunities. As each screenwriter we interviewed for this book demonstrates, how an individual travels the various paths of his or her journey is unpredictable and truly unique. For example, twenty-six-year-old Tony Bui (*Three Seasons*) knew as a teenager that he wanted to be a filmmaker, and the way in which he would tell his stories was greatly impacted by a trip to his birthplace in Vietnam. Thirty-seven-year-old Ed Bernero (*Third Watch*) was a Chicago cop for ten years before turning to writing in his spare time. Forty-eight-year-old Anne Rapp (*Cookie's Fortune*) worked on film productions as a script supervisor for fifteen years before uncovering her passion for storytelling. Although all of these writers started in different ways and have very disparate styles, they have something important in common—an honesty in how their characters tell their own particular stories, no matter what the genre.

Although each screenwriter's journey is unique, there are common experiences shared by most who have dared to claim this dream. These experiences often involve the need to take enormous risks and to challenge the many myths surrounding the film and television industry. Most books on the topic address the craft, but few delve into the actual experience of being a screenwriter. When Marie-Eve and I first discussed the idea of writing this book, it seemed like a great opportunity to explain, explore, and honor the screenwriting journey.

In *So You Want to Be a Screenwriter,* we offer many questions that you can use for self-evaluation regarding your own personal journey. We also describe ways in which to create meaningful stories and believable characters, citing specific examples. And we talk about the power of collaboration, which we know well from our own collaborative experiences.

Marie-Eve suggested that I also share personal vignettes of the screenwriter's life. Thus, my alter ego, Donna Flint, was born. Her journey, which you will read about at the beginning of each part, is really a reflection of my own fears, hesitations, and victories. They are certainly a part of my history.

Coauthoring this book and remembering my own journey through Donna's presence has been a great way for me to ponder and evaluate my travels through the creative maze. I recently ventured into the Badlands of the Anza-Borrego State Park in Southern California. The treacherous, unearthly canyons and gullies reminded me of the road I had already undertaken as a screenwriter. Near the Badlands is State Route 86, which cuts a line straight between the park and the Salton Sea. Cars on this road, where the horizon is visible from miles away, drive at incredible speeds. Occasional markers indicate a journey's end for the road traveller—one that has most likely been safe, predictable, and rather tedious in between some amazing views. I'm still in the Badlands, walking a path that I know will lead me to even greater heights and, at the same time, plunge me into deeper abysses than I have ever descended. A risk taker at heart, I will continue to hike this trail with wondrous anticipation, as I discover all of the exciting unknowns that lay ahead. I know that I'm not alone out there—I hope we have a chance to meet somewhere along the way.

●

PART I

The Screenwriter's Journey

DONNA FLINT

Memoir of a Screenwriter—The Hook

I first began screenwriting from an old log cabin in a West Virginia holler, having married into a long line of natives of this Southern state. An urbanite at heart, my nuptial rosy cheeks soon turned a pale shade of gray as I endured one of the strangest times of my life.

The greenery in West Virginia was savage. It took hold of everything, including the cabin we literally unearthed to move into. Foliage cascaded down hillsides like tangled ropes, ready to ensnare anything in its path. I lost a cat there and always wonder if he isn't mummified in the upper branches of a tree, encased in long, leafy tendrils.

From inside those dark cabin walls, I was writing a masterpiece, the kind that would surely set Hollywood on edge. The kind that was also sure to justify my existence in this damp, unnerving hell.

Although I was new to screenwriting, telling stories had always been part of my life. As a young child, I created a cartoon strip about a fat cat who did everything in his power to eat well and avoid physical exertion. I also illustrated stories about orphans wandering the rat-infested alleys of a cruel metropolis in search of their parents. Another story involved two children crossing Australia and encountering aliens.

At school, my head was always in the clouds. A history class would trigger daydreams of living with Native Americans or following the Oregon Trail. I once had a science teacher hurl a blackboard eraser at my head while I was on a microcosmic journey to save mankind. That sci-fi fantasy abruptly vanished into thin air, along with chalky clouds bouncing off my skull.

As a child and teenager, I had no motive for writing and illustrating my stories other than the sheer pleasure of it. I never thought of it in terms of a career goal. It was just something I did.

In college, I spent my first year as an English major. Most of my friends were studying business and computer science. They asked me how I could make a living as a writer. The more I thought about it, the more an idea blossomed—I could always do writing on the side, so why not pursue something more stable? I drifted into the film and television department and ended up with a communications degree. After I graduated, I moved to Chicago and worked as an industrial video producer, while my notebooks of stories collected dust on a bookshelf. Almost ten years went by.

One day, I attended a writing workshop sponsored by my company. The workshop leader gave a basic presentation on screenwriting, including information on the three-act structure, character arcs, and plot points. My mind started wandering on ways to tell a story in this format. I took laborious notes and began contemplating interesting characters and conflicts. Suddenly, my old, rusty interior furnace was reignited. That night, I pulled out my notebooks, scanned the contents, then shoved them back on the shelf. The stories were juvenile and inappropriate for film. I could surely think of something better. And so, while journeying into marriage and a new life in a new town with my doomed cat, I began my first screenplay.

Now, as I sat in my West Virginia cabin, I was writing the "real thing." I labored over the trials and tribulations of my central character, took part in her journey, savored her conquests. But when I showed my first draft to my husband, my beaming smile did a one-eighty as he told me, in a roundabout way, that it sucked. I was deflated, having worked so long and hard on it. I began to wonder if I lacked the necessary talent, not to mention those interesting and worthy life experiences to draw upon. My stubbornness kept me going.

Writers cling desperately to their first work, so impressed with their ability to complete it in the first place. Probably the best advice I ever received in those early years was from the late screenwriter, Carl Sautter, while attending an American Film Institute workshop in New York. All the participants were novice writers, with only one or two scripts under our belts. Carl told us to take these labors of love and throw them onto the floor. Of course, that meant separating my masterpiece from my breast. But I did as he asked and became even more horrified when he told us to forget these scripts and move on to new projects. These first efforts, he explained, had been a good exercise in writing. It was now time to continue improving our craft. Say what? Wasn't this the script that was going to shake up Hollywood? Reluctantly, I took his advice and began a new screenplay. Looking back on that "masterpiece," I now cringe at the memory and am eternally grateful that I showed it to so few people.

As time passed, I realized that pretty much everyone has a screenplay, or at least an idea for one that they intend to write when they have more time. Even the guy behind the counter at my local coffee shop had one. I wondered what differentiated him (and me) from the "successful" ones. You know, the writers who attend Oscar parties and make six-figure deals around Malibu poolsides. Was it purely a result of their talent? Or did they know tricks of the trade that I didn't? Were there certain truths about Hollywood that I should be aware of? Was the fact that I'd completed a "communications" degree at a Midwestern college instead of a "film" degree at a prestigious film school going to hurt me? Since I had no connections in the film industry, would I be an outcast from the "inner circle"? Would agents reject me because I didn't live in Los Angeles? Was I too old for such a youth-oriented industry? Would I have better luck with a sex change? It seemed pretty hopeless. Despite these odds, I'd read about gurus in the film industry who (for a price) would share the Hollywood truths, allowing me to walk down an enlightened path to stardom. If I could find the right consultant or workshop, I could get an agent, sell a screenplay for gobs of money, hobnob by those Malibu pools— just one good deal, and I'd be set for life.

●

CHAPTER 1

Why Have I Chosen
to Be a Screenwriter?

There are some people who will try to do their best to discourage you from screenwriting. If you don't have that deep knowing about who you are, and what you want, then you will go away from it.

Carmen Brown

It is a human quality to want recognition, to be seen and heard and appreciated. It is also part of the human spirit to feel a need to contribute one's creativity in ways that can impact others. Writers like Donna Flint chose screenwriting as a way to express their creativity. Her initial experience was not unique, and the questions she posed were understandable.

Like Donna, it is easy to get sidetracked in the writing process, getting lost in what might happen rather than in what is actually happening. The truth is, there is no "right way" to become a successful screenwriter, and no gurus (or even consultants) can prove otherwise. Although you can stack up certain odds in your favor (e.g., your chances of meeting someone in the film industry who can help your career are greater in Los Angeles than in Topeka, Kansas), the journey you take will be unique to you, a result of your dreams, your history, your aspirations, your willingness to take risks, and your ability to not buy into worn-out myths about the film and television industry. Those myths can be powerful tyrants that can cloud your judgment.

Donna would often experience those moments when she would be stifled by the hold that the myths would take on her creativity—myths that made her believe that she could not be successful because she was a woman, did not live in Hollywood, was over thirty, and had not tasted enough life experiences to be worthy of creating a screenplay. But it is almost impossible to venture into new arenas without fearing that we will fail or fall flat on our faces. Donna had bought into a number of myths, which only worsened these feelings. She would eventually realize that the myths would stop her progress unless she found the strength to use her own voice in her writing.

Screenwriter Adam Rifkin believes that there is no such thing as failure. "So many people are operating out of fear. I'm afraid to sit down and write a script because, what if it's no good? I'm afraid to quit my job and move to Hollywood because, what if I don't make it? As hard as it is to succeed, I firmly believe that there's no failing in show business. You can't fail, because there are as many opportunities as you can create for yourself. You can only quit. You can't fail."

Despite difficult moments, Adam has practiced what he preaches and refused to quit. After writing twenty-nine scripts, he struck gold with number thirty, the enchanting comedy *Mouse Hunt,* which starred Nathan Lane.

Somewhere, somehow, Adam had prepared himself for his screenwriting journey and committed himself to refusing to believe that he could not succeed. His determination and perseverance would be the cornerstones for the future paths that he would travel.

We often resist knowing exactly why we have chosen to follow a specific profession. Was it really our choice? Were we being impetuous in our decision-making? Exactly why had we decided to become screenwriters? Perhaps asking these questions may seem simplistic and a waste of time. Perhaps you are one of those fortunate ones who has always known that you wanted to become a storyteller.

If you are like most others, however, asking these questions will encourage you to affirm the reasons why you have decided to choose this career. Are the answers you come up with reason enough to propel you to the next step? Do your answers supply you with the strength you will need to forge ahead and accept the inevitable rigors? Does your response include something like, "I must do this, no matter what." Are you certain of your motivations, and have you acknowledged that you are the one setting forth on this journey, not someone you would like to be or that someone else wants you to be? Do you know the reasons why screenwriting is a must for you, why it excites you, why it is meaningful and something that you must accomplish? Is it the process of writing that makes your heart beat a mile a minute, or the rewards that successful screenwriters can attain? Remember that you can have both the rewards and the immense joy that writing stories provides, as long as you are willing to question, ponder, and listen to your inner muse, which demands that you be true to your vision.

It is important to realize that we sometimes choose paths that are not quite right for us. We are impacted by what we believe and imagine is waiting for us at the other end, such as tremendous personal, professional, and financial rewards. We see the quick overnight successes and are seduced into believing that this is the ultimate goal.

Asking the Difficult Questions

It is not often that we give ourselves the opportunity to ponder and ask why we are propelled to do what we do in our lives. It is not often that we give ourselves the permission to soul-search and to affirm the choices we have made in the pursuit of our personal and professional dreams.

Throughout this book, we encourage the process of questioning in order to help you to crystallize your thoughts and feelings regarding your choice to become a screenwriter. For many, asking questions can be extremely intimidating, even when it is done in privacy. The ability to question our motives and to become introspective helps in gaining the awareness needed to make creative choices. The questions at the end of each chapter regarding the fears, myths, and risks associated with different aspects of the screenwriting process are designed to inspire new ways of affirming your decision to become a screenwriter. They are meant to make you question old assumptions that you may not even have realized were so much a part of your everyday decision-making.

When we give ourselves the time to stop and speak to the inner part of our being, answers may emerge that may come as a great surprise. Allow yourself to take the time to answer the questions we have posed and to perhaps even marvel at what you discover. Using these questions as a guide for journal writing may serve as a catalyst for a future story or a newly-developed character, which may, in turn, ignite your imagination to new heights.

If you become discouraged as you are asking these questions, use those moments for further exploration. Nothing about the awareness process is negative or destructive. It is simply a new path that is brought in front of you in order for you to gain new insights.

Aspiring to become a screenwriter will involve the asking of difficult, thought-provoking questions along the way. The answers may demand further questions and may even lead to feelings of frustration. There will, however, be no lost moments. As each phase of the journey is accomplished, new awarenesses will emerge that will help guide your next decisions. Layer upon layer of questions and answers will form the foundation of your creative path. The writers who truly want to make a contribution as the powerful storytellers they perceive themselves to be will accept the premise that probing and questioning are a natural component for attaining success. They are not satisfied with making assumptions, but rather are challenged by the perfecting of their craft. They have been willing to view their screenwriting journey as a process, not an end in itself. They will relish the visibility and connectedness they had dreamed about. The arduous path and the moments spent "interviewing" the inner self will be well worth the joys of accomplishment now being experienced as each new script is in the making.

No creative pursuit is a linear process. With each new set of successes, new questions will inevitably be brought into consciousness. Take the time to write down the questions that resurface. Noting the pattern of your responses can be extremely helpful in recognizing the hesitancies, the fears, and the doubts that can so easily creep up as the journey proceeds. What happens to the questions that are left unanswered? Was it a purposeful decision to "skip" over them, or were they too provocative? What are you discovering about your resistances, your excuses, or lack of information regarding your personal creative process? Do not allow yourself to despair about the answers, which may come as a total surprise to you. They are just wonderful fodder that will bring you new and important information that is crucial to your chosen journey. Accept that you will probably ask yourself the following types of questions more than once throughout your screenwriting career. They can serve as a starting point for your inner probing. Do not treat the questions you encounter throughout this book as the enemy. Have the courage to face each one head on. Know that you will be awarded new and powerful information upon which to base your next steps.

- What is it about screenwriting that excites me?
- Why do I think that the screenwriting format is the best way in which to tell my stories?
- What peak experiences have reassured me that I am on the right track?
- What fears are inhibiting me from pursuing my dreams?
- What myths do I have to confront to claim my voice?
- What risks will I have to take to make my dreams a reality?

Not everyone who sets out to become a screenwriter will achieve wealth and fame. Although people from all walks of life become screenwriters, most who stick to it over time seem to have a few things in common, including their passion for the writing process itself, not just for the elusive pot of gold at the end.

"I think that everyone who wants to be in this business needs to ask themselves why," suggests Ed Bernero, a cop turned television writer of shows such as *Third Watch* and *Brooklyn South*. "What is it that they think they're going to get from it? Five years ago, I was writing for myself in my basement. And I kept writing even though nothing was selling. There were things that I wrote that I never even sent out. So for me, it's about writing. Luckily, it's a job in which you can get paid pretty well. But I really believe I would do it anyway."

Those who do not enjoy the writing process, but rather have sought screenwriting simply as a means of gaining visibility, usually become frustrated when results do not come quickly. The writing part becomes a chore, while the marketing of a screenplay occurs prematurely, causing frenzy and inner chaos. Such writers are often focused on trying to tell a commercially appealing story, rather than one that comes from their heart.

"I've had friends who have given me scripts that are so clearly written with the goal of making a commercial sale," says Noah Baumbach, who penned and directed *Mr. Jealousy* and *Kicking and Screaming*. "Rarely does that work. Unless you have an innate commercial sensibility, I think it's a real mistake to try to break into the business that way. Often, the best way to get noticed is to write something personal and original."

You need to have the courage to ask if writing is what you truly want or if you have chosen it simply as a means to try to become important and famous in the world. Asking yourself the tough questions can help provide the answers that will help clarify your path. Is it possible to become a successful screenwriter, be visible, and reap the rewards that the industry can generously provide? Absolutely! For some, like Ed Bernero and Noah Baumbach, it is exactly what has happened.

It is those writers who have been willing to periodically stop and listen to their inner voices, as well as to be true to their unique vision, who will not only attain success and gain recognition, but, more importantly, will gain the joy of being connected to a larger purpose through the creation of their stories. Screenwriter Sharon Y. Cobb has become very attuned to her inner voice, especially in moments of crisis.

"I had a crisis of faith about a year and a half ago, before getting the Danny Glover deal (*Return of the Sweet Birds*). I have this kind of weird little process that I do when I question if I'm doing the right thing. I close my eyes and look at my path and ask myself what do I see in front of me. So a year and a half ago, I went, My God, I'm killing myself out here. I'm exhausted. I don't have a real life. I make okay money, but just enough to support myself from month to month. So I did that little process, and you know what? There was nothing else on my path. And I trust my intuition enough to know that if there was anything else I would have been able to see it right then. So I knew, fine, I'll keep going. And I did."

In determining whether the screenwriting process truly fits what your inner voice is telling you, responding to some hard-hitting questions will enable you to clarify your motivations and bring you closer to your own truth. Do you have the courage to discover if you really want to write and, in particular, if screenwriting is the appropriate medium for you? The journey for most screenwriters involves walking on bumpy roads with a smattering of downhill slides and unexpected perils along the way. It is much like the journeys you will create for your characters. You will ask them to take enormous risks. You will have them go blindly into the night without safety nets. You will ask them to have courage and passion and excitement around the decisions they make. Are you willing to do the same?

In contrast, there are many writers, particularly those just starting their journey, who are determined to go through it unscathed, with no bloody knees to report, no twisting and turning helplessly at night with feelings of being totally overwhelmed. So what happens to the writer who is convinced that all he has to do is write another *Rocky* and his life will be coming up roses, but instead finds that the majority of his query letters go unanswered and the few scripts that are actually requested are returned? What does he feel like when all the time he had planned to spend writing is eaten up by his job, family, and other time-consuming aspects of daily life? What happens to the writer who has vowed to succeed, or else? And that to do so he must move to Los Angeles, where the action is, yet he does not have the money to make the move? What happens to his self-esteem, his energy, and his will when he reads about other writers who have become overnight successes? How does he feel when he realizes that, at some level, if he does not act on his goal to become a screenwriter, it will feel as if something inside of him has died?

We are constantly bombarded with messages that reinforce that pain is unnecessary, that pain is bad and to be avoided at all costs, and that the pain we feel when we have given up listening to our soul's voice must be numbed.

There is no question that the screenwriter's journey is not a smooth and easy one. And there is no question that even those writers who have taken risks were not exempt from feeling pain, disappointment, and self-doubt. Anyone who has the courage to claim a dream, whatever the dream might be, is not free from travelling a difficult path. There is no such thing as a free ride when we take risks to liberate our creative voices. It is precisely the process of climbing the mountain that will stay with us forever and bring pride and fulfillment, along with the possibility of feeling great connectedness with a bigger world outside of ourselves.

"You have to have a reward above Hollywood," says Anne Rapp, a former script supervisor who has had two of her screenplays directed by Robert

Altman. "My reward is that I've done something that touches someone else's life. It enhances my own life. I learn something every time I write a story. I see myself in every character. I would like to think that I'm actually in the character. I think of someone like Altman as a true artist, because he never does what someone else thinks he should do. He never does what he can make the most money from. He does stories that are part of who he is. He constantly told me to go out there and go to the edge. That's the great thing about him. I was never afraid that I was going to make a fool of myself and he was going to read it and think, oh God, this is terrible. He allowed me to be courageous. It was the best thing he could do for me."

Perhaps Anne never consciously asked herself why she had chosen screenwriting as a way to tell her stories, but somewhere along the way, it is certainly a question that she was able to answer and to employ as she proceeded forward. Asking yourself the following questions may help you move forward along your screenwriting path.

- How does screenwriting give meaning to my life?
- How would my life be affected if I could not claim the screenwriting dream?
- How have I committed to doing whatever it takes to claim my dream?
- In what ways does the script format provide a structure that will help me to really expand my story ideas?
- What attracts me to the idea of becoming a screenwriter?
- If I have I entertained other writing forms, why do I return over and over again to screenwriting, feeling like I've "come home"?

When lecturing, Sharon Y. Cobb asks her students why they have chosen to write.

"The students who say they're compelled to write, that's the thing. I didn't choose screenwriting, it chose me. I was compelled. It was clear that I must do this. They have that kind of desire, that flame within themselves, and they're writing every day, writing when they get up, writing before they go to bed, writing like their life depends on it, because if you're a real writer, it does. That's the truth of the matter."

Understanding your choices and accepting the risks rarely happens without some form of questioning. The questions put forth in this book are intended to stimulate and help you to better understand your unique journey, whether you are just starting out or your career as a screenwriter is already underway. These questions will help you to understand aspects of this journey that may be new and, at times, seem overwhelming, as well as a little frightening, yet forever challenging and exciting.

The process of asking questions will enable you to dig deep inside yourself and come closer to hearing, with more clarity, that truth that lies inside you. When you are willing to ask the difficult questions along the way, you will be more prepared to strip the layers of rationalizations, defenses, and excuses you may have encountered. These untruths may have clouded your thoughts and feelings and kept you from realizing your ability to activate your amazing creativity.

Will it be your destiny to bring us stories that will have the power to impact and stay with us forever? Will you have the determination and resilience to challenge the myths, face the fears, and take the risks necessary to find the success you dream about?

Confronting the Fears

Fear is paralyzing. Fear takes our breath away and is the poison that has the power to stop us from moving forward. It is also a great motivator and can help us to come to our senses.

As a screenwriter, your journey will not be very different from the writers whose voices you will hear throughout this book, as they share their personal stories, their trials, and their triumphs. They will speak about the myths and fears they have encountered and were able to surmount through wit and wisdom.

As you claim the screenwriter's dream, you will hopefully discover the courage to be seen and heard in a way that brings you to the attention of a larger audience. Many have not had the determination to be visible in this way and have preferred to silence their creative voice rather than to take the risks and experience the fears, which can certainly cause discomfort, yet when challenged, bring tremendous inner fulfillment.

In choosing the screenwriting journey, you have also chosen to be a part of an industry that can be demanding, at times cruel and seemingly inhuman, and sometimes very discouraging. As a screenwriter, you have ventured into competitive territory, where, more often than not, decisions about what scripts get purchased are extremely subjective. You may at some point on the journey have to depend on the judgment of others, the opinions of those who have never met you, do not know who you are, and who will ask you to alter your scripts or will hire others to rewrite your story. They may even ask you to forego your own voice for the sake of involving "bigger voices" on your project. The journey you have chosen is not devoid of anguish or without moments of frustration and disillusionment. Expressions of anger may be triggered and utter discouragement felt. Playwright and screenwriter Josefina

Lopez has already travelled a journey full of pain and success. Growing up as an undocumented immigrant in East Los Angeles, Josefina became a prolific writer at a young age. She won an Emmy for a play she wrote at seventeen and optioned another play to Warner Brothers by the age of twenty-one. Despite these and many other accomplishments, Josefina has battled many personal demons, including attention deficit disorder and intense feelings of inadequacy.

"I feel like I've been on an obstacle course, and I've had to fight so many dragons to even be allowed to fight the big one," says Josefina. "Forget the luxury of actually writing. It's like, how many dragons do I have to kill on the way here. I remember growing up with people knowing I wanted to be a writer. I remember how cruel these kids were. One girl read one of my poems and said my dog can write better than you. It was so hurtful, but I remember thinking, well, you must have a very talented dog. As an artist, people will put you down because you're a dreamer."

Despite her parents' resistance to her educational choice, which they worried would lead to an unstable career, Josefina completed a bachelor's degree and is now attending UCLA's MFA Screenwriting Program. However, she believes it takes more than a diploma to become a screenwriter.

"You can go to school and learn how to write a well-structured screenplay that moves and is exciting, but that thing, the soul, that's something you have to go find. You have to go on your own journey to be able to tell a story about a character who is on a journey of their own. Having gone through one myself, I look a lot at the dark side of myself and at the stuff that is really so painful. Because I finally looked at it, I can now retell stories about how I actually got to where I am."

Like Josefina, your journey will have the power to take you to great heights, and at the same time drop you into the abyss with your heart pounding. Your path may offer you tremendous joy, passion, and excitement, and at the same time, can stop you in your tracks with those demonic, negative thoughts and fears.

Carmen Brown gave up a gourmet cookie business in Chicago to pursue her dream of screenwriting. One of the hardest things she learned to face was rejection.

"Rejection makes you question if you really have what it takes," says Carmen. "It makes you question what you're bringing to the table. Now, you're asking yourself, do I really have what it takes to make it? And from that point, it's a constant stream of no's. 'No' becomes a very big word. At times, I just pull myself away from it all and ponder, who are these people who are rejecting me anyway? You need to ask yourself—why do I want to become a screenwriter? If you want to make money and become famous, then why put yourself in harm's way. It's a long, hard journey, and you must have backbone to survive. It's a prerequisite for the screenwriting life. You should know beyond a shadow of a doubt that the screenwriting life has chosen you."

When you have asked the questions, probed, and been willing to struggle with the answers, you will be much more ready to face the fears that have a way of creeping in no matter how well prepared you are. If the answers point you in new directions and you decide to change your original course of action, then use these questions as a compass to guide you along the way. The key is to claim your own truth, to visit the depth of your knowledge, and to become your own prophet as you travel on your creative journey.

Will I Face the Fears?

Starting a creative venture is not an easy task. Putting yourself on the line and making the decision to go forward means developing a strong interior, so that when the path becomes steep, your footing will be sure. Becoming a screenwriter can be an extremely exciting and audacious decision. Do not expect that you will avoid being afraid from time to time. The fears may grip you by the throat, yet they will also have the power to guide your next steps if you allow yourself to feel the fear.

Most of us do everything possible to ward off feeling afraid. We expect ourselves to take huge risks without experiencing any anxiety. As you confront the fears listed throughout this book, it may be helpful to recognize that fear need not become a deterrent to the dreams you wish to attain. The power of fear comes from our belief that we will fail, be shamed in some way, and be rejected. When you think about your worst nightmare as a screenwriter, what does it look like? Our fears are based on some form of truth we have experienced, yet when we are willing to look at each one closely, what we discover is that we have somehow forgotten to trust our inner voice. We have ceased to look at our ability to make productive decisions and have given up our power to someone else's voice, someone who we believe can rule our ability to become successful.

In looking at the list of ten common fears below, you will see that they are based on assumptions that:

- You can't make good decisions.
- You have given up trusting yourself.
- You have lost your own voice somewhere along the way.

Ten Common Fears About Becoming a Screenwriter

1. I'll look like a failure if I don't sell a screenplay.
2. I won't have the drive and endurance to make it.
3. I won't be able to convince agents and/or producers to consider my work.
4. I won't be able to finish my script.
5. I'll have to give up too much to pursue my writing.
6. I'm afraid to really go after what I want in case I don't get it.
7. No one will take me seriously.
8. My family/friends will tell me to get a "real job."
9. I don't have anything interesting to write about.
10. Everyone will think that I failed if I change my mind about being a screenwriter.

- The "adult" part of you has given up and let the "child" take over.
- You have forgotten what you claimed as your dream and need to go back to basics.

Addressing the fears you have internalized will become an ongoing task as you take on the risks necessary to meet your goals. You have countless opportunities to challenge your own truths versus succumbing to the voices that may be impacting your success.

At the end of each chapter of this book, a section on fears, myths, and risks will invite you to discover how you are holding yourself back from claiming your full potential. The fears we all experience on the creative path are a part of the beliefs that no longer suit our professional purposes, yet occupy a great deal of our thinking. As you are introduced to the multitude of ways in which fears stymie your purpose, your task will be to take the time to challenge them, one by one. The fears that seem to have overtaken you need no longer do so. Your mission is to become more acquainted with all of the ways in which you are stopping yourself from moving forward. Risk-taking will have to become a part of your journey if screenwriting is your dream.

As you read each chapter, it might be helpful to take the time to add your own personal fears, myths, and risks to the existing lists. The more aware you can be of the elements that hinder your progress, the more satisfaction you will gain from the process of introspection. Reaffirming what your own creative voice really sounds like will be a lifelong process, yet one in which great satisfaction and growth can be the outcome.

Will I Challenge the Myths?

Our fears are often based on the myths, beliefs, and assumptions that we have "taken in" as universal truths. Have you ever stopped to question why you believe certain things you have heard regarding the screenwriting profession? What about your own definition of success or what it takes to "make it" in Hollywood? When you think about your personal and professional dreams, do you stop in midstream and begin to hear opposition?

Without realizing it, we have all, at times in our lives, bought into other people's messages about what they believe reality to be. The danger lies in running our lives according to a set of rules and beliefs that belong to someone else. There is no greater detriment to the creative process than incorporating into our own spirit that which others claim to be the truth.

At the end of each chapter, you will find myths presented that will offer you an opportunity to rethink and reevaluate whether or not they belong to you. It will be crucial for you to decide whether each myth is a belief you wish to uphold or one that you want to challenge. Unless you are willing to scrutinize these messages throughout your screenwriting journey, they will have the power to crush your dreams.

As you proceed on your creative path, you may come across people who are envious of your ability and determination to honor your dream. They will wonder what makes you able to propel yourself forward while it seems impossible for them to do so. They may even use expressions like, "Is that really realistic for you to do? How will you ever manage? What does your family think of all this?" You may find yourself becoming very defensive and going into a great deal of explanation, as you experience more and more frustration. You may even begin to question yourself and the decisions you are making. Projections can be lethal, and other people's fears and trepidations are the poison that can kill your creative spirit . . . if you allow it.

As you are introduced to some common myths at the end of each chapter, give yourself the opportunity to ask if they belong to you or someone else. Allow yourself to recognize how you may be buying into these messages. What do you need to incorporate into your own creative process in order to dispute what is not yours? No matter what level of development you have attained, when you are in a vulnerable state of being, when doubts are creeping in faster than you can stop them, it is at this time that the myths gain their power.

It is important to recognize your support systems, the people in your life who applaud your successes no matter how small. Anyone who has had the courage to claim the screenwriter's journey will be constantly challenged to question the myths along the way in order to find his own truth. As you take

Ten Common Myths About Becoming a Screenwriter

1. My first script will make millions and I'll be able to retire.
2. If you have to work hard at screenwriting then you must not be talented enough.
3. Only the "gifted" few get to do what they really want in life.
4. Writing what I know is not interesting enough for a script.
5. If I don't go to seminars and workshops led by the "masters," I won't know how to get my script sold.
6. Successful screenwriters lead glamorous lives.
7. It doesn't take special qualities to be a writer—anyone can do it.
8. I have to know somebody to make it in the film business.
9. I have to live in Los Angeles to sell a screenplay.
10. I can't sell a screenplay without an agent.

the time to explore the myths below, you may discover that you have already been able to challenge some of them, while others remain present in your life. They may appear and disappear without warning. What will remain constant, however, is your commitment to meet your goals and create the stories that lie inside you, ready to come to life. One question remains—will you meet the challenge to listen to your own voice? If so, how will you do this, and what tools will you employ to make your screenwriting dream come true?

Will I Take the Risks?

When we choose to do something we love, we do not always consider that we will have to engage in taking risks in order to accomplish it. We often think of risk-taking as some horrible feat, something we must do that is fraught with danger.

Often, it is not until we decide to claim our destiny that we are faced with the true meaning of taking risks. It may seem difficult to give an unequivocal "yes" to becoming a screenwriter if we feel like venturing on this road is a luxury. It may seem unattainable and at times impossible for us to succeed at doing the very thing that makes us feel alive. As you proceed through each phase of your journey, there will probably be people who will be unable to accept your decision for reasons of their own. There will certainly be the lonely and isolated times when no creative juices will flow. You may be witness to others reaching the success you dream of and wonder if you will ever be in the same arena. Question after question will emerge, and the process of rationalization will drive away any sense of trust and intuition.

It is precisely during these frightening moments that all the energy you have will need to be spent regrouping and going back to your original purpose. Taking the risks will come in your determination to move forward, no matter what your intellect attempts to say. You must be willing to accept a basic human tenet, that without our creativity we have nothing. To face the fears, to challenge all the negative messages, and to move beyond the doubts will remain the greatest risks you will be called upon to make. You will be tempted to stop dreaming about your journey as a screenwriter. You will be driven to be "practical" and, in so doing, leave wonderful and exciting options by the wayside. You may tire of the rigors and convince yourself that you do not have the emotional strength to travel on this path alone. You may have great internal tugs-of-war that will leave you exhausted and ready to attempt anything other than going after your dream.

Without risk-taking, our ability to claim our dreams is nonexistent. It is our dreams that give us the raison d'être and that provide inner fulfillment and enrichment in our lives. Achieving your dream of storyteller will mean facing the fears, challenging the myths, and taking the risks necessary to transport you on your journey.

Am I Willing to . . .

1. Ask difficult questions along the way that may cause internal conflict and lead to confusion?
2. Work through the moments of frustration rather than give up?
3. Ask for help when it may be the last thing I would ordinarily do?
4. Persist no matter what others may say or do?
5. Take the long road versus the shortcuts that may seem easier or more exciting in the moment?
6. Take time to regroup and go back to the basics when panic strikes?
7. Challenge the word "reality" when it applies to projections others have placed on me?
8. Admit that nothing is accomplished alone and that I need affirmation and support if I am to be successful?
9. Live in the present and avoid attempting to know the future?
10. Learn the craft of screenwriting without shortchanging the process?

●

CHAPTER 2

Delle Chatman: An Architect of Communal Dreams

I believe that screenwriters are the architects of communal dreams. If as a culture we dreamt better dreams, we might have a better reality.

Delle Chatman

Little did Delle Chatman realize, at the age of five, as she peeked from behind her father's living room chair watching as Dr. Frankenstein performed his scary "magic" on a small black-and-white TV set, that the soul of a screenwriter was being born. Delle was a child of a military family, always on the move. Creating characters through writing, Delle found a way to have companions who were ever-present in her fantasy world, giving her stability and solace in her constantly changing real world.

Throughout her life, Delle would remain true to her own voice. To this day, she has been able to evaluate projects, write stories from the heart, and be true to the spirit of the stories she wants to create. Free of Eden, *an original story that she cowrote with Yule Caise, was her first produced feature film that aired on Showtime Television. Starring Sidney Poitier, Phylicia Rashad, Robert Hooks, and Poitier's daughter, Sydney Tamiia Poitier,* Free of Eden *is a compelling story about a teenager's desire to have a better life by leaving the projects.*

Full of diversity, wisdom and strength, Delle has flourished as a screenwriter, a novelist, a television series writer, an actress, a university professor, and a mother. Her path has been (and will continue to be) a challenging and exciting one. Here, in her own words, is her journey, as well as messages of inspiration for other writers travelling on similar roads.

The Journey Begins

I became entranced with film and television at a very, very young age. I was five years old when my parents finally allowed me to stay up late and watch television on Friday nights with the rest of the family. I had no idea what they were watching, but it was a big family event. And it turned out they were—are you ready?—horror pictures on late-night Friday nights. *The Mummy, Frankenstein,* and *The Werewolf.* And, of course, I was absolutely terrified. But I was also entranced and captivated by the thought that somebody could turn off all the lights in the living room, and there would be this little box that would put up these black-and-white pictures and have this spooky-sounding music, and you'd watch these men (they're usually male characters) be transformed into creatures, and you'd be dragged into a world you didn't really want to visit, totally against your will. I was famous for running behind my dad's chair yelling, "Change the channel! Change the channel!" as soon as the monster showed up. But I was hooked. I was fascinated by stories specifically told through images with music and with passions that were really rather extreme. By the time I was twelve, I was writing short stories in school. I actually wrote my first screenplay when I was twelve years old. My father was in the Air Force; we travelled a great deal. So my personal environment shifted and changed. There was a continual turnover of people and personalities in my life. So in a sense, the fictions I created were the one great constant.

That screenplay I wrote at twelve—I requisitioned my dad's Kodak movie camera, and I cast it. Costumes were made. The school counselor at the junior high school I was attending heard about this production and called me into her office and told me I was "too young" to make a movie. And I think at a very early age, it instilled a fear of the front office. And I like to think it wouldn't happen these days, but I'm not so sure. It forced me to take the story out of the screenplay form and into the prose form. I knew if I wasn't going to be allowed to collaborate and produce this story in a communal fashion, I still had to get it out. I still had to express it. I still had to explore it. I give myself credit for not letting go of the spark.

That same story that I had worked on from the time I was twelve until I was about sixteen or seventeen years old was first a screenplay, then a novella, which I burned only to return to it in the mid-80s. This story resurfaced, and I wrote it as a novel. It wasn't until I'd finished the first draft that I realized it was an adult translation of that very first story. It went from being a story that was set in biblical times to a story that's now set in the future, so go figure. Imagination is a strange thing.

Life in Hollywood

After a stint as a television reporter, Delle landed a dream job as a staff writer for a PBS television series. Although life in Hollywood would be enthralling, seductive, and financially rewarding, it would force Delle to look in the mirror and dig deep into her soul.

It was very exciting to begin with. For one thing, as soon as I went to work, my first job was as a staff writer on a series called *The Righteous Apples,* which was a dramedy produced by PBS about a high school set in Boston that had recently integrated. The Righteous Apples was the name of a music group that was made up of a black guy, a black girl, a Jewish guy, and a white girl. It was literally a rainbow group of young people. That job put me in the middle of a production staff. It introduced me to a more social way of being a writer. It was my first professional writing job in this arena, although I had been a television reporter before then. But even TV reporters are lone wolves. Writers working on television are very much a part of a team. So, in a sense, [it was] the first time the creative process became a group effort. That was exhilarating, but it was also frustrating. It became more frustrating as the years went by, and it became clear to me that until I became an executive producer who was creating my own series, I would essentially be taking other people's characters down paths that were not of my own choosing.

I ended up on staff for a series called *Snoops.* It had a great premise, but I often said we were already in intensive care before the first episode even hit the airwaves. It just wasn't working. I had written a couple of stories and one script for the show. The executive producer had just been replaced, because, as I said, the whole series was in a lot of creative turmoil. I remember two specific events. One was that I'd written a script that was given to another writer to be rewritten. The series was a murder-mystery show, and I'd created this wonderful character for a costarring role. The character was a black woman from South Africa who I thought was really a heroic figure. She was turned into the murderer in the revision, because, as the rewriter said, "No one would ever guess she'd be the bad guy." I remember thinking, I gotta get out of here, because this is antithetical to a whole lot of things I really, really believe in. That was one bell going off. The other bell that chimed was on a more personal note. It was on a Friday evening, late, like 7:00, 7:30, and I had a friend flying in from out of town, someone I was supposed to pick up at the airport. And there we were sitting in a story meeting without a fresh idea among us, just staring at each other. I thought to myself, do any of us have a life? A real life outside of this room? Is there a life outside of this office? Is there a life outside of this series? Don't I need to have a little bit more room for Delle? Not just creatively, but just personally, in order to feel good about my life. A balance. Hollywood is not a culture that's big on balance.

The year from 1988 to 1989 was really difficult for me. In 1988, the Writer's Guild went on strike. The odd part was that I was making more money than I had ever made. In a way, it was the syndrome of the "golden handcuffs": You've achieved a certain professional level where you're remunerated handsomely for your efforts. You look to your left and you look to your right, and you see friends who envy the job that you have and the salary that you make and the profile that you're gaining. Yet, you have no sense of being about your own specific, God-ordained work. It was during that period that I moved out of the little humble Hollywood apartment into my West Los Angeles apartment, which, of course, demanded that I continue earning a certain amount of money to support this industry lifestyle. The lifestyle of success in Hollywood is extremely seductive and extremely expensive. I was also at a moment in my life where I felt that at this age, I should have all of this, because I'd been raised to think that way. My parents expected their daughter with the college degree to be secure in the middle class; enough of this bohemian stuff. They expected me to knuckle down and get serious. So I did. I bought into that.

The strike was the first time in a career that had been very full, rewarding, and remunerative that I had a moment to stop and realize that it had been about three years since I had written an original "Chatman." And so, in a sense, I had lost that therapeutic part of the writing process, the exploration of issues that I have on my mind and in my heart. That realization led me to leave and to put the television staff work behind me.

Life Out of Hollywood

In 1990, Delle broke the "golden handcuffs." She moved to Chicago, where she had been invited to teach courses on writing for film and television at Northwestern University. She became increasingly concerned with how her students viewed the screenwriting process and was committed to helping them to find their own reasons why they had chosen to follow the screenwriter's journey.

I have watched young writers over the last half-dozen years become increasingly impatient with the process—not only the process of writing, but the process of building a career. This particular generation of young people seems to be much more results-oriented than process-oriented. They are often looking more to the prize than to the experience of writing. I find that vexing at times, I have to admit. I believe that this generation is less self-aware than my peers and I were at that age. Young people in general are afraid of not being accepted and even more afraid of not being recognized, appreciated, and, down the road, hired. Down the road can mean six months; they believe that being hired is more important than anything else. They're so young and have so much consciousness about something of which they have no control.

What surprised my students the most is what I called upon them to think about on the first day of class. I gave them what I call a Writer's Test. They were asked to answer a list of ten questions in their notebooks in private. I never saw the answers. The questions ranged from the external consideration of how they assessed other people. Is it through their behavior, their dress, their conversation or gossip? And then I would go from these external questions to internal questions, such as, What kind of person do they like? What kind of person are they attracted to? What kind of person do they love? What kind of person do they wish they could fall in love with? And if there's a difference between these answers, why? They had to analyze their fears and their parents' greatest strengths and weaknesses. As they moved past those questions, they were called upon to explain why they wanted to be filmmakers or screen-writers. I realized for many of them that it was the first time that they've thought about this stuff.

It really was amazing. In bringing this to the first day of class, I was telling them that this is the fabric out of which they are going to be creating a story. It's not a question of merely writing about what you know, because I feel what each of us individually knows is really quite limited. It is what we feel that is so fathomless. So I encouraged them to really dig deep to find what it was that mattered to them. What were the stories they felt they were born to write—not the ones that they thought would sell, but the one they felt they were here on the planet to write. They needed to recognize that the world would be a colder, darker place if they didn't get those stories told. It meant finding out things about themselves that they might not really want to know. There's always the risk that maybe people won't like it, or it won't sell for a long period of time, or it may not be precisely what people are looking for. I also told them I'm a good deal more experienced than they are, and I fight the same battles. I have to ask myself the same questions every time I sit down to start something new. I know what it's like to look in the writer's mirror and see something I don't recognize, and I don't ever really want to go back to that space. Because that space is a space that's really hard to die with. You know how you say things are hard to live with? It would be hard to die with. Over the last several years, since 1994, mortality has become much more of a fac-tor in how I make decisions. I watched a number of people very close to me literally die. I know the kind of self-satisfaction and peace that I want to be a daily part of my life. Being led by the nose by the marketplace simply does not permit you to develop and enjoy that.

Building Bridges

In the early 1990s, Delle wrote, directed, and edited a 16mm/video futuristic narrative called Madame Secretary, *which won an Award of Excellence in the National Fine Arts Competition as well as a First Place in the Broadcast Education Association Competition. Like many of Delle's stories, this film brings together characters from diverse racial, social, and economic backgrounds, representing themes that are of great significance to her.*

The themes and circumstances that I create serve, first of all, my own personality and my own identity. Second, they attempt to build a bridge—not just between myself and the world, but between certain segments of society. You know, many of my stories deal with people of different colors blending together—people with different philosophies, people from different economic and educational backgrounds. This is probably an outgrowth of being an African-American who travelled extensively all over the country and among many different social circles. In fact, one of the poems in my upcoming one-woman show is called, *The Black Girl Who Travelled in White Circles.* Since my father was an officer in the military at a time when most other African-Americans were noncommissioned officers, the pressurized environments in which my brothers and I were raised put the racial integration of society and the internal integration of the individual very high on my list of issues that had to be examined on a regular basis. I believe that my writing, first of all, serves me and my spirit, and second, tries to address the issues that pertain to the wider society.

Free of Eden

Delle scripted Free of Eden *in 1991, and it would take eight years before her vision would be realized on the screen. Although many writers might have given up, Delle's faith kept her focused and able to sustain her love of writing through periods of discouragement and frustration. Her early training prepared her for such moments in her screenwriting journey.*

I wrote the first draft of that script in 1991. It aired eight years later, when the world was ready for it and the marketplace created the right niche for it. I could have been severely vexed by that delay, or I could believe that the themes and the truth I was chasing in that story in 1991 were so powerful and so universal and so timeless, that they would be just as ripe and true eight years later as they were in my imagination so many years ago. There's a certain kind of patience that's required, I believe, and an inner understanding of timing and a rightful moment in which a project will find its audience and visibility.

The Journey Continues

Even with the Free of Eden*'s success, Delle knows that she will continue to face challenges on her journey. She must still probe deeply into her decisions. Delle realizes that there will always be moments when she will have to work to balance what success means to her and what the prices are that one must pay for such success. Can she change the silhouette and remain true to herself?*

I'm asking myself a lot of questions right now. Because in the wake of *Free of Eden*'s broadcast and the success of having that film so well produced, directed, and performed, there are new opportunities that also challenge me to define myself or redefine myself. With every piece of work produced, your personal and professional identity shifts one way or the other. Because I have an interest in themes that include and also transcend black culture, there's always the danger of being pigeonholed. *Free of Eden* is actually the first and only all-black story I've ever told, and I know, talking to my manager and attorney, that the expectation from the industry is, of course, for more of the same. And so the challenge becomes, how do I capitalize on this success without being controlled by it?

This is an ongoing challenge for any screenwriter, any creative artist. As you know, it's not intrinsic to me. Bruce Willis has this problem; Kevin Costner has this problem. Every time an artist puts a piece of work out there, in a sense, he changes his silhouette in the world, in the industry, as well as in the minds of the public. If he wants to operate yet again, his responsibility is to make the proper choice. In terms of a writer, is this the right choice? What's the next story I'm going to tell? The one-woman play I'm working on is an attempt to dodge all of that. I am dying for the opportunity to do something creative that is not dependent on somebody saying yea or nay. Or here's the Delle Chatman we believe in. Be her.

One of my favorite visual aids that I used in my class was to talk about Kevin Costner, who won the Oscars for direction and best picture for *Dances With Wolves*. When *Robin Hood* came out two months later, they were talking about how his hair was getting thin and the Sheriff of Nottingham was acting him off the screen. Follow that with some personal tragedies in his life, and then a couple of films that don't work, and suddenly the world wants to know, who is this guy? In a lot of ways, he has become the very favorite whipping boy of many industry pundits. This culture is ruthless, full of a lot of extremes and spiritually treacherous.

I multitask my way through the labyrinth. In other words, I don't believe in closing any doors. I just met with a producer who has the rights to a novel that I would very much like to adapt. It's not an all-black novel, but it is certainly about a black protagonist going through a predominantly black experience. I am not at all afraid to make that my next gig if I get the assignment, because there are many aspects of the assignment that really intrigue me. I don't believe in running away from anything. I believe that I have to first ask myself what story is perched at the edge of my imagination, ready to come out, because that's going to be the easiest for me to write. At the same time, I have to be able to put my ear to the ground, not just the ground of the industry and the commercial agenda, but my ear to the ground in terms of my audience, to see what stories are ready to be told. I do believe that as artists, in a way, we are called upon to be ahead of our time.

For Delle, it is ironic that Hollywood is beckoning now that she no longer lives there.

You know what I kind of relate it to? It's sort of like a boyfriend who, the more you try to dump him, the more he chases you. I've experienced that; we all have. The more ruthlessly you treat him, the more he wants you.

Parting Words

I would like to remind writers that screenwriting is an art form in its infancy. It is new. Poetry, theater, prose, sculpture, painting—these arts have been around for centuries upon centuries upon centuries. Screenwriting is not even a hundred years old. Film is a hundred years old, but the first films didn't have scripts. So this is an art form in the cradle. If I could, I would get on my knees and beg people who believe they want to write films not to let commerce rule their imaginations, because that shortchanges the art form. It shortchanges audiences, and it shortchanges the artist. Unfortunately, because it costs so much money to get films made, and because there's so much money to be made from films, it's easy for screenwriters and screenplays to become agents of prostitution. Frankly, that breaks my heart. It makes me desperately concerned for my daughter, who loves movies already and will be going to movies ten and twenty years from now. I want her to be able to go to the theater and see not just stories that paint rosy pictures, but stories that give her an opportunity to understand something about life—to get a firmer grip on life and understand that life is meant to be celebrated and, at times, endured. Life is always a worthy experience. So much of what I see demeans what I feel this storytelling mode is capable of accomplishing and becoming. So I think my number one appeal is for screenwriters to let their imaginations and their souls rule their muse rather than their bellies.

●

CHAPTER 3

Am I Prepared for the Screenwriter's Journey?

If you stepped back and looked at it rationally, screenwriting is a completely
insane notion. You're on the edge of a precipice ready to jump and you have
no idea where you'll land—if you'll land—or splatter at the bottom.

Ken Mader

Have you considered if and how you have prepared for your journey into the world of screenwriting? Do you have an awareness of what skills you will have to perfect and what inner changes you may have to make? As we undergo any journey, personal or professional, we are called upon to prepare along the way. Some people believe that preparation is not necessary and that the desire for something is enough. Others believe that preparing will take the thrill away—they would rather be spontaneous and take what comes.

Nothing is a certainty in life, but one thing is true: important endeavors demand a commitment of energy, spirit, and declaration. Have you spent time learning about your own power of determination and ability to persevere, no matter what forces tempt you to wander away from your dream? Do you look for quick fixes and run out of energy when a project does not flow easily? Are there questions that you have left unanswered and are sure that somehow they will get taken care of, even though you do not have the slightest idea of how that will happen?

Ed Bernero hated being a cop, a career he felt duped into in the first place. "My wife and I were married at seventeen. I spent the first four years of our marriage in the Philippines in the Air Force, because it was the only job I could get at seventeen that could support a family. I wanted to be an air traffic controller and was actually screwed into becoming a cop. I went into what's called Open General. I didn't go in with a guaranteed job. The recruiter told me, you just tell them what you want to be when you get there. But by the time I was there, they had made me a cop, which is what they make everybody who goes in without a guarantee."

Although he did not recognize it at the time, Ed's ten years as a police officer would become part of his storytelling preparation. The people he met and the behaviors he observed would become the fuel for the stories he would create. The characters would come alive because of the experiences. Did Ed realize that all of his experiences would prepare him to create powerful stories and characters? Perhaps not on a conscious level. However, there is no question that as the cocreator of the television series *Third Watch* and as a staff writer for *Brooklyn South,* Ed brought all of his risk-taking ability, inner drive, and creative vision to the formation of his stories. As he so astutely expresses, everything in his life has been a preparation. In his case, he accepted the challenges even though he did not know exactly where they would lead him.

"If I look back, I think that almost everything in my life has prepared me for this," says Ed. "That's why I would suggest to other people to embrace every experience they have, because at some point, it's going to help them."

Despite youth-oriented myths surrounding Hollywood, there are writers who have had the courage, wisdom, and perseverance to challenge what so many others have chosen to believe. Ed was in his mid-thirties with three teenage children by the time he started writing for television. Perhaps his career as a police officer gave him the impetus to fight for what he wanted, and perhaps the support systems he embraced contributed to his ability to make the decisions that would bring him the success he is now experiencing. Whatever the order, preparation was the ultimate criteria for taking him to each new step of his journey. His respect for his own history and the life experiences he encountered encourage all who hear his story to believe that it is certainly more than luck that brings us to the table of success.

Forty-eight-year-old Anne Rapp, who began her screenwriting career only five years ago, believes that accumulated life experiences are essential for telling meaningful stories.

"Today, you see so many filmmakers manufacturing style. Listen, somebody who is twenty-two years old has to do a little bit more manufacturing than I have to do. They haven't had time to have their hearts broken or fall on their faces as many times as I have. This sounds a little corny, but I think I've already lived a full life. I'll never run out of stories to tell."

Anne's preparation for her own unique journey is something that is of great importance to her. Her willingness to honor her own voice, to use what she has learned about life and the adventures she has so ardently embraced, has already brought audiences the wonderfully human and interesting stories that lie in her imagination. Audiences are fortunate that she did not allow herself to buy into the worn-out myths that discourage many women past their twenties from claiming their dreams.

Screenwriters often do not believe that their histories, their observations, their life experiences, and their willingness to take risks are sufficient precursors for the screenwriting journey. Unfortunately, luck is too often credited for our success and accomplishments. Remember Donna Flint and the cartoon strip of the fat cat who loved to eat and hated to exercise? She was, at an early age, already putting images and words together almost like a storyboard, basing them on her own imaginative way of incorporating her life's adventures.

Almost all of the writers interviewed in this book had similar ways of presenting their stories as children, from creating comics to making Super 8 movies. While Donna had not openly uttered her aspirations of becoming a screenwriter, she would have specific childhood experiences that would influence and direct her screenwriting journey.

Adam Rifkin, on the other hand, was acutely focused on his goal at a tender age.

"I knew from the time I was a very little kid that I wanted to be a filmmaker," says Adam. "I loved movies all of my life, and I always wanted to make them as my job. I made movies as a kid with my friends and a Super 8 camera. I went to the Academy for the Visual and Performing Arts High School of Chicago and studied visual arts there. I used that as another place to make films. I made Super 8 movies there and continued to teach myself about making films."

Regardless of when you decided to claim your dream, you can be assured that you have already attained a certain level of preparation through your life experiences. It is critical to understand and accept that preparation for the career you wish to obtain is an ongoing process, no matter what level of success you have already reached. The more willing you are to ask the pertinent questions, the more you will be able come to grips with your concerns and recognize the challenges that will be yours to face.

Answering the following questions may encourage you to respect the inner preparation that you have already undertaken and help you evaluate the next path and the decisions you will be required to make as you proceed.

Ten Common Fears About Becoming a Screenwriter

1. I'm afraid to take my desire to be a screenwriter seriously.
2. I won't be able to share my plans with others without feeling embarrassed and awkward.
3. I'm not sure I have the necessary skills to go to the next step of the journey.
4. I'm not a free enough spirit to take my show on the road and be flexible when doors close and I must find alternative routes.
5. I won't be able to block out the expectations that others may place on me as I declare my mission.
6. I'm afraid to do the networking necessary to get ahead.
7. Jealousy and envy are always around the corner and can attack at any time. I'm not sure I'll be able to keep to my course if those I trusted no longer offer me support.
8. I'm not sure I'll be able to commit to the writing process on a consistent basis.
9. I'm afraid I won't be able to forge ahead when there seems to be nothing but obstacles in my way.
10. I'm not sure I'm the kind of person who can accept options that are not my first choice.

Will I Face the Fears?

In preparing for the journey, you have already taken some important steps in acknowledging that you are interested in pursuing the profession of screenwriting. You may have begun asking pertinent questions and found yourself marveling at the answers that evolved. With each step that you take toward the next goals, you will discover new questions that may cause confusion, doubts, fears, and hesitation. Preparation means taking the time to ponder, go inward, and be willing to listen to the answers that will surface and confront the fears that may arise.

Will I Challenge the Myths?

The beliefs which have been the foundation of how we live our lives often need a complete overhaul. They are the familiar messages which have guided our behaviors, yet they have often, without our even knowing it, brought tox-

Ten Common Myths About Preparing for the Screenwriting Journey

1. I have to have a degree from a prestigious film school to succeed.
2. There's no need for me to learn more about the craft once I understand the basic screenwriting format.
3. According to the trends, my real life experiences are too dull for the screenplays I want to write.
4. Taking the time to be a screenwriter means being lonely and separated from friends and family.
5. Since I have not been a writer all of my life, I have no right to think I can start now.
6. All I need in order to succeed is a good concept and the right contacts in the industry.
7. Anyone can write a script.
8. Most successful screenwriters got their breaks through pure luck.
9. I have to be young, white, and/or male to make it in the business.
10. I have to start this profession at an early age or I might as well forget becoming successful.

icity and discouragement in such large doses that very little creativity could emerge. The task of claiming the screenwriting journey is to replace these old, worn-out thoughts with new ones in which you will define yourself. The process of preparation will demand a great deal of energy in order to reestablish your inner truth.

Will I Take the Risks?

You have examined the fears and the myths that can interrupt the energy needed to write creatively. The preparation phase of the screenwriting journey means your desire to be seen and heard through your creative work must be taken seriously. Unless you are willing to push forward and put yourself in the arenas that will bring about visibility, the result you are seeking will not be activated. Reaching well beyond what you think is possible is your only hope for success. The gratification of having crafted a unique and powerful story can be yours if you are willing to take the risks.

Am I Willing To . . .

1. Solicit the help I need, even if I may be turned away?
2. Make the phone calls, write the query letters, and network on a consistent basis no matter what else is going on in my life?
3. Change the way I think about my creative abilities?
4. Learn everything I can about the screenwriting process?
5. Entertain many ways of being involved in the writing community?
6. Visualize being successful even when deterred by others?
7. Set the goals I need in order to succeed?
8. Take the time to celebrate the small accomplishments even if I haven't yet struck gold?
9. Disengage from people who project their negative thoughts on me rather than offer their support?
10. Walk the path alone if necessary?

●

CHAPTER 4

Ed Bernero: Writing for the Love of It

There was a lot of anxiety and fear. But for me, the bigger fear was not
doing it. I was terrified of being seventy and looking back and saying, when
I was thirty-five, what would have happened if I would have tried that?

Ed Bernero

The Journey Begins

*Ed Bernero married at the tender age of seventeen and soon became the father of three.
Since his job as a Chicago police officer didn't pay much, he often worked additional
jobs to give his children the educational opportunities he thought they deserved. In his
mid-thirties, Ed went on the midnight shift. When he came home in the morning, his
wife would be going to work while his children would be heading off to school. Ed suddenly found himself alone with time on his hands.*

I really had nothing to do, and people always told me, you should write a
book, you've got all these great stories. So I thought I'd give it a try. I tried to
write a novel, and it was tremendously bad. I found that I rambled. I would
start out telling the story I wanted to tell, then I'd find myself forty pages later
going, What the hell is this? It's not where I started. I was complaining to
another policeman, who's also an actor in Chicago, and he asked if I'd ever
tried to write a script, because you can't ramble in that format. So I got Syd
Field's book, *Screenplay,* and tried it and found that I really enjoyed the structure of screenwriting, because it kept me focused on what I had to do. I sort
of naturally took to it. I've heard a lot of people complain about structure, but
for me that's the whole reason that I do it. If I didn't have that structure, I

would find myself rambling again. I think at some level, I need the discipline of the structure to keep me on track.

Connecting With Others

Ed took a basic screenwriting course to learn formatting skills and read Syd Field's book on screenwriting. The more he worked at his craft, the more he wanted to make screenwriting his life's ambition. Nevertheless, hours upon hours of writing in isolation can be a lonely occupation.

Something that was very important, since I was trying to do this thousands of miles from Los Angeles, in a place that doesn't really believe in it, was a screenwriting network that I started. It was very encouraging to me to find that I wasn't the only person sitting in my basement trying to write a movie. I realized that there were other people doing this and that I wasn't tilting at windmills, and that it wasn't impossible, because there were other people who believed they could do it as well. This was greatly helpful to me, and I would recommend to anyone around the country, in a place that's not Hollywood-oriented, that they seek out other people who believe it's right, too, because there are times when it's very discouraging sending things out and having things come back or being ignored. Usually you never get anything back, you just never hear anything. That can be very discouraging if you don't hear other people saying, Hey, I'm going through that, too.

That group directly led to my being here in Los Angeles. One of the other founding members had met the NBC vice president at Northwestern University. She sent one of my scripts to him, and he called me to say they were interested in optioning the script, which they ultimately didn't do. But he asked me if I had ever tried writing a television script, because of my background as a policeman, and oddly enough, I had never even considered that television actually had scripts. When I sat down to write, it was always a feature. You never think you're going to write a television show. I told him that I hadn't, and he said, You should give it a try.

Testing the Waters

Ed proceeded to write a spec episode of Homicide *and sent it out. A week later, he had numerous agents wanting to represent him. He soon ventured to Los Angeles to "take some meetings."*

The biggest benefit to having been a cop starting out is that people will take meetings with you. You're different, I suppose. People go, Oh, he used to be a cop. Sure, I'll meet him.

There was a point where I came out in August of 1996 and had some really nice meetings with executives for studios and television shows. It was all very nice, but the unspoken thing was, But you don't live here.

When Ed returned to Chicago, he reflected on his life. He had worked on his craft, received good feedback on his work, and was ready to move forward on his journey. Although risk-taking is inherent in screenwriting, his greatest fears had to do with his job as a police officer.

My fear was going past ten years as a policeman. I really hated that job. I would sit in my underwear at the dining room table trying to figure out how not to go. I mean, I really hated it. And I sort of felt like ten years was a magical place you crossed over when you were thinking about retiring. You've been in a job over ten years, this is where you're going to be forever. And I actually left the police department a few days short of my ten years.

So that's when my wife and I had to decide whether or not we were going to take the step to move to Los Angeles. We ended up moving out here with no job. We had to take a leap of faith, not only that we believed in my talent and that this was something I could do, but we also felt that because she was a nurse and I was a policeman, we could both get a job here if necessary. We took the step in October of '96. We just quit our jobs and moved to Beverly.

Ed was fortunate to have a family that rallied around his decision, providing him with a very important support system.

The thing that astounds me about my family is that my wife quit her job and moved across the country with faith in me. I told her I don't believe I could have done that. I don't believe I could have given up everything I had and moved across the country with faith in somebody else. I did it because I had faith in me, which I think is infinitely easier than to put your trust and faith in someone else's ability. All my kids were in high school already, and I was asking them to leave their friends and to leave their whole lives and my daughter's soon-to-be graduating class. They were very resistant to it at first.

Policemen don't get paid much money, but we wanted them in private schools and to have whatever we could give them, so at times in their lives, I had four or five jobs. I would sleep maybe an hour before going to another job. So several days after we talked about a move, they sat me down. They told me they had gotten together and decided that because I had done all that for them, they would do this for me. I was crying. It was unbelievable. They said, All your life you've given up stuff for us, so we'll do this for you. They've actually become quite happy with it. I'm a much different person than I was then. I'm a much happier person. Our standard of living has changed quite a bit. Two of my kids are in college now, and I don't know how we would have paid for it if we weren't here.

Before leaving Chicago, Ed's large, extended family planned a going-away celebration. Although the event was full of hope and happiness, there was also some trepidation.

We had this terrible fear the day my family had a huge party for us in Chicago. People came from out of town to go to this party. My parents rented a hall, and at one point during the party, my wife and I were alone. I said, You know if this doesn't work, we're going to have to come back. My father was good about that. He said, If this doesn't work, don't think you can't come back here. They were all just impressed that we actually did it. Another reason for us to have done this is, we both want our children to see that it's important to follow a dream. Because it's sort of a unique way of making a living, or not something that everyone thinks is the way you should go. But if it's your dream, you have to follow it. Maybe it will work and maybe it won't, but at least I know that if this hadn't worked, I wouldn't be an old man saying I wish I would have tried.

Life in Hollywood

Shortly after moving to Los Angeles, Ed worked on an episode of Steven Bochco's NYPD Blue, *after which he was added to the writing staff of Bocho's* Brooklyn South. *In 1998, Ed moved on to the John Wells (*ER*) drama* Trinity *for NBC, where he was a story editor and writer for the show. Currently, Ed is a producer and writer for NBC's* Third Watch, *which he cocreated with John Wells.*

John Wells, who has become a very good friend of mine, certainly knows how to do medical drama. So with his doing a lot of the paramedic stuff and me doing the cop stuff, it's a great marriage. The show is like *ER* outside. Everything that happens before *ER*.

Ed acknowledges that there are certain rigors inherent to television writing. If a writer is not prepared to meet stringent deadlines, problems can ensue.

Right now, we're in the point in our season where it's pretty easy. We haven't started filming yet. We start filming in two weeks. So we have sort of this lux-ury time where we're working on four different episodes. Now, a month and a half or two months from now, we'll be thoroughly under the gun. Every eight days, we'll have to come up with a new script that's able to be shot. If a member of our staff is not able to do that, it's apparent very quickly, and it's very problematic, because then the other people on the staff have to fix what they do.

Despite the rigors, Ed loves his profession. While many writers for television aspire to write features, he takes an opposite point of view.

One of the side benefits to having the success I've had in television is that I've been offered movie work. I'm sure I'll do some, but right now, I'd rather focus on this. I'm one of the only people who works for television that doesn't wish they were writing for films instead.

Ed believes that writers will have a better chance of success if they are truly prepared for the opportunities that may arise. He's had the courage to say "no" to potentially lucra-tive opportunities, because he felt such decisions would better serve him in the long run.

This year, a company wanted me to develop a show of my own. And I told this company that I'm not ready. It wasn't an easy thing to say, because it's very ego-stroking. Hey, you could start your own TV show. But I firmly believe that if you do something that you're not ready for and you fail, you're not going to get another chance. Instead of being at the bottom of the stairs, you've put yourself in the basement. Now, you have to get back up to the bot-tom. So I had to say I'm not ready. I don't know enough about the business side of running things to do it myself. I know it's a tremendously hard thing to accept, but I think some writers would be much better off waiting to take on certain things until they're really ready.

The Need to Keep Telling Stories

Ed has no doubt that his destiny was to tell stories, regardless of whether or not he had achieved his current success.

Being a storyteller is something I have to do. It's become my therapy. I found in looking back over old things that I've written that I was telling stories I didn't even know I was telling. I was telling stories about my childhood, I was telling stories about my parents. If I were still in Chicago, still in a patrol car,

I would still be writing. I would be sending things out and hoping I could be doing it as a living, because the family has to eat. But unless someone can honestly say that if they never make it they would still do it, then they shouldn't do it. They should look for something else. One of the greatest highs I've ever gotten was the first time I wrote "The End." I was never good at finishing things—I'm the consummate starter. And the first time I wrote "The End" was an even bigger high than getting my first job in this business. It wasn't a very good script, but it didn't matter. It was a story I wanted to tell, and I sat down and I told the story. Unless you can look in the mirror and say that that is supremely satisfying to you, then I think you should look for something else. I've met with unbelievable success in this business. I mean, I've been so lucky, but I still get kicked in the balls all the time. If I didn't have the joy of what I was doing I would be unhappy. So unless you can find that joy in your own work, in your own art, get away from this business, because there are days that are really bad. But even those are still better than my best days as a policeman!

Parting Words

It doesn't matter where you're from. This entire business starts with writing. If you're a talented writer and believe in yourself, just keep sending stuff out and they will find you, because they have to. It's not a choice; they have to find you. It's almost like scripts are all diamonds, and this town is mining and mining and mining, and if you'll just be patient, they'll find yours.

I'd probably like to leave with my favorite quote of all time. It's by Eleanor Roosevelt. "The future belongs to those who believe in the beauty of their dreams." That is how I've tried to live my life and how I want my children to live and how I think everyone should live. If you believe in your dream and follow it, at some level, you will achieve it. It may not be exactly what you think is going to happen, but you will get there as long as you don't lose sight of it and don't stop believing in it.

●

CHAPTER 5

What Lies Ahead If I Continue the Screenwriter's Journey?

I think you always have to hope against hope. I'm as upset by rejection
as the next person. Just don't take it personally and move forward.

Noah Baumbach

Does the process of preparation ever stop? Is it enough to have declared that the screenwriting journey is for you? Declaring yourself a screenwriter can be the most difficult thing in the world. You have now made yourself visible. It is an awesome responsibility fraught with people's projections of how "only a few talented ones will make it." How could you imagine that you could be successful in such a competitive field, without an advanced degree in film? Of course, you will have to relocate to Los Angeles and heaven knows how expensive that will be! How will you support yourself?

Question after question will bombard your mind, and well-meaning friends and family will only add to the confusion you are experiencing. The critics and those who envy your ability to claim what you really desire may find ways to make you question what you believed you really wanted. Those closest to you may not take you seriously and may even attempt to sabotage your every effort with their skepticism and pessimistic view of what it takes to succeed. Although they may want you to achieve your goals and be happy, they may be struggling with their own fears for your safety and well-being. Others may tell you that you are being unrealistic and may propose that you write as a hobby, since it is so difficult to make a living as a screenwriter.

What lies ahead are multiple opportunities to reject the negative messages that have a way of taking over your creative energy. There will also be an understanding of the importance of networking and of forming and belonging to support systems that can affirm rather than destroy. You will need to recognize that reaching out to others can make a tremendous difference, although it may be awkward and perhaps even intimidating at first. Isolation can breed discontent and is usually the downfall of any creative process. As you proceed on your journey, it will be important to remain connected with those people who are truly interested in your success.

Stories have always been the powerful connectors of history and the connecting links to recognizing what we all share as human beings. Writers who keep themselves "shut out" from opportunities to meet others who share similar goals will, in the long run, face more restrictions and will experience fewer moments of being supported, and may even find themselves retreating further and further away from the stories and characters they dreamed of creating.

All the writers in this book have had to face specific rigors as they claimed their dreams. The challenges were similar, the fears apparent, and the risks they knew they must take were almost universally felt.

"Probably the biggest belief I had to challenge coming from the Midwest is that nobody there thinks this is actually a job that you can do," says Ed Bernero. "Here in Los Angeles, it's sort of a company town, and if you tell people you're a television producer or a writer, it's like saying you work at a car factory. But in Chicago, that's completely unheard of. Yeah, sure, you're going to write movies. I think almost any artistic endeavor is like that. If you want to be a sculptor people will go, Oh, that's cute. Go sculpt something. Just don't quit your job."

Ed's declaration was out in the open. For some, the declaration must be kept quiet, for family traditions preclude such visibility. Screenwriter/filmmaker Paul Wei had to face this very different challenge, as he was unable to admit his passion for writing to his own family.

"For a long time, I was not working," says Paul. "I was just doing an odd job here and an odd job there in order to finish my screenplay. I didn't tell my Dad I was out of a job. So every day, I would have to pretend I was going to work, and my Dad would ask, Are you working today? And I would say, Of course I'm going to work. I would go out to the library to finish my screenplay. If my Dad knew I was out of work and not making any money, then he'd really be worried. It made me write faster, because I wanted to get the script done. So it put a lot of pressure on me to write as much as I could. He never found out, but when he talks to his friends, he always feels more humble than he should. He feels kind of embarrassed. A lot of Chinese people who come here, within a few years, they become very, very successful. They've bought a house and this and that, or have their own business. And here's his son who's still struggling and living at the minimum."

Vietnamese-born screenwriter/director Tony Bui shared similar experiences.

"The parents that I had were like, You can't do that stuff. You need to make a living. Who do you know that's a filmmaker? No one. They would always say, You're an embarrassment with our friends. All their kids are going to Berkeley and Stanford and all that stuff. All their friends had kids doing something else."

Despite the negativity, Tony was determined to claim his vision of becoming a filmmaker. As his dream became realized through the success of his films *Yellow Lotus* and *Three Seasons,* starring Harvey Keitel, Tony's parents became very proud of his accomplishments.

Each person who will find the courage to claim his creative voice will, like Don Quixote, find the windmills he will fight. All of the writers we interviewed told us, with overwhelming echoes, of the importance of connecting with others who would have the ability to mirror them and to bring them words of encouragement when they were the most needed.

"I think it's really important for writers to have support, and who better to give you support than other writers," says Ken Mader, who now heads the Chicago Screenwriters Network originally founded by Ed Bernero. "We all go through the same things while we're writing, and it's helpful to have a little community like that. We've also structured our group as a networking entity. You never know who in the group is going to become successful, which has happened. It continues to happen. So we're constantly expanding our network, which is beneficial to everyone in the group."

Perhaps the most traditional preparation comes in the form of studying our chosen craft, whether formally or independently. For writers like Josefina Lopez, the next step in the creative journey meant a formal educational commitment.

"I didn't want to study it formally when I was an undergraduate," says Josefina. "There were people getting their masters in playwriting, and I thought, Why don't you just do it? If you're an architect, you need to learn it. But a writer? It can come easily without studying. But I'm so glad I'm studying it now instead of just staring at a blank page going, 'Come out! Come out!' Those magic moments no one can teach you, but at least, if you have the structure and you take yourself to the edge, maybe it will come easier."

By the time Sharon Y. Cobb moved to Los Angeles, she felt that she had a strong foundation upon which to build her career.

"The craft of screenwriting is totally different than any other form of fiction writing," says Sharon. "But I had a real solid base. I'd been writing for several years before I came to L.A. It gave me the foundation I needed to build the house on, so to speak. Once I came to L.A., my background in marketing and public relations assisted me a great deal with networking. The networking is everything out here, especially in the beginning. That's really where the key to my success has been. Not only do I love the writing, and I write fast and I write well, but the networking was so, so important."

When she was a university professor, Delle Chatman urged her students not to move to Los Angeles unprepared.

"I've advised students not to go west until they have two screenplays under their arm that they would live or die by," says Delle. "If their dream comes true and Screenplay Number One sells, the very next question's going to be, 'What else have you got?' And if they don't have anything, in a sense, they look a little less serious than if they've got more than one script to which they are committed. I don't discourage them. I don't encourage them. Because ultimately, I think people have to carve out their own path. I urged them to get into a writer's group, so that they have some place other than the marketplace in which to check out their ideas and try new things and a way to receive feedback on their work. I want them to continue writing, to be willing to develop a network of fellow artists whose opinions they can trust. It's important that their support system be understanding and provide a safe place for them to explore and examine what they want to write."

Although Ed Bernero has never participated in workshops and has only taken one basic screenwriting course in his life, he does believe it is important to learn the craft if you are serious about developing it as a long-term career.

"Because of the occasional well-publicized spec script that gets sold for millions, people think that that's the thing to do to get in this business," says Ed. "Most of the people who have long careers have prepared for the business by learning the craft, learning what we do, taking the time to watch everything that they can possibly watch. We had an interesting period when we first got to L.A. and my agent told me that my job was to watch television. This led to very interesting conversations with my wife—'I have to watch television, I'm working.' Which is not a bad gig, I'll tell you. Though I have to say, some of it was pretty bad!"

As writers progress along their own unique paths to success, each will find new and expansive ways to prepare for the steps ahead. As we heard from

Josefina Lopez, obtaining an MFA seemed like the most natural decision for her to make. For Ed Bernero, his continued learning came in the shape of watching many and varied television programs and integrating the styles and nuances that give the powerful shows their magic.

Many writers believe that the best way to improve their craft is to keep writing. Paul Wei adheres to this philosophy and is committed to his own screenwriting progress.

"If you do want to write, you just have to keep writing," advises Paul. "Nothing will come out unless you keep writing and keep writing. And don't feel defeated if you cannot write for one day or two days or even two weeks. Sometimes, you just have to stop for a while and then pick it up and do it again. Just never get discouraged."

There will, of course, always be the writers who declare that screenwriting is important to them, yet somehow they cannot find the time to actually sit down and write their stories.

Betty Hager grew up in a small Alabama shrimp-boat town called Bayou La Batre. She wrote a wonderful children's book series based on her experiences of growing up in Bayou La Batre in the 1930s, which she later adapted into screenplays. Betty describes a young woman she knows who has stories to tell, but finds all the right reasons not to do the work of writing them.

"I know a young girl who writes well, but always has to work to make a living. She hasn't learned that somehow, you have to make the time to sit there at your computer and write. She says, I'm going to write, I'm going to be a writer someday. But she's not doing it. I know she gets tired after working all day. It's difficult to do that. On the other hand, there is always time if you make it, even on a Saturday or Sunday. It can also be the most uplifting thing you can do. Probably some of those things that are worrying her a great deal in her life would go if she kept writing."

Is it really fair to expect that one's creativity will flow continuously without end? When the writing does not come easily, or the challenges ahead seem too daunting to proceed to the next step, is there a way to pause without giving up? These questions are dealt with more specifically in Part III.

It is important to remember that wanting to accomplish something worthwhile will necessitate hard work and the willingness to experience struggles from time to time. There can also be the gratification of knowing that you have been able to make difficult decisions. To fulfill what you envision for yourself is a process that can last a lifetime. It is the determination to fight for what is your true voice, for the mission you have set, that can bring immense satisfaction and a renewed belief in your inner strength.

Claiming the dream, preparing to travel on the many roads that will be

Ten Common Fears about Continuing the Screenwriting Journey

1. I need to know what lies ahead, or I won't feel in control and won't be able to manage any surprises.
2. If I write scripts that aren't popular, I won't make an impact.
3. I can't commit to an entire life of writing if there is a possibility I will never succeed.
4. I will never be recognized as a serious writer.
5. I'm afraid to be too optimistic about my future success.
6. I won't be able to do all of the work required to reach my goals.
7. Somewhere along the way, I will lose my own voice and be tempted to write for the trends.
8. I am not a competitive person and don't feel comfortable asserting myself.
9. Because I'm not a patient person, I'm afraid that waiting for results will really burn me out.
10. Some people can live with anxiety and do very well. Since I need a lot of calmness in my life, maybe this isn't the right career for me.

presented to you, and going forth with very little knowledge of what the future holds are requirements for any creative venture.

It may not be easy to face the mirror and ask the difficult questions we have presented throughout this book. It is, however, a necessary component of the process of discovering and evaluating your screenwriting career. You may initially be discouraged, for some of the questions will not have immediate answers. These questions are meant to help you to reaffirm your decision to write meaningful and powerful stories. They are designed to encourage you to fantasize and luxuriate in your imagination. Each of your answers will stimulate additional questions, which will elicit answers perhaps never before expressed. You may discover new and creative ways of problem-solving and awaken your sensitivities to what lies ahead on your amazing journey.

Will I Face the Fears?

You have already taken several monumental steps in realizing that screenwriting is the joy of your life and that writing stories from the very depth of your being will be the way in which your passion will be felt. There will be a great temptation to want to know what lies ahead. You will want to go faster than you are prepared to, and taking it step by step may lose its luster after a

Ten Common Myths About Continuing the Screenwriting Journey

1. Once I've declared my dream, I have to write a winning script.
2. You can only make it if you were born to be a writer, as opposed to someone who chose the profession of writing later in life.
3. If I take a break from writing, I can never come back to it.
4. If I'm really committed and talented, I should not feel so many hesitations.
5. If many of my scripts are rejected, I should reconsider my choice of becoming a screenwriter.
6. Writing groups will only remind me of all the competition I have to face.
7. Sharing my fears with others will make me look weak.
8. Other writers who aren't connected or successful can't help my career.
9. I can't make screenwriting a priority if I have family and/or financial obligations.
10. Instead of writing new scripts, I'll have more of a chance for success if I put all my energy into marketing the first one.

while. Living in the future will add to the anxiety, intensity, and misgivings that creep in and often occupy a space that is much too close for comfort. Dread may wipe out those glorious feelings, and there will need to be a way in which your voice can become stronger and stronger. Remember that fear is a natural component of the human condition. It is only when it paralyzes us and we can find no release that it must be questioned. When you reach for the stars for the first time, expect that frightening moments may accompany you—not forever, just for a brief moment as you travel to what lies ahead.

Will I Challenge the Myths?

During this phase of the journey, your biggest challenge will be to put the future expectations aside as you strive to stay in the present. There will be many times when you will feel compelled to hurry the process. You will have had enough of sending script after script to people who you do not know and wondering if they have ever received them when the responses were lacking. You will feel angry at the futility you may experience, and you will need to know where to reach for the support systems to fill up your creative and emotional gas tank. You will have to combat envy and jealousy, as you hear about the instant successes. The biggest myth you will have to face head on is the one that insists that only the "lucky" and "the chosen few" will succeed. You have claimed your desire to be a screenwriter. Now, you must confront the old beliefs and go forward, setting goal after goal toward attaining what you have stated is the most important venture of your life.

Will I Take the Risks?

You have written your first, second, or maybe third script and feel like you have "arrived." You feel that now you deserve to rest and wait for them to be accepted. You are not certain if you want to keep putting forth the effort to keep writing unless someone gives you the go-ahead. It is hard work to write a screenplay. Life is short, and you do not have a lot of time to waste.

Unfortunately, the first few scripts are just the beginning. Many writers often believe that after the first screenplay has been created, the risks have been put to rest, and now it will become a waiting game. As any successful person will tell you, taking risks is part of an ongoing process, not an end in itself. Each creative venture you take will introduce new risks. Every time you put yourself on the line will be a test of your stamina, both figuratively and literally. It's the line that's drawn between those who will succeed and those who are not willing to take the necessary risks to claim the dream that they really desire.

Am I Willing to . . .

1. Choose writing over an easier way to make a living?
2. Relocate if it means empowering my next steps?
3. Ask questions during the writing process?
4. Rewrite a script as many times as necessary to attain my desired story?
5. Stay with a story and not relinquish it when I get stuck?
6. Face unpredictable and overwhelming challenges?
7. Regroup and go back to basics when necessary?
8. Check out assumptions that are told as truths?
9. Seek help when stuck, discouraged, or doubtful of the next step?
10. Accept that trying to know all the answers ahead of time is not necessarily beneficial or possible?

●

CHAPTER 6

Tony Bui: From Inner Vision to Outer Dream

If you don't follow external influences, your interior
will give you a much more powerful film.
Tony Bui

The Journey Begins

Tony's initial interest in films and filmmaking began when he was in high school. As
he went on to college, he developed some unique perspectives on the process of writing
and directing.

I would read other directors' bios, and I'd find out they had been interested
in films since they were eight years old. Sometimes, I feel like I got into it late
in the game, only because I was already in high school when I kind of knew
what I wanted to do. But at the same time, I was only fifteen or sixteen. I
definitely had the confidence to know what I loved and had the confidence
to do it. But no one shared my interest. Even now, none of my friends work
for film or television.

I grew up reading novels and books, which has been an influence on me.
I often write stories before I do screenplays, so I can do my own adaptations.
Really, the screenplay to me in and of itself is not an end. It's a means to get
to an end, when I actually get to make the film. The screenplay is just a way
to show how the scenes will occur. It's a blueprint for what will be shot, and

I don't really enjoy reading them. I'm sure people who have spent their lives writing screenplays will totally disagree with me.

When I went to film school, I fell in love with European films and lesser-known films. Those films were so different. As scripts, there was probably nothing on the page, but certainly there was a vision that was part of a whole process. It wasn't like the script was totally written out and then they made the film. That's one thing about film school—the films you get to see have nothing to do with the films that you go pay eight dollars to see. Not only is there a passion, you feel like there's a voice, and you can tell the voice is different.

I always thought of myself as a filmmaker. It was all linked together. If I came up with an idea, I did eventually want to see it on film, so it was natural for me to sit down and write out the idea and then eventually go make it. But I never thought, Okay, I'm a screenwriter. The same for directing. I would never take someone else's work. I remember graduating from college and going out into the world and people saying, Okay, what do you want to do? Do you want to be a writer, do want to direct? I was kind of confused by that. It was all one thing to me. It was all one linear process for me. It wasn't like I felt obsessed with writing and wanting to be a screenwriter. In fact, I actually stay away from screenwriting books. I'm afraid of ruining the process that I'm comfortable with. I don't write in any kind of linear fashion. I've maybe taken two screenwriting classes that I sort of had to do. It really comes from the fact that most screenplays that I read bother me.

Tony shies away from traditional screenwriting formats and structures, instead focusing on the core issues of his story.

There are screenwriters who are worried about the first act, the second act, and the third act. I know a lot of people who position their pages so that the first forty pages is act one, whatever's act two, whatever's act three. They even break it down to, at this point something happens, at this point something happens, a character arc happens. I don't know what those acts mean to me. It becomes too clinical, and I would never get into that.

Often screenwriters spend more time trying to get that formula to what they think is the right formatting, the right number of words, and all that kind of stuff, and they think that's what will make a successful screenplay. I think a better avenue is to give up spending all the time thinking about the "how-tos" and spend more time thinking about what they're actually writing about. Trying to say things on a personal level, to get in touch with your own life, or to try to have your own voice. Of the many scripts that I've seen through classes when I was at the University or that friends have sent me, at least 80 percent of the people seem to be trying to find that formula for success, and to me, that's a weird thing to do.

A Sense of Identity

A turning point for Tony came in 1992, when, at the age of nineteen, he returned to Vietnam for the first time since he was a young child. It was an event that would change his life and impact his whole perspective of filmmaking.

That trip really changed my life, because it suddenly made me care about different things. It suddenly gave me a sense of identity. It gave me a sense of a voice and gave me the confidence to use my own thoughts. I'd never left home before that, so it was the first time I had travelled outside the United States. It's a very poor country. There's no water, no electricity.

After the first trip, I would return every six to eight months. As that was going on, I was watching all of these wonderful films in college, in which the filmmakers' personal voices were very apparent. That's what really made it happen for me, when those two things converged. I was able to find my own voice and have the confidence to proceed. I think that if I'd never gone back to Vietnam, I would be a totally different filmmaker right now. I'd be making shoot-'em-up films or action films.

All of those experiences really came down to one thing. It all came back to something that spoke a truth that I identified with. That's what I found was the most important thing, to be true to myself in watching others do it in their work. That's the strongest thing I've carried with me.

Facing the Fear

Tony prefers to do his writing from midnight until six in the morning, while the rest of the world sleeps. Although not traditional in many regards, Tony shares a common element with many other successful screenwriters—the courage to step into the unknown.

One thing that's worked for me as I go through the process, which I think I carry into my life, is not being afraid to go into that which you fear or to venture into the unknown. I find myself, especially now, getting into genres I've never written before. I'm very fearful of it, and yet, that fear has really engaged me and is part of why I want to try it.

I meet so many people who are afraid to take a step into areas that they don't have confidence in. Whether it's writing in a different genre, whether it's a collaboration, or writing about a particular subject matter. I think a lot of people are held back by fear. I find it very rewarding to really embrace that fear and actually feed off of it. With my current writing and future things that really make me scared, I think, Gosh, I'm scared of that, but I still continue to walk into it. You can be empowered by it, you know. Look around and see what you're really afraid of in the process, whether it's the genre or whatever. Then really go for it.

Parting Words

As Tony expressed earlier, he did not always have the support of his family behind him. Nevertheless, he feels fortunate that he was able to start out as a young man with few responsibilities.

I was able to start out at an early enough stage where I was able to put it all out on the line. I was very fortunate that I didn't have a family to support. My family would say, But you're dirt poor, and I would say, You know, I don't care. I don't care about having to work minimum wage to support doing what I love to do. I don't have any dependents to worry about. I have only myself to take care of. And when you have nothing to lose or no one to support, that's very empowering, because it allows you take risks and put it all on the line.

I was twenty-three years old when I wrote and made *Three Seasons*. I remember thinking afterward, Wow, how did this thing ever get made? You're in America, the film is eighty percent in Vietnamese, you're shooting in a foreign country where no one had ever shot before. How are you going to get insurance, bonds, actors that want to be in it, and interest studios to put money into it? I think I was young enough not to know any better, young enough not to care. I had nothing to lose anyway. I was able to do what I wanted to do. For all the people out there who are young and just starting out, this is the time to really take these risks, when you think about it.

Summary

What is it about someone who has claimed his dream that makes us sit up and take notice? Is it all that rare, or do we just come in such little contact with this type of person? We do not often give ourselves the permission to stop and ask ourselves if we are doing what we really want and love to do. Why is that? What elements exist for those who seem to have the courage to do anything they choose, while others struggle and can't seem to release their creative energy?

All the writers included in Part I shared unique ways in which they decided to claim their dreams. No two writers have experienced the same journey, yet there was a common thread—they had to write! They were not willing to sacrifice their love of writing for very long. They felt empty without it and knew that nothing would really make any sense if they had to compromise on their dreams. For some, the journey has been lonely and isolating. For others, strong support systems were in place, making risk-taking more manageable. Nevertheless, they all agreed that the screenwriting journey means facing the fears that often loom larger than life, as well as needing to keep a constant check on the myths that can be so paralyzing.

Most of us have experienced the kind of fear that makes us feel as if we're on the edge of a precipice. But does the alternative, although apparently safer, really feel any better in the end? How does someone who didn't dare to claim his dream feel when he sees others pursuing and achieving theirs? As Ed Bernero expressed, such a person may end up haunted with regrets.

In Part I, we addressed the importance of asking questions in order to uncover the meaning of what the screenwriting journey holds for you. Without the desire to probe and discover your personal truths, it is more than likely that you will miss the importance of the process of your own inner discovery. The questions we raised are meant to help stimulate new ways of discovering the meaning that writing has for you. Delving into the purpose of screenwriting and evaluating your motives, determination, and ability to struggle through hard times will provide you with new awarenesses and answers that will help guide your next steps.

You have been asked to evaluate your own inner strength, the resilience you will need in order to be successful, and the courage you hold inside of you to know your own truth. You have been given an opportunity to crystallize your thoughts about this exciting journey, and have been offered survival tools for those challenging moments when you feel alone and scared about the future.

Dare to ask yourself the questions, and know that within you lies the answers that will bring you to the destined place of your self-expression.

You, like the writers who have shared their journeys with us, have stories that must be told. They will have the power to help us to feel connected and linked. They have the ability to entertain, to make us cry, to honor our vulnerabilities, and to inspire us. What could be more meaningful than that!

●

The Screenwriter's Journey: Questionnaire for Self-Evaluation

The following questions are meant for introspection and affirmation. They are proposed for the benefit of clarity and a better understanding of how to proceed when approaching the "stuck" places and those moments when reevaluation is needed.

1. Why have I chosen screenwriting as my profession?
2. How do I intend to reach my goals? What training do I need, and what resources are available to me?
3. Am I considering this career on a whim, or is this the most important dream of my life?
4. What are some of the sacrifices I may need to make now and in the future?
5. What adjustments do I need to make to find the time and place in which to write productively?
6. What have I been willing to do to prepare for the length of time it may take to become a known entity in the screenwriting world?
7. In what ways am I determined and willing to work hard at my craft without relying on assurances about when or if I will find success?
8. How will I cope with the moments of solitude and loneliness I may experience during my journey?
9. What will I do if my scriptwriting falters and I have nothing to fall back on?
10. How will my decision to become a screenwriter affect other areas and relationships in my life?
11. If I have to turn to others for support, how will I feel about being dependent on them?
12. I have always operated well alone. How will I feel if I need to go out of my way to connect with other writers?
13. If I pursue the screenwriting journey, how will I be able to pursue my goals in the way I want?
14. What will happen if I decide to quit my job and give scriptwriting my full concentration? What will happen if I don't make it or find that I don't like writing in this format?
15. How will I maintain the staying power to deal with the rigors of this profession?
16. How will I be able to handle waiting for weeks, months and maybe even years before selling a script?

17. How will my personality traits help or hinder the attainment of my goals?
18. How will I stay true to the genre I love, regardless of popular trends?
19. How will I adjust to the fact that in the film and television industry, nothing is certain and everything is subjective?
20. If I decide to move to Hollywood, how will I cope with the competition that exists everywhere?
21. What are the benefits of staying where I am and perfecting my writing skills on my own versus moving to Los Angeles prematurely?
22. How will I face the fact that I may have to give up friends and relationships that are providing only negative reinforcement?
23. In what ways am I flexible or rigid when it comes to creative problem solving?
24. What strengths can I draw upon from my past to give me the courage to face the moments of difficulty and struggle that the screenwriting journey may present?
25. What commitments am I willing to make to claim my dream, no matter what obstacles may arise or what challenges I may need to face?

PART II

Creating Meaningful Stories and Believable Characters

DONNA FLINT

Memoir of a Screenwriter—Act I

I never did find the guru who could propel my career to stardom. I did, how-ever, manage to disentangle myself from the savage greenery of my West Virginia holler. My husband and I moved to Chicago, where I soon joined a screenwriting group. Connecting with other writers brought me a certain sense of comfort—if my dreams were so crazy, at least I wasn't alone. Was I hanging out with a bunch of kooks, or were our ludicrous aspirations actually possible? Fortunately, we never tested the possibilities under a full moon.

I became a fairly prolific writer and managed to complete a number of screenplays. My writing improved with each new script. I had the format and structure down to an art and would beam with pride whenever my first act break hit precisely on page thirty. No doubt about it, I was becoming a pro.

One day, I attended a workshop in which the presenter stressed that our best work would come from writing what we knew. What I knew was that this bozo had his head up a dark crevice. Duh, like I could really get anyone interested in a script about dullsville in the holler! Maybe I could call it "Mystery of the Disappearing Cat." I rolled my eyes at another workshop par-ticipant. For some reason she didn't smile back, instead giving me the old raised eyebrow. I immediately pegged her as a novice.

Later a group of us went out for drinks. Everyone else seemed really inspired. I sipped my frothy brew and contemplated my own work. I had recently written two homicide thrillers in which I had put endless hours of research at the library and had talked to several police officers for the sake of authenticity. But what did I really know about being a cop? Not the job description, but the essence of the profession? What did it feel like to put your life on the line every day? My biggest danger was realizing I'd forgotten the diaper bag an hour from home when my two-year-old let go of a stink bomb.

A cold, dank feeling crept into my being. The more I tried to push this discomfort down, the more it bobbed to the surface, along with the ugly truth—although my scripts were well-written, they were not unique. They were not drawn from my personal experiences, and they were certainly not written from the heart.

When I got home, I was utterly depressed, thinking I should stick my scripts in the diaper bag for road emergencies. I sat down in front of my computer and stared at the blank screen. Then something caught my eye. The old notebook of stories I'd written when I was a child was tucked in a bookshelf to my left. I pulled out the dog-eared thing and flipped through the pages. I realized in looking through the stories that I tended to write the same kinds of plots over and over again, just with different characters and locations. They were essentially stories about lost or abandoned children trying to find a home.

I'd moved around a lot as a kid and had always longed for a sense of place. I was one of those rare nonmilitary brats without a hometown. As an adult, I'd kept moving from here to there, always feeling the itch, but never scratching that place I could call "home."

That got me thinking. Were there other people who roamed the world feeling isolated or disconnected from others? What made them like that? More importantly, what made me like that? Yikes, now I was really starting to sound like the kook. But what if . . . just what if there was this character who was searching for a sense of place? Maybe on one of her stops, she begins to get close to someone and it scares her, so she decides to move on again. . . .

It sure didn't sound like a Hollywood story, but the next thing I knew, my fingers were skipping across the keyboard, and I wasn't even thinking about what should happen on page thirty.

●

CHAPTER 7

How Believable Characters Give a Story Its Meaning

The first draft is like a slab of clay that I throw together in some kind of form. In the second draft, I keep adding and gain more clarity. Clarity comes as you know what your story is. It's wonderful, but also frightening to start something, and it's easy to go, 'Oh, God, there's nothing there!' But you keep writing new drafts, knowing it will come together somehow.

Josefina Lopez

We are living in a time when people are feeling less connected. Technology has advanced faster than our minds can comprehend, often leaving us more isolated and confused. Out of the need for more human contact and communication, people are scrambling in desperation to the technology that promises more, but does not deliver what the human spirit is crying out to experience. The human presence seems to be a smaller and smaller commodity that is being rapidly replaced by the automated "human" voice—the robotics, automated answering services, computers, e-mail, voice mail, etc. Comfort and convenience now steer the services that, in the past, allowed for human contact. These technologies relentlessly promise to soothe, to comfort, and to ease life's complications. In truth, they drive people further away from one another.

As the promise of progress through technology invades everyday life, it becomes more evident that people are searching for ways in which to connect to one another. The more technology, the more the need to be seen and to be heard. It is a cycle that has many people longing for the visibility that seems to have eluded them.

There is a great need for human connection and for ways in which we can all experience the joy of knowing that others truly understand us and accept the human qualities we represent. It is not an accident that more and more people are seeking films that offer the opportunity for "mirroring," which is so desperately needed. Whether this mirroring is done through comedy, suspense, drama, fantasy, or adventure, people are responding to the stories in which they can, in some way, relate to that which parallels their own lives.

Technology is a powerful tool that offers the gift of improving the quality of life. It also has the power to alienate and to make people believe that they are unimportant and without value. There is no question that nothing replaces the human voice and absolutely nothing will ever replace the human touch.

Fortunately, there are a number of filmmakers who have demonstrated an ability to reach us in the ways we are craving.

"I think what we've lost with computers and the technology age is the ability to listen," says screenwriter Anne Rapp. "We don't have time to listen anymore. We do e-mail so we don't have to make a phone call and listen to someone's voice. We've made it possible to cram in as much as we can, to get everything over with as quickly as we can, so we can hurry on to the next thing and then get that over with just as quickly. People don't listen to each other anymore. People don't touch each other any more."

Perhaps the operative word in Anne's message is "touch." People are starving for a sense of belonging, to be understood and honored. Storytellers who can take time to observe and have the courage to write what they see and know will, indeed, have formed a meaningful partnership with their audience. They will provide moments of recognition so often desired. Their characters will have the ability to connect us to something familiar.

Films do not have to be heavy-laden with deep, obscure philosophical agendas to be meaningful, and they do not have to hit us over the head with jargon meant more to impress than to reach us. With the complexities that often rule our lives, escapist, fantasy-type films can play an important role in helping to release the tensions of the day. Being able to laugh at our own foibles can help us to not take everything too seriously.

Nevertheless, films all too often have the tendency to offer cinematic quick fixes instead of presenting believable characterizations that give a story its value. Screenwriters often belittle their ability to impact audiences. When they create stereotypical characters and plots, as well as write for the current trends, they do not realize that audiences may leave the theater feeling cheated and devalued. However, whenever they have the courage to write from the heart, honoring the soul of the story, those same audiences will feel grateful for what they have seen, which, in some intangible way, may have offered them great meaning.

Unfortunately, the film medium all too often reinforces the concept of pat solutions to complex human problems and concerns. Films have the ability to provide us with a better understanding of the human spirit, and there is a need for a greater in-depth understanding of the psychological nuances that impact relationships. Filmmakers often hesitate in presenting the moviegoer with the intricate issues that often exist for all of us as we travel on our unique journeys. No matter what the chosen genre, most people who love the medium of film will appreciate the stories in which they find a familiar thread that in some way reflects their lives. Reinforcing that human beings are terribly interesting and have fascinating ways in which to experience life's adventures can be a wonderful goal for the screenwriter who is devoted to the art of storytelling.

Presenting characters in the extreme is certainly an option for storytelling. However, doing so often has the effect of discouraging people from understanding the multitude of complexities that exist as human beings go about the business of living their lives.

For writers to understand what influences human behavior is a goal worth reaching, for it can give a story its power and the characters their believability. Bringing forth the conflicts, the paradoxes, the secrets, and the vulnerabilities that lie within each of their characters can offer us the moments of recognition that lend value and a deeper understanding of the stories we are watching. Somehow, we can leave the theater knowing that the story we have experienced is not far from our own truth, and we can feel comforted in the connection that has taken place.

Contrary to some who believe that moviegoers will watch anything simply to be entertained, audiences today are not seeking to shy away from gaining new insights into the behaviors of the characters who are telling their compelling stories. Writers tend to believe that their characters have to act in extreme ways for them to be credible—a kind of "bigger-than-life" mentality. Exaggeration in either direction—overextended versus underdeveloped characters—takes away from the power inherent in a good story. *The Green Mile,* written and directed by Frank Tattersall based on the novel by Stephen King, is an example of a film that is entertaining, yet loses its believability. Paul Edgecomb (played by Tom Hanks) is the head guard at the Coal Mountain Louisiana State Penitentiary's death row. Day in and day out, he is faced with issues of death and the execution of inmates who have committed horrendous crimes. Throughout the film, Edgecomb seems to be able to maintain his cool, while another guard exhibits typical abusive behaviors often depicted in prison films. Edgecomb never loses control, and at the slightest urge to react in a human way, he stops himself in Herculean fashion. From the audience's perspective, this could be a bit of a stretch. Is it really possible to be a part of a prison system—death row, no less—and not feel a very normal desire to leave it and escape the cruelty that lies within its walls? Does it not wear down the human spirit to be in the midst of so many who have made manipulation and cruelty their life's mission? We have to ask whether the lack of credibility in this film exists because whenever we see Edgecombe, we realize that unlike a real person, he does not have a mean bone in his body. Is the choice of actor the problem, or is the writer unable to give us the full range of a character who can feel immense anger, even a slowly-developing disgust for his job, and at the same time represent a basic trust for humanity? Or is it both?

Films can offer characters who present us with complex paradoxes and dualities. The challenge for the writer is to give us characters who have something to say, in a manner that makes sense and offers some percentage of reality. As a matter of fact, the films that have gained the greatest recognition have often been the ones that had the courage to present characters as full-blown human beings—imperfect, often very lonely, and striving for understanding, fulfillment, and love.

When a character's behavior is presented in the extreme, the ripple effect is that people are discouraged from understanding what is really taking place within the character's interiority. Characters depicted in the extreme tend to leave issues unresolved, are often frenetically attempting to understand what has taken place in their lives, and are given robotic and trivialized experiences. Audiences are left perplexed and confused. They have not been given the perspective of what has triggered the rage, the sorrow, the numbness, the cruelty, or any of the behaviors that the characters may be taking for granted, but for the audience are bewildering.

The War of the Roses, directed by Danny DeVito and written by Michael Leeson based on the novel by Warren Adler, is a good example of such a film. We see an idyllic couple moving up the ladder to success. They have fallen madly in love, married, had children, and slowly, but surely, become alienated. We are not witness to what has really been happening in their relationship and can only make educated guesses as to how the manner in which they were seeking money and success might contribute to a great sense of disconnectedness. It seems that the writer wanted to show us a very common theme in marriage—the husband's traditional role of breadwinner, alongside the wife's ever-growing discontent and developing insecurities.

Did he take the time to ponder the slow erosion of a relationship and the ingredients that tear people apart? It is more the exception than the rule that overnight unhappiness can terminate a loving relationship. The extreme descriptions and behaviors take away from the potential power of this film. We see the hurt turned to fury, revenge, and cruelty. No holds are barred, and what the audience is privy to is a caricature of a dissolving marriage. We see only momentary expressions of genuine sorrow and sadness. We see expressions of emotion that are off the continuum. There is no hope for this couple, and it is only going to get worse before it ever has a chance to get better.

In the end they destroy one another. What could be a greater extreme? There are many real-life relationships that end in disaster, but few of them get caught in the straight path of the hurricane. In real life, there are subtleties, confusions, and movements back and forth into the world of indecision. We see none of this in *The War of the Roses.* Once the die is cast, there is no turning back. Although the writer appropriately avoided the Hollywood happy ending, the process of what was really happening to this couple was cut short in the path of their self-destruction. Rather than seeing realistic behaviors of sadness, regret, confusion, and even self-doubt, we saw their lives only in the extreme.

Magnolia, directed by Paul Thomas Anderson and starring William H. Macy, Julianne Moore, Jason Robards, and Tom Cruise, is another film in which the characters have a host of inner conflicts and play out their pain in ways that alienate rather than connect to audiences. Tom Cruise plays a rageful son who has felt betrayed by his father and has lost a beloved mother through her death. His hatred of women takes over his life, as he becomes an internationally-known leader in teaching men a multitude of ways to take charge and control the women in their lives. Once again, we have a story where a man has been deeply wounded and turns his pain into destruction. He has shut off the valve that allows his own compassion to flow. He is bent on only one thing—destroying those who have hurt him the most. Cruise plays the role very convincingly, yet the stereotypic message remains: When men are hurt they will turn to rage and cruelty.

We never see the middle ground of this man's experience. We gather, through assumptions and a limited use of backstory, that he has been left to his own devices growing up. His father has been unfaithful to his mother, and the son blames him for her death. As his father lays dying, we wonder what it will take to bring reconciliation between them. This film would not have suffered if it had presented with fewer stereotypic devices and more well-defined characters.

Perhaps the greatest flaw of films that turn to the extreme for their message is that they offer only one high-voltage level of intensity. Writers need not resort to this manner of storytelling to give us their intended ideas and creativity. Life is not lived on one cylinder. It takes variety and nuance in writing to present us with believable characters. A powerful story is not synonymous with showing characters in the extreme. Researching the subtleties of human behavior is well worth the effort if the script is to have meaning and validity to the moviegoer.

The more that audiences can relate to the characters in a movie, the more connected they will feel, and the more powerful the story becomes. The relationship between the story, the characters, and how committed the audience will be to understanding what is transpiring needs to be taken into consideration if the writer expects the film to be successful. It is a key ingredient if the story is to enjoy long-lasting popularity.

Waiting to Exhale, directed by Forest Whitaker, met with audience approval, for it addressed the essence of what women and men struggle with in attempting to define love. In this film, four women are searching for a time in their lives when they can finally feel connected to another person and experience the power of love that they so desperately need in order to feel enriched. Many women who see this film probably share similar feelings, desires, and questions about the meaning of love. How do meaningful relationships happen? What does it take to attract the "right" person, and what do we do when that individual never appears? Why do we have an inability to connect with a partner who will help to empower us, not devalue our very essence? Although the film succumbed to some stereotypical characterizations, audiences responded to the issues that resonated the very same dilemmas they often face in their search for everlasting love. The writer has provided us with food for thought and has fueled our imagination.

Moviegoers want to travel on a journey with characters who are alive for them. They want to participate in the action, the turmoil, the conflicts, and they want to be witness to every detail, as the characters attempt to resolve their dilemmas. No matter what the venue, whether viewed on the big screen or on television, audiences remain fascinated by what propels the characters' behaviors, thoughts, and interior motives.

Unlike many screenwriters, who would prefer to write scripts for features over television series, Ed Bernero is delighted to tell his stories on the smaller screen, because it gives him better opportunities for developing meaningful characters.

"Television is a much better medium for me, because you get to know the characters over a number of weeks," explains Ed. "Most movies focus on just one aspect of the character's makeup. If they could make the movie ten hours, I'm sure the character would be much more interesting. I think movies are far more story-driven than character-driven, while television is character-driven. If you never get to care about the people in a television show, it will never work. I really don't think you're going to get too many shows where you really don't care about the characters."

It is a challenge for writers of feature films to create interesting and believable characters within the accepted script format of 90–120 pages.

Screenwriters often complain of feeling restricted from being able to fully develop their characters and stories within this framework. They feel the pressure of attempting to hold the audience's attention for a specific period of time. It is also a difficult task to build the tension and conflict that are needed in order to drive a story forward. If writers want us to fully appreciate the stories, it is crucial that their characters are given the voices necessary to bring the viewer into their worlds. It is important that screenwriters accept the premise that most moviegoers today are interested in knowing why the characters have come to behave as they do. What has brought them to this part of their journey that we are now witnessing? What will be the result of the decisions they are making? Will we be privy to their personal challenges and motivations? Will their stories be told truthfully and unabashedly, so that they will resonate with us and, in so doing, allow us to honor our own humanness?

Movies do not have to reach Oscar status or have won other prestigious awards in order to impact us. Many films that leave us with strong images and universal themes have the ability to ignite a deep connection and tie the threads linking us all. For example, *Eve's Bayou* and *Shall We Dance* are two very different stories, coming from varying traditions and heritages, that brought audiences a unique view of relationships, family life, and what it means to feel lost and scared.

Eve's Bayou, written and directed by Kasi Lemmons, is an eerie, complicated family drama that takes place in the Louisiana bayou in the summer of 1962. The film delivers an extremely powerful view of betrayal and confusion that exist in ten-year-old Eve Batiste's heart when she realizes that her father is not the perfect man she had thought he was. We are frightened for Eve, as she uncovers dark family secrets, and wonder how she will choose to live with the truth. There are mesmerizing moments when we are being exposed to the deepest of intimacies, and we are faced with a relationship that is crumbling in front of our eyes. The torment, the guilt, the witnessing of an innocence lost are issues that impact us at a very deep level. Audiences are reminded that parental love is an entity unto itself, and they travel with Eve as she is challenged to accept that parents have human frailties and are often susceptible to life's seductions, which have the power to destroy a child's innocence.

Coming from a very different part of the world, *Shall We Dance,* written and directed by Masayuki Suo, introduces us to an unusual view of one man's attempt to deal with the various pressures and monotony of his life. Shohei Sugiyama's life is a cycle of commuting to and from work and laboring his way up the corporate ladder to make enough money to pay the bills. On one of his commutes home, he is drawn to an ad for a dancing school. It is a moment that changes his entire view on life.

This Japanese film gains its strength due to Masayuki Suo's willingness to write believable images of what men experience when their very rigid and predictable lives become utterly devoid of spontaneity. How many middle-aged businessmen sitting in the audience have not known similar moments, wondering what their lives are all about? Having attained security, a "good" job, a house, a wife, and kids, they often ask, Now what? Or, Is this all there is? How many of us, men and women, have not yearned to break free from such lifestyles, but were not able to find the courage to do so?

Storytellers who can bring us characters that give us a better understanding of ourselves will enable us to gain a new appreciation about the journeys we are on, the relationships we form, and the imperfections we must accept along the way.

There have been a number of films that have helped people to develop a more sophisticated understanding of the human condition and exactly what influences affect the decisions we make.

Fatal Attraction, directed by Adrian Lyne, is a story about a successful attorney with a loving family who indulges in a one-night stand. He soon regrets his actions when the woman refuses to release him of their relationship and becomes more obsessive about him the more he rejects her. Although some of the behaviors were shown in the extreme, this film gave audiences a closer look at the intricacies surrounding obsessive love. It gave us a clearer understanding of what happens when human beings lose control and will stop at nothing to satisfy their need to be loved, no matter who is destroyed in the process.

Pretty Woman, written by J. F. Lawton and directed by Gary Marshall, is a fantasy fairytale about a chance encounter that results in a prostitute being rescued from the streets by her Prince Charming. Although it is a film that presents remedies that are not commonly inherent in real life, it became immensely popular in its portrayal of the magical events that can happen if we are just in the right place at the right time. Unexpected events can, as in this story, bring us untold joy and fulfillment. They are often the most dreamed-about moments that can come about when we least expect them. Audiences love happy endings and powerful stories. When they are created with truthfully represented characters who can fulfill our desire to believe in goodness, beauty, and everlasting love, the equation is complete. The key is not to avoid the fairytales of life, but to portray the characters enacting the stories as real and believable human beings who experience a multitude of human emotions.

Secrets and Lies, a film by British writer-director Mike Leigh, is an emotionally-charged story about Cynthia, a cockney woman at the end of her rope when her daughter Hortense finds her way back into Cynthia's life. All the characters in this troubled family have their facades slowly and painstakingly scraped away as the lies, secrets, and collusions are exposed. Profoundly moving and deeply memorable, this film demonstrates what happens when fear overpowers us and our lives become foreign, even to ourselves. Unfinished business from the past is the poison that dominates Cynthia's life. Mike Leigh did not spare us from witnessing the dread, bewilderment, and alienation as the characters tell us of their anguish. As the events unfold, we are mesmerized, because we have been allowed to enter their very private and excruciatingly painful worlds.

Shine, the much-acclaimed Australian film directed by Scott Hicks, documents the true story of former child prodigy David Helfgott, a once-promising concert pianist who spent a decade in numerous mental institutions following a nervous breakdown. We learn that David was raised by a domineering father, a Polish-Jewish refugee whose parents and siblings were killed in the holocaust. Determined never to lose his own children, the father smothers them with a pathological and obsessive love. When David develops an amazing skill on the piano and is offered a scholarship to Juilliard, his father refuses to let him go. Paradoxically, the father also insists that David become a great pianist. On the one hand, David is forced to excel, yet on the other, not allowed to develop and refine his craft. These inner conflicts are the seeds that lead to his eventual emotional collapse. Nevertheless, David eventually learns to reconnect with the world around him. With the love of an astrologer who inspires him to greatness, he rediscovers his immense joy of music, which he had so long ago abandoned, and is once again acclaimed for his talent.

This film demonstrates how psychological and physical abuse can eliminate our ability to reach our full potential, and that when we allow true love, gentleness, and kindness into our lives, healing can take place. Audiences were moved by this powerful story, which proved that courageous human beings, if they dare, can beat the odds.

Sling Blade, written and directed by Billy Bob Thornton, invites us into the unique world of a man who is willing to stop at nothing, even killing, to protect the child he has come to love. The inherent torment and isolation are a powerful reminder of what can happen when we are allowed to be shut off from human touch, kindness, respect, and affirmation. This film is a wonderful example of how silence, a carefully-scripted backstory, and unrelenting focus on character development can empower a story. The story of Karl, a mentally-challenged adult institutionalized for murder, unfolds as he is being interviewed by a young girl who is working on an assignment for school. The interview serves as an introduction to the abandonment that Karl suffered as a child. We find out that he was shamed, made to sleep in the shed, and treated cruelly by adults as well as other children. His mother taught him the laws of the Bible, yet could not protect him from the ravages of his world. He kills his boss, Jessie Dickenson, when he believes that his mother is being raped. The tone and manner of the mother's response, "Why did you kill Jessie?" makes him realize that she was not being raped, but participating in consensual sex, and he proceeds to kill her as well. What makes this film so ardent, powerful, and complete is its ability to tell us who the characters are and what lies below the surface of their behavior. We learn a great deal about Karl throughout the story, for each person he meets elicits more pertinent information about his history. Frank, a young boy who befriends Karl once he is released from the mental institution, becomes his protector. In turn, Karl fills a void and becomes the father that Frank so longs for. They form an immediate bond, one of respect and admiration. Karl's silence, his demeanor, and the pacing of his words carry great strength. We are allowed to see the story unfold without extreme stereotypical devices used for effect. Each character in the film is integral to the story.

Frank's mother, Linda, is in an abusive relationship with Dole, an alcoholic played expertly by Dwight Yoakam. His character flaws are realistically portrayed, without resorting to the typical manner in which alcoholism is usually depicted in film. The story builds to a crescendo when Karl realizes that Frank and Linda will be harmed if they remain with Dole. He will, once again, protect who he has come to love, no matter what befalls him in the process.

Over and over again, *Sling Blade* gives us amazing subtleties in portraying the life of a silent man whose emotions run deep. We are allowed to feel compassion, respect, and great admiration for his strength and have been given many opportunities to connect with him. Billy Bob Thornton took the time and energy required to write a script that is filled with a powerful view of the complexities that make us human.

Affliction, a film written and directed by Paul Schrader and starring Nick Nolte, Sissy Spacek, James Coburn, and Willem Dafoe, is a tale of one man's attempt to redeem his abused soul. Long-divorced, Wade Whitehouse (Nick Nolte) is estranged from his young daughter. A snowplow operator and policeman, Whitehouse suspects that a wealthy man killed in an apparent accident was actually murdered. The investigation offers him a chance to right some wrongs and to find some self-respect. But as the mystery unravels, so does Whitehouse.

This is another example of how important a film can become if we are allowed to get to know each character and their inner stories. The backstory and histories in this film are presented through narration, as William Dafoe's character recounts the story of his brother Wade's slow, but certain demise. We learn about their father's alcoholism, abusive treatment of their mother, and about the decisions they each made that led them down very different paths. Wade's alcohol abuse, his inability to love, and the alienation of his daughter bring him closer and closer to self-destruction. In contrast, William Dafoe's character has made the conscious choice not to drink, and so becomes the onlooker to the tragedy awaiting his brother, once his childhood protector.

Through cleverly-spaced flashbacks, we gain a deep understanding of the patterns and legacies that families pass down, one generation to the other. We witness the ravages of Wade's anger-turned-to-rage and to what happens to his human spirit when all of the compassion has been whipped out of him. This is not an extraordinary film, yet it is realistically portrayed. Dialogue and characterizations are well-developed, and happy endings are not sought for relief. It is a true depiction of a very common family dynamic when the whole system is out of control.

All of these films provide us with inner histories that are intense, perhaps seemingly extreme at times, yet very real. They not only dare us to enter the private hell and suffering of the main characters, but by the very nature of their themes prove that stories depicting the many faces of human suffering both attract audiences *and* bring us ever closer to connecting with one another and ourselves.

While we cannot expect all films to help sensitize us to our feelings, superficial dialogue and trite interactions demean what human beings are seeking when they want to relate to the fantasy movie, love story, drama, or even action/adventure film experience. The use of one-dimensional characterization also keeps audiences separated from each other by reinforcing stereotypes about people, genders, and races.

What is the writer's responsibility in providing the audience with the inner history of his characters? Is it critical to know what motivates specific behaviors? What techniques can be used effectively to help us connect with each character's story? First, there has to be a good reason to include a character in a story. What information will they provide, and how will they move the story forward? What information does the writer need to make the character believable? To answer these questions, you must be willing to research the psychology of each character in the story. Who are these people you are writing about? What are their desires, goals, emotions, and personal histories? When you know what your own motivations are for your behavior, you can pass along this gift to your characters. What makes you angry, sad, or confused? What role do your emotions have in your life? Have you become adept at shutting down your reactions? How do you express your feelings, and how does this compare to the way in which your characters will express theirs? If you do not believe that knowing a character's emotions and history is crucial to your story's strength, then it is more than likely that your story will be left with "unfinished" information.

Screenplays offer a multitude of ways in which a character's history and background can be included in the format of the script. Our goal is not to discover the ways that work best for you, but rather to encourage you to probe your own interiority to find the reasons that encourage certain behaviors. The more information that you gain about the persons you have chosen for your story, the more substantial they will become. Characters are people, not abstractions. They are human beings with inner conflicts, vulnerabilities, fears, needs, and dreams. If you treat them as flesh and blood rather than view them simply as characters you do not know, they will come to life. Would you like them as friends? Do you like what they stand for, or would you have countless debates over your differences? Examine them and think about what they were like as children. What took place in their lives that brought them to their current position? Who were their parents? Where did they live? What were the major events that helped to form them? The use of self is the strongest and most congruent tool you have. Take the time to uncover the secrets your characters may hold and the ways in which they are protecting themselves from the world. Take the time to use your awarenesses, your secrets, your peak experiences, your dreams, your emotions, and the ones you may be afraid to expose, in forming your stories. Stop at nothing to find your character's voice and to show us the power of their words and actions.

"Screenwriters have to acknowledge and accept the power of the form in which they have chosen to write," says Delle Chatman. "The power and the reach of it is immense. I would hope whatever gender they are, whatever color or race they are, whatever creed they believe in, that they would make an extra effort to be inclusive in their storytelling. It is crucial that we don't continue to see cinematic stories that are segregated. Human beings are human beings. I strongly believe that screenwriters, in a sense, must be conscious of that and assume some responsibility for showing the world what is possible."

Screenwriters who choose this path will be challenged to bring us the stories, themes, and characters about which they feel passionate. Whether it be through humor, turmoil, suspense, romance, and even the unspeakable, writers must have the courage to tell their stories truthfully and directly. Storytellers are the keepers of the universal threads that have the ability to connect us in unforgettable ways. When effectively told through the written word, and realized through powerful images, the screenplay can touch us and promote shared understanding.

Ten Common Fears about Character Believability

1. I won't know what to do next if my characters, whom I spent a lot of time researching, don't turn out the way I envisioned.
2. I'm not sure I can write scripts with characters who express their emotions in ways I prefer not to express my own.
3. I have always been turned off by psychological analysis in character development. I'm concerned that this will pose a hindrance when writing my stories.
4. I'm afraid to spend a lot of time on character development if I'm writing an action/adventure film. I feel I should spend my time concentrating on high-paced, thrilling scenes, and special effects.
5. I'm afraid that character-driven films are considered too heavy-laden and don't attract large audiences.
6. I have never studied psychology, so I don't know enough about human behavior to create believable characters.
7. I don't know how to present subtleties in the characters I create, which makes them seem shallow and one-dimensional.
8. I'm afraid that if I delve too deeply into my character, what I discover will necessitate having to rework my entire story.
9. I'm afraid that if I spend too much time developing my characters that I will never get the actual script finished.
10. I'm afraid to seek help from experts to better understand human behavior, because I may have to expose too much of myself to them.

Will I Face the Fears?

Screenwriters today do not have an easy task, for audiences are, more than ever, demanding to see films that have meaning and personal significance. They continue to love to be entertained, yet desire to see characters who speak their language. They are not thrilled when they have left the theater with nothing to hold onto, no messages of any substance. The pressure is on the writer to create stories with the characters who can, in some way, impact the viewer. Will you write scripts that adhere to the trends, yet which have no meaning for you, or will you have the courage to write what you feel is important from your heart, not guided from your pocketbook?

Ten Common Myths about Character Believability

1. If I don't know enough about the depth of my characters, then I should relinquish writing my script.
2. If I want to write important and meaningful stories, I will have to "give up my life" to spend all of my spare time researching my subject matter.
3. Using simple, true-to-life themes is synonymous with writing boring stories.
4. If my scripts don't adhere to the formats I have been taught, the story lines and characters will falter and lose their significance.
5. If my scripts don't adhere to the popular formulas, agents and producers will not be interested in them.
6. It is better to show emotions sparingly, or audiences will be turned off.
7. Only women are interested in character-driven stories.
8. You don't have to worry about character depth for children's stories. You need simple, uncomplicated characters, or children will not understand them.
9. I will have a better chance of success by coming up with high-concept ideas, rather than spending my time researching stories and characters.
10. It doesn't matter if my characters don't have a lot of depth. The right actors will make them work.

Will I Challenge the Myths?

If you are experiencing difficulty in creating meaningful stories and believable characters, perhaps you have bought into debilitating myths that are handicapping your progress. If your subject matter is of interest to you, what is making it impossible for you to proceed with your script? The most powerful myths are the ones that cause screenwriters to question their own motives, abilities, and skills. Challenging the messages that may have already swayed you into believing that there is only one way to become successful will be an ongoing task. Over and over, you will be faced with the opportunity to reaffirm your own ideas and refute the opinions of others. Writers give myths their power when they are not committed to responding to their own wisdom. As you challenge the myths listed below, allow yourself to recognize their faulty premises and their negative messages.

Will I Take the Risks?

What are the biggest risks you believe that you will have to take in creating characters that are believable and stories that will influence those who see your films? If you have taken the time to study your craft, if you have committed yourself to screenwriting as your profession, what will you need to do in order to complete your screenplays? It is always a risk to take chances, to gamble on writing stories that fascinate you, without any assurance of how others will receive them. You can compromise and perhaps even sell a script you do not feel was well-conceived. You can also become rather famous writing in a genre that may be enjoying current popularity, but is not the genre of your choice. The bottom line will always be, to what extent will you go to honor the stories and characters you hold inside of you? What compromises will you make, and will they eventually erode your creative spirit? Nothing that is worthwhile and that we wish to accomplish happens without risk-taking.

How Can I . . .

1. Give myself permission to write my own stories in my own way?
2. Trust that I have the ability to find my characters' true voices and present them as believable human beings?
3. Obtain the necessary resources and learn more about my characters when I do not know enough about their interiority?
4. Find more ways in which to honor my own wisdom and worthy life experiences in creating my stories?
5. Solicit the help I need if I cannot move my story forward alone?
6. Come to terms with the premise that even a simple story, when well-written and well-researched, can have a powerful impact?
7. Elicit from my characters the core messages that I am attempting to convey?
8. Effectively write the themes and emotions into my story so that audiences will feel connected to them?
9. Fully explore my characters' inner histories, so that I can give them believable reactions to the events they will encounter?
10. Use my characters' inner histories to create powerful tension and conflict in my story?

●

CHAPTER 8

Harold Ramis: Nothing Human Offends Me

I encourage writers to use real experiences in their writing. It's your only chance to make a unique statement, because the only thing we have that is truly unique is our own identity.

Harold Ramis

The Journey Begins

Harold Ramis was drawn to the performing arts at an early age. A keen observer of life's interesting twists and turns, he learned to appreciate the humor that exists in most human experiences. Harold graduated from Washington University in St. Louis during the tumultuous mid-sixties, a time when young people had to make significant life choices, such as whether or not to fight in Vietnam. Milestones in Harold's life always seemed to coincide with significant social events. He was working as a substitute teacher in Chicago's impoverished Robert Taylor Homes when Martin Luther King was assassinated, igniting tensions in a racially divided city.

I have always felt a certain synchronicity with major events. In 1962, I was a substitute teacher in the depths of an inner-city ghetto of Chicago during the riots. I was also eminently draftable during Vietnam. I made myself completely countercultural by resisting the draft. I didn't do this in any heroic way; I just weaseled my way out of it by claiming to be as antisocial as one could be, which was the homosexual-drug-addict ploy. I thought that this would definitely brand me and I would probably never work for the Defense Department or any straight American corporation. Nevertheless, my friends and I had made a pact in college that was to do only what we liked with our lives, and that certainly didn't include these types of jobs.

Harold's countercultural experiences would become fodder for antiestablishment themes that would appear in many of his films, such as the mockery he made of fraternities and stodgy academia in Animal House. *They also helped mold his philosophy against stereotyping based on ignorance.*

By the late sixties, I had leaped off the diving board of life and had become a long-haired hippy who dressed like a medieval jester. I was very inspired by the cultural radicals of the time, from Bob Dylan and the Beatles to Abbie Hoffman and others who were turning the world as we knew it upside down.

Around that time, I promised myself that I would not make any moral or value judgments about others without experiencing life completely and fully myself. I think it was Balzac who said, "Nothing human offends me." That expression is about judgment. It's about looking at people as they are and trying to understand them.

From Second City and SCTV to the Big Screen

Harold's start in comedic acting and writing came in 1969, when he auditioned for Chicago's famed Second City.

The audition for Second City was terrifying, as such an experience is for any new performer. You're not certain of your craft or of your talent. Getting in front of people and risking rejection can initially be a terrifying thing.

Despite his anxieties, Harold was accepted into the theater troupe, where he learned to master one of the most difficult methods of performance—improvisation.

With improvisation, writing is improv and improv is writing. At Second City, they used to caution us against "writing on stage" as a process, which means trying to control what other people are doing or having a fixed script in your head. One great thing about Second City is that it teaches you to fail. You're on stage night after night, and sometimes you really bomb. There you are in your worst nightmare, standing on the stage without any lines. The audience doesn't like what you're doing, and you can't find a way to get off. If you do that for a thousand nights, pretty soon it stops hurting. Once the terror is gone, failure has no real consequence. When I went through a rational checklist of all of the reasons to be afraid, I realized that it was the circumstance that was causing the anxiety, not anything specific that I had to fear.

In 1974, Harold moved to New York to help write and perform in The National Lampoon Show *with fellow Second City graduates John Belushi, Gilda Radner, and Bill Murray. By 1976, Harold was the head writer and a regular performer on* SCTV.

At Second City, we were taught a great principle, which was to never say "no," but to say "yes, and . . .". One person offers an idea, and another person takes what was good about it and follows it with "yes, and maybe XYZ happens." That was how the skits grew. As comedy writers, we band together, because it's the nature of the genre. You need someone to laugh at your ideas to know that they're funny. I did lots of collaborative writing in the late 1960s at Second City and then at the Second City television show (*SCTV*), where I was the head writer.

I learned that the greatest service I could provide as a head writer was to discover something good in everyone's contribution. For example, if someone came up with a scene that seemed too long, I would say, Maybe there's something we can do with the premise, or, The character is good, or, The scene has some good lines of dialogue. I always got a lot of cooperation from the other writers, because even if their work was rejected, it wasn't in a critical way. I always tried to be constructive and to salvage something from their ideas.

When I first started making films, the style tended to be pretty broad and wacky. The challenge for me was to find some meaning in these stories. The messages in most of my early films were very simple. *Caddyshack* was about social classes and a young man trying to identify with the right adult role model. Certainly the thematic content isn't what people remember or take away from these films, but I needed to define it in order to write the scripts.

Harold's breakthrough film was the blockbuster comedy National Lampoon's Animal House, *which he cowrote with Doug Kenny and Chris Miller in 1978. He then cowrote, produced, and/or directed a string of hits, such as* Meatballs, Stripes, Ghostbusters *and* Ghostbusters II. *He made his directing debut with* Caddyshack, *which was followed by* National Lampoon's Vacation, *starring Chevy Chase and Beverly D'Angelo. He also cowrote and directed* Club Paradise, *starring Robin Williams and Peter O'Toole, and in the same year, cowrote and served as executive producer on Rodney Dangerfield's* Back to School.

He went on to cowrite, direct, and produce Groundhog Day, *starring Bill Murray and Andie MacDowell, which won Best Original Screenplay in the 1993 British Academy Awards, as well as Best Comedy Film in the 1993 British Comedy Awards.*

Harold's most recent film, Analyze This, *starring Billy Crystal and Robert DeNiro, is not a project he was originally drawn to as a writer/director.*

Robert DeNiro's company financed the writing of the script as a project for DeNiro, though once it was written, they were no longer interested. An executive from DeNiro's company moved from New York to Los Angeles and took it to producer Paula Weinstein. Paula liked the concept and hired another writer, who was unable to move it ahead, so his script was dumped. This happens a lot in the movie business. Finally, screenwriter Peter Tolan was hired when Billy Crystal became interested in the premise, which was a story about a Mafia leader who has a nervous breakdown and goes to see a psychiatrist. Peter finally got the script to a place where people could really see it.

At this point, I was asked to direct the project. I didn't have time to read the script, because I was working on something else. All I heard was that Billy Crystal was a Mafia boss's psychiatrist, which I thought sounded formulaic. I read the coverage, and it didn't move me. Then, my agent called and asked if I would be interested in the project if Robert DeNiro was playing the gangster. Suddenly, I saw it in a totally different way. DeNiro's name communicated a grounded reality and intelligence, which made it seem like a whole different movie.

Although Analyze This *was a comedy, Harold wanted to make sure that, like all of his films, it contained meaning and significance. He also wanted to give the film realistic tones that were drawn from his own experiences and thorough research.*

Making films is a huge effort, so they better matter. I want to make sure that my films are saying something that I can be proud of for the rest of my life. I gave *Analyze This* a lot of thought before rewriting the script. As soon as I put DeNiro in my mind and started to think of all of the possible psychological constructs, the project became very meaningful and potentially funny to me.

I have many friends who are psychologists, and my first job after college was working as an attendant in a locked psychiatric ward. I have also been in therapy in many different combinations—with my wives, my parents, with all three of my children, with my brother. My wife and my ex-wife even went to therapy together. I believe in therapy, and I didn't want to see it trivialized. One thing I learned was that when a person starts "acting out," the question the therapist asks is, Why is he doing it now? So I thought of the "why now" for this particular story. Asking this question made me see a great roundness for DeNiro's character. He would have been an adolescent, just coming to manhood, when his father was murdered. That would have been around 1957, the year of the Appalachian, when the Mafia was riding high. Now, as the millennium is dawning, the Mafia is in total disarray. In a sense, the Mafia has had a nervous breakdown. The bosses are going to jail, and the old rules don't apply anymore. Everything we say in the movie about the Mafia is true. One thing that wasn't working in the earlier drafts was that the Mafia was being portrayed in the mythical tones of *The Godfather*. I was much more interested in the more realistic tones of a Scorsese film. I knew that if we portrayed the Mafia as the Godfather, then the film would start in an unreal place and could never be real.

Another big mistake in the old script was that it didn't have any social significance, and it was too melodramatic and unrealistic from a psychological point of view. The symptoms of the Mafia boss's anxiety were totally inappropriate. I've been with people who have had panic attacks, and I've taken them to the emergency room, so I know exactly what it looks like. Unlike what existed in the old script, I wanted to show the natural evolution of what brings DeNiro's character into therapy. I thought it would be so funny to see this tough guy who would rather think that he's having a heart attack than believe he could be suffering from an anxiety disorder, which he equates with fear and weakness.

At one point, I gave Robert DeNiro the DSM-IV™ (*Diagnostic and Statistical Manual of Mental Disorders*), which describes the symptoms of anxiety and panic disorder. I told him about some cathartic breakthroughs that I had experienced. The crying that was described in the script seemed like a joke, but I explained to DeNiro that I once had a big breakthrough and cried uncontrollably for days on end, never knowing what would trigger the tears. DeNiro seemed fascinated by this, because it came from real experience, and all his characters are strongly rooted in reality.

Analyze This has a great through line about fatherhood. It was in the earlier script, but it wasn't fully developed. I had spent about four years in a mythopoetic men's group. I spent a lot of time reading Robert Bly and thinking about maleness and fathers and inheritance and initiation. Bly had said something to the effect that our society no longer knows how to initiate young men. Therefore, fatherless young men turn to gangs to be initiated, and since the gangs can't really fill that void, they end up botching it. I was talking with a psychiatrist and expressed my opinion that it would be natural for someone in a profession like the Mafia to develop an anxiety disorder. He said it would actually evolve in the opposite way—that such a person would start with the anxiety and then become a gangster, thinking it was the antidote. Hanging out with tough guys makes you feel safe, but of course it isn't the answer.

All of these things contributed to the final meaning of the film for me—that it's possible for men like Robert DeNiro's character to get in touch with their grief, their rage, and their anxiety. If men like that could learn to deal with issues on the feeling level, then we could reduce the level of violence in our society. For me, it became the film's reason for being.

Regardless of all of his success, Harold still encounters moments of fear and faces times when he must still take enormous risks. His maturity has helped him to understand that perhaps these risks aren't as fearful as he might have once thought. He has also realized that you don't always have to have all the right answers to do good work.

There's no risk without loss, right? You wouldn't consider something a risk unless there was something to lose. As I've grown older and have gained more experience, I realize that I have so little to lose now.

The greatest thing I learned along the way was to say "I don't know." My wife recently went to see the Dalai Lama. She said that the most delightful thing was when someone in the audience would ask a very complicated question on a serious issue, and the Dalai Lama would respond with "I don't know." Then he would laugh. As a film director, I've learned that although everyone expects you to know everything—and most directors are so bound by their own egos that they feel they need to have the right answer all the time—it's a great relief to be able to say "I don't know." It allows me to shut up and listen to people who do know the answer or who might have good ideas to contribute. In the end, I get to make the final decision, so it's not like I have to sacrifice my authority by listening to other people.

What's Next

Frank Capra said a wonderful thing once. He said, it's a tremendous responsibility to speak to people for two hours in the dark. There are so few opportunities to make movies. Very few get made, so I feel lucky. I've made seven films in twenty years, so chances are, at the rate I work, that I won't make many more. So to me, it's crucial to keep discovering important themes. One of the new projects I plan to do is to remake a Stanley Donen comedy from the sixties called *Bedazzled,* which starred Peter Cook and Dudley Moore. In it, the devil grants a desperate young man seven wishes in exchange for his soul. I want to give my version a more contemporary slant and identify what are the most commonly wished for things in our culture. It could be very funny and still be full of meaning.

Parting Words

I remember a discussion I had with a friend. She was talking about what she wanted to do, but she was expressing herself completely in terms of dreams and wishes. It occurred to me that there is a difference between a dream and a goal. The dream is that you're doing what you normally do, and suddenly you find yourself transported to another place in life as if by magic. Someone lifts you or elevates you or taps you on the shoulder and says "You're a screen-writer" or "You're an actor." That's the dream. Goals are measured steps that get you to where you want to be. There's no magic involved.

●

CHAPTER 9

What Makes Characters Do What They Do?

Connection between the audience or reader with the emotion of
the character makes a story powerful. If you study real human behavior,
you'll be able to create real character behavior.

Sharon Y. Cobb

Every character you create has a past history, a theme that runs throughout his life, a set of legacies and programming that impacts his behavior, and a specific role from which he perceives his world and the events in his life.

Creative storytelling involves forming characters who are prompted to act in specific ways. As a reaction to the backstory that accompanies the behaviors, audiences can be introduced to the character's full range of motivations, getting to know why that person acts as they do and what purpose the behavior serves.

Audiences deserve to know why the character's behavior is what it is. None of us comes to an event in our lives completely empty or neutral. There are reasons why we are inspired to take a certain course of action, even if we are not fully aware of what it is.

If a character, perhaps a serial killer, finds that he is now living to kill, to control, and to gain power, we need to understand that there are very significant reasons why he has been able to shut out his conscience and feel entitled to take a life. There are reasons that he has given himself permission to kill people he does not even know. If the writer chooses this as a major theme, then it will necessitate giving us some idea of who this person is and how he came to this point in his life. Including at least a brief history or backstory of the character who dominates a story is crucial if he is to be understood and believed.

Los Angeles writer Betty Hager sums this up well: "You need a balance in your character, even if he isn't a balanced character."

Screenwriter/director Paul Wei was determined to give his serial killer the appropriate balance to create a sense of identity, while maintaining realism. This involved extensive research.

"I did so much research on all the serial killers and what makes them unique. Maybe they also have a human side, though inside they are a serial killer. Maybe they have something different. Something just like you and I. So I would do all this extensive research to find out. Without this kind of research, you would write something just like everybody else. I want to write something different, so the characters are different."

In most films that entertain this theme, we see the behaviors, but we rarely get a glimpse of what influences have impacted the killer to behave in this way. We could make assumptions about the "whys." However, more often than not, we are left knowing nothing substantial about the character's interior processing.

Each character comes to the story with a complex personal history and experiences that have helped in forming his identity. What has impacted him? What what was his heritage, and what role is he now fulfilling? What is his family like? How have they affected his current status, his decisions, his aspirations?

Empty characterizations contribute nothing to the value of a script. A story that allows us to get to know the character indicates that the screenwriter has researched and taken the time to get to know the people in the story. Achieving a script's entertainment value does not require your characters to be simplistic caricatures, empty vessels with no history or prior influencing factors that have had an impact on their lives.

There are hundreds of films in all genres with rather simple premises that are still gripping, entertaining, thought-provoking, and memorable. Their success lies in the way in which their characters speak to us as full-blown human beings. One such example is *Gattaca,* directed by Andrew Niccol and starring Ethan Hawke and Uma Thurman. This film takes place in a future world of genetically perfect elites. Vincent Freeman (Ethan Hawke) is a man with a dream—to venture into outer space—a dream that is hindered by the fact that he was not a product of genetic engineering. He circumvents this handicap by posing as a one-time star swimmer and perfect genetic specimen who has been crippled in an accident. His disguise allows him to become one of Gattaca's favored astronauts, though his dream is suddenly threatened when he becomes a prime suspect in the murder investigation of a Gattaca executive. The lead investigator is his genetically perfect brother.

This story gains its value as the result of the information we are given about the unique relationship between two brothers who are born under very different circumstances, one being genetically perfect and the other having a "weak heart." Through his words, Vincent walks us through some of the most important moments of his life, helping us to form an immediate bond with him. We can relate to the dream he struggles to make a reality, no matter what handicaps he is challenged to conquer. He wants to go into space, to witness Titan, and recognizes that in order to succeed, he will have to fight the establishment of Gattaca, to go beyond what others believe about what it takes to "make it." By going into the past, the film gives us a much broader understanding and appreciation of who Vincent is, as well as what forces have given him the strength to strive for his childhood dream. If the writer had not taken the time to give us a profile and history of these brothers, this story would have become just another superficial and meaningless sci-fi of the '90s. It provides audiences with thought-provoking moments—questions that are answered and that give us an opportunity to examine the human will and expressed passion for the fulfillment of a dream. As *Gattaca* shows, knowing the thoughts and history of the protagonist most definitely helps to make a film memorable.

Creating backstories need not become laborious nor bog down the momentum of a script. It simply means that the screenwriter needs to take the time to really get to know the characters and to explore creative ways in which to share what is discovered about them. The more that you know about the people in your story, the more interesting they will become for the audience. *Gattaca* could easily have become a boring film if no information had been given about Vincent or his brother, yet we are given the best of what had been found out about determination, stamina, and the dreams of a little boy who yearned to travel into space. We are not left without answers about Vincent's motivations, his family influences, the competition he shared with his brother, his loneliness, and his personal victories. As you proceed in having a full understanding of your characters, after all of your research is completed, you will have valuable options for inclusion as backstory information. Since screenplays are typically restricted to a certain page length, you must be select in choosing the most pertinent information that will expand your story. Take the time to have well-defined characters with histories, backgrounds, and human involvement that will give significance to your plot and story lines. Remember that a character becomes real when he can share his emotions, thoughts, conflicts, and turmoil with us. When audiences can feel what your characters are experiencing and when those characters can speak their own truths, we will be reminded of our own human qualities, and what could be more powerful than that!

"I respond to movies that seem honest and have a real personality," says Noah Baumbach. "Particularly stuff coming out now, because so many movies seem put together by committee. Even if I don't like a movie, if it's really somebody's vision, I respond to that. Ultimately, I'd like to have the experience that everyone hopes for, and that is to identify with the people on the screen and go through their experiences with them."

In order for audiences to connect with the characters, it is imperative that writers take the time to let us know what this person is thinking and what their past histories have been that have brought them to this current point in time.

When a Man Loves a Woman, written by Al Franken, is about a family coping with the impact of alcoholism, through the stages of drinking for fun, abuse, detoxification, and recovery. The parents, Michael and Alice Green, are a seemingly happily married couple. Their two daughters are outwardly happy and give us the impression of being well-adjusted, yet they have seen, firsthand, a very different side of their mother. They have lived with a woman who has surrendered to the many pressures in her life by turning to alcohol.

Although this film presents us with many honest and important themes, we learn very little about what brought Alice to the point of severe alcoholism. What has caused her to use alcohol as a way of dealing with the pressures and inner pain she is experiencing? Was there a history in her family of using alcoholism to cope with problems? What is causing her distress, and from where does it originate? Does anyone else know about her history? Is her habitual drinking separating her from those she loves, and how can they reconcile her self-destructiveness? Did the writer or other creators of this film really understand how alcoholism has the power to cause havoc on a family unit?

The audience could spend hours surmising and attempting to find the explanation, but that would be making assumptions that the writer may not have intended. Although this film presents many honest and important themes, we are left disconnected from Alice, as she escapes from telling us more about who she really is. As a result, a potentially significant story is diminished in its ability to impact us.

Another character battling similar demons, though in the final stages of alcoholism, is the protagonist in *Leaving Las Vegas,* directed by Mike Figgis. Other than knowing that he once had a family and a successful career, we know little else that explains his pain and the reasons for his self-destruction. We see him slowly killing himself, yet lack a clear understanding of why he has chosen this path. What, or who, has caused him to want to die, to have nothing to live for?

Many writers believe that good stories should be laced with intricate plot lines and complicated characters. The simplest story can give us the greatest depth of character, which, in turn, empowers the story. When screenwriters have taken the time to become acquainted with each character occupying a place in the script, the story will hold the power it needs to bring the messages intended.

Fear as a Powerful Motivator

Creating believable characters means being willing to show the full range of their emotions, as well as the qualities that make them unique to the story. In western cultures, we are programmed to believe that human suffering is a weakness. Mass media messages reinforce that to feel something other than happy is unacceptable. Many writers believe that to make their scripts successful, they must shy away from perfectly normal human responses and reinforce happy endings.

In every story that has significance, it is evident that fear has taken its toll in some way and has helped move the characters in a direction that perhaps they could not have gone without it.

Shilo, scripted by director Dale Rosenbloom and based on the best-selling novel by Phyllis Reynolds Naylor, is an uncomplicated story that embodies powerful aspects of fear and how it motivates human behavior. This family drama is about a young boy named Marty, who befriends a little beagle. The dog's owner, Judd, is a totally shut-down man who abuses his dogs, lives outside of the law, and drinks too much. He is afraid of allowing anyone a glimpse of his past for the shame it has bestowed on his entire life. We learn from Marty's parents that Judd's father used physical abuse in order to control his children. We are given a vivid picture of how Judd had been "programmed" not to trust anyone, and rather than risk getting close or befriending Marty for any reason, he feels safer remaining isolated and alone.

Dale Rosenbloom has painted a realistic picture of the pattern of abuse that can be passed down from one generation to another. He has not been underhanded in offering us a valid reason as to how Judd has become the cruel man his father was.

Marty, meanwhile, wants the little dog so desperately that his fear of not having this dog is greater than his fear of confronting the man everyone is afraid of. Judd makes a verbal and written agreement with Marty requiring that he perform certain tasks in exchange for the dog. Marty is able to meet his end of the contract through his immense determination to own the dog. Judd, however, finds it perfectly acceptable to go back on his word, stating that the written agreement had not been witnessed. He thinks he has won out and the boy can do nothing about it. Without the background that Rosenbloom has given us, none of Judd's behavior would make any sense in the scheme of this film. It would just be a superficial way of looking at a cruel man being unkind to an innocent child. The interaction between Judd and Marty is clearly understood, since the writer supplied us, in a very uncomplicated way, with vital information that answers questions we might have had about Judd's behavior and what has caused his isolation. We know that Judd has become what his own father had been—abusive. He has not been willing to go beyond the patterns that had existed in his own family history. Trust had been compromised for him by his own father, and now it has become too scary for him to allow himself to trust others.

In *Shilo 2—Shilo Season,* Dale Rosenbloom reintroduces us to the issue of alcoholism and the grave influences that Judd's family of origin have had on him. Marty's mother believes that Judd drinks to excess because he is so unhappy. Marty and his mother talk about the outcome of drinking without limits and remark that perhaps Judd is not a "bad apple" and that he may yet be able to change the legacy that was passed onto him by his father. The writer has chosen to give us a realistic view of the destruction that alcohol abuse can have on the human spirit. This information is shared within the context of the story in a manner that is plausible and offers the audience believable characters. It does not have to be a convoluted process to offer deeper perspectives of a character's history, and it can certainly improve the quality of a script in any genre. Perhaps all it really takes is for screenwriters to accept that moviegoers value knowing who the characters are and how and why their behavior may be the result of the familial and environmental influences that impact them. This means that scripts that are intended to be remembered must have characters who are memorable. Characters who present real-life issues must also have had a past that is carried into the way in which their behaviors and decisions are demonstrated in the present. Screenwriters who take the time to learn what this past is have the ability to create extremely interesting and unique characters.

Contrary to the popular myth, all stories do not need happy endings to be interesting and to appeal to audiences worldwide. Rather, if stories are to represent human experiences, the screenwriter needs to acquire firsthand knowledge of what drives people and what forces exist in their lives that have the greatest impact. Fear is a great motivator. It makes us choose to do, or not do, many things in life. Judd's fear of getting emotionally close to another person was greater than his fear of solitude. In the end, he remains alone, angry, holding on tenaciously to the memory of his father, who had betrayed him in his cruelty.

Remains of the Day, directed by James Ivory and based on a novel by Kazuo Ishiguro, is a powerful film that demonstrates the impact of fear in determining what paths we will choose to travel and what experiences we will choose to reject. In this film, fear has taken its toll and will direct the characters to make decisions that, in one brief moment, will reverse the natural course of events and affect their lives forever. The central character is Stevens, a tragic individual who, like his father before him, places his duty as a butler above all else in his life. As the chief housekeeper, Miss Kenton, enters his world, slowly but surely, we see a change in Stevens' demeanor. We know that something very significant is about to happen to him, and we witness his resistance to accepting the stirring of emotions he is experiencing. We see the strong affection he is developing toward Miss Kenton and the effort with which he fights it.

In a brief, but powerful moment, we are brought into the inner conflict Stevens is about to experience. He will make a decision that will continue to keep him emotionally detached, for he has let the fear guide his next steps. Choosing love is not part of his life's theme, or so he has decided. It is in that moment, when Miss Kenton attempts to get show him the attraction she holds for him, that we are suspended in space. At that precise moment, the audience wonders if he will choose to love her and to make the decision to go beyond his family legacy, where only loveless relationships reside. Instead, he turns away and rejects the moment. The reasons for his actions become clearer as the story unfolds.

When his father has a stroke and is dying in his room, Stevens is presiding over an important banquet for diplomats at Darlington Hall. Stevens spares only a moment to visit his father. Trying to set the record straight before he passes on, his father divulges a secret. He tells his son, "I loved your mother. I loved her once. Love went out of me when I found her carrying on." He continues, "You are a good son, proud of you. I hope I've been a good father to you. Tried my best."

Stevens wants to comfort his father by touching his hand. His father cannot tolerate the closeness, nor what he senses as his son's pity, and abruptly asks him to leave. In an instant, we are witness to a powerful moment between a father who has been out of touch with his son and a son who has become adept at shutting out his pain. We can assume that the father's admission was probably the only intimate moment they have ever shared—a dreadful moment at that. What was Stevens to say or feel at such a disclosure? What was he to do with the shock and pain he may have allowed to creep in for a solitary moment? Yes, he had wanted to show his father some measure of affection, and once again, his father could not stand to be so close.

Later, while Stevens tends to a self-pitying French diplomat, Miss Kenton comes to inform him of his father's death. Since Stevens will not leave his duties—for duty is his life's motto—Miss Kenton delicately asks permission to close his father's eyes. Through these scenes, which illustrate the very private world of two men, father and son, we are brought closer and closer to their isolation. We see how the legacy of emotional solitude has been passed from one to another. The father loved once and was unable to accept his wife's infidelity, and thus shut out all of his feelings for the remainder of his life. Stevens has now become his father's son in his inability and refusal to express and accept the love now being offered by Miss Kenton. We walk the tightrope with him, as we are given clear signs that he is truly attracted to this woman who has burst into his life. He clearly needs and wants love, but his fear of accepting and trusting such intimacy has won out. Like his father, being alone, safe, and living in emotional isolation is preferable to facing the fear of loss if he chooses to love. Had he known, at some level, of his mother's wanderings? Had he felt the distance between his parents and the disillusion that was to follow? Had the separation of his father and mother influenced his present decisions?

In viewing this film, we realize that Stevens' actions and demeanor all make perfect sense. We are grateful to have been connected to a moment in this story when we can "connect the dots." We have been given valuable information regarding the characters and their histories. We have been given knowledge of how past behavior and role modeling has influenced their current decisions. Family secrets are never really totally secret. In some way, perhaps Stevens had some awareness of what had transpired between his parents, even though he may not have been able to recognize it on a conscious level. What is true, however, is that his father had also kept his pain and deep emotions to himself. "Like father, like son" does not get lost within the context of this powerful story.

In every story, there lies the element of fear. We are witness to characters who will evolve, stay on neutral, or stagnate because of fear. Writers who take the time to look at the role of fear in motivating a character's behavior will be able to bring a truthfulness to the story that will strengthen the messages intended. Whether the story demands a happy conclusion or not, audiences will appreciate the writer's courage in bringing us characters with whom we can relate. Accepting that fear is a strong component to how we make life decisions, and giving value to how it motivates behavior, is a realization that will give writers, their characters, and their stories an extraordinary ability to impact.

This is demonstrated in such powerful films as *Breaking the Waves* by Danish writer/director Lars Von Trier. This fervent love story unfolds in the early 1970s in a small, tightly-knit community on the remote north coast of Scotland. The central character is Bess, a young girl who lives with her family in the confined world of strict Calvinism. She falls in love with Jan, an oil-rig worker and "man of the world." Despite local opposition, Bess and Jan marry, but soon after, he must return to the rig. As Bess counts the days till their reunion, she is convinced that their love is made from Heaven, especially since she believes she can communicate directly with God. When an accident renders Jan bedridden, he pleads with Bess to prove her love and devotion by continuing with her own life. Bess, as with everything else that has happened to her that is negative, blames herself for Jan's paralysis. She believes that the only way that she can bring him pleasure is to sleep with other men and share these experiences with Jan, so that he can feel some passion in his life, which has thwarted his sexual energy.

Little by little we observe that Jan is responding to Bess's stories of her sexual exploits. Bess seeks more and more of these experiences and will stop at nothing to relieve her husband's pain. In desperation, she decides to sacrifice her own life, literally and symbolically, to save her husband from his deepening depression. Her life becomes meaningless, as she enters into elicit encounters to bring joy to Jan, who has begun to look forward to her stories. Bess believes that it is God's will that she surrender everything for the man she loves and accepts it as her duty. She will do anything to accomplish her mission, to respond to Jan's requests, and to prove her love. She is an amazing example of what one woman will do, in altruistic surrender, as she succumbs to her extreme need for love. The more that she sees Jan's arousal as she relates her sexual episodes, the more she will seek higher and higher levels of sacrifice to keep his pain away. We experience her slow demise into mental instability, to the death of her spirit, and finally, to the actual death of her body.

Like many women, Bess has been worn down and feels a sense of worthlessness. She believes that her life holds value only in living for another. It gives her life its very essence—living for the sake of another person is her role and the goal that holds the most value. She had never been given the tools to claim her own identity. This film is an extremely painful example of fear taking hold of a person's life, and with its force, destroying everything in its path, even a human life. How many women have been willing to give up everything in their own world, believing that the sacrifice was synonymous with love? How many women watching this film continue to jeopardize their professional lives and personal dreams in order to serve others? How many people have entered the very same kinds of "contracts," resulting in some form of self-destruction? *Breaking the Waves* gave us an opportunity to walk the path with such a woman and to feel her anguish and her dread of losing love, as each of her decisions brought her closer and closer to her death. Although the themes of suffering and fear were prevalent, it was the premise of how Bess viewed love that made the greatest impact. Bess was brought to life with credibility and honesty. The portrayal of this woman's ultimate self-sacrifice took no shortcuts, no quick remedies, nor did it necessitate a happy ending to attract audiences and leave them speechless.

Sharon Y. Cobb echoes for many the questions that writers must ask themselves as they progress on their writing journey.

"One of the first things I do when I write is ask, What does my character fear?" says Sharon. "I like to start with getting to know what my character fears. Or in a scene, Is he or she allowed to do this? What are their secret desires? And another one I always love is, What do they do when they're alone that they don't want anybody else to know?"

Any character you create will carry a host of emotions that will drive the story. Being willing to address the issue of fear is critical to developing congruency between the character and the story your characters are telling. If you have the courage to recognize and use your own fears as a guide, your story will have the potential of gaining tremendous significance.

Ed Bernero believes that stories will not have the power to touch audiences if the writer is unwilling to draw from personal experience.

"You have to live to work in this business," explains Ed. "If you spend all your time watching television or movies, you end up just copying movies. You have to live. One of the problems in this business is that people go to film school and come out and want to work in this business, but they've really got nothing to say. I'm certainly not suggesting that they don't go to film school, but it's more important to live."

"If you haven't had the life experiences, then you don't have anything to draw from," concurs Chicago writer Carmen Brown. "Sometimes I wish I could have started writing when I was in my early twenties. Who knows, maybe I could have really gone somewhere, but then I realize I hadn't had the experiences to put on the page."

Marvin's Room, adapted by the late Scott McPherson from his own successful stage play, is a film in which many audience members will feel connected. In this story, a terminally-ill woman tries to cope with her troubled nephew, estranged sister, and dying father. Despite an impressive cast (Meryl

Streep, Diane Keaton, Robert DeNiro, and Leonardo DiCaprio), the film lost some of its significance as a result of not showing us the conflicting emotions that can surface when a person has accepted the responsibility of caring for a parent who is loved and who is slowly leaving consciousness. The story line was predictable, and there seemed to be very little understanding of the stressors, inner conflicts, and pain that are prevalent whenever we are forced to watch the slow demise of a family member. For audiences viewing the frenetic caretaking amidst the tension between the sisters, a great deal is left unsaid. It is hard to believe that an adult child, herself facing a terminal illness and having been the "responsible one," would not, at some point in her daily routine, experience a host of emotions. Why are we not witness to her feelings of anger, frustration, sadness, anxiety, and, of course, guilt for having all of these feelings? What lies ahead for her? What will happen to the father she has so adoringly and sacrificially cared for every day of her life? Will the sister from whom she has been alienated be able to share in the next crucial decision regarding her health, as well as facing their father's physical and mental deterioration? She is forced to face her own mortality, her lack of bonding with her sister, and the necessity of coping with her current anguish and life's newest complication—her impending death.

This film introduces us to monumental issues that are wearing to even the most evolved of us. They are real-life occurrences, yet the one-dimensional characterizations diminish the power of this story, which contains themes with which most moviegoers could certainly identify. We are never allowed to see the protagonist's fears or her concern for the future. We only get a momentary glimpse of the reasons as to why the sibling relationship has deteriorated. In this film, the "good" sister is too good, and the "bad" sister is painted in the extreme. Relationships are never so simple, and it would have given much more credibility to the characters if we could have been given more information about how these sisters were brought up, and how and by whom they had been assigned their respective roles.

Human beings are not simply empty shells with limited access to their emotions, and if they are, then it is up to the writer to let us know, in some creative way, how they came to their lack of expression. A meaningful story will never be enhanced by characters who are not allowed to be expansive. In *Marvin's Room,* the frenetic caring for the parent amidst the negative energy shared between the sisters offers few clues, and a great deal is left unsaid. The audience members attempt to sort it all out, to connect with what they are being shown, and leave the theater rather dissatisfied and disappointed that a story full of potential was told by such shallow characters.

"It goes back to your underlying reason," says Chicago screenwriter

Carmen Brown. "Are you doing this for fame and money? I feel that the most powerful stories are the ones you can relate to and simply believe. You can always go and research a subject, but are you being true to self? Why are you doing this? That's what you have to examine."

Fortunately, many films have been created by writers who have taken the time to examine the pains, inner conflicts, fears, and the multitude of ways in which human beings are challenged to own their own humanness. These writers were not embarrassed to show us the depths of the human condition.

The hit comedy *The Full Monty,* a feature debut for both screenwriter Simon Beaufoy and director Peter Cattaneo, challenged many myths about male behavior. The story involves six men who are unemployed steel workers in Sheffield, England. They are all having difficulty coping with their unemployment and feelings of uselessness.

One of the men, Gaz, is amazed to discover how much women will pay to watch male strippers when the Chippendale dancers come through town. He thinks that if the Chippendales can pull in that kind of money, why wouldn't he and his friends be able to do the same? Although the film eventually leads us toward its hilarious finale, its core theme is centered on the friendships the men develop and the ways in which each will help the others to deal with their emotions, their losses, and the anxieties they have been facing. What a wonderful exposé of what transpires within the male psyche! How rewarding for all of us to be given new ways to better understand what men must confront when they lose their identity and must look inward to discover their hidden creative resources.

It seems all too often that the "big" films have the tendency to bypass the characters' emotional interiority. When the characters allow us to glimpse their true selves, it is usually done in the extreme, either as numb and stereotypical cardboard cutouts or characters who are hell-bent on violence and revenge. The audience is rarely given the opportunity to really understand why the characters are behaving the way they are, other than through simplistic and superficial backstories. We never find out about our heroes and their Achilles' heels. Thinking that these scripts can be churned out in the least amount of time possible, many writers continue to be swayed by popular trends. They follow the script formats that often encompass the big film mentality, offering stories and characters who leave us cold and who we will probably forget soon after leaving the theater.

"I think a lot of people believe that writing a 'commercial' script is the shrewdest way to break into the business," says Noah Baumbach. "But I think the best way to get noticed is to write something personal and original. What

I've discovered is that, in a lot of cases, the studios want more unique scripts. Later, they may water them down, but in the beginning they like to think that they're making something sort of different."

Chicago writer Ken Mader believes that the best stories are those that the writer feels most passionate about.

"Write stories that involve you and that move you," he suggests. "Whatever it is that gets your juices flowing you should write about. Don't worry about what the hot new trend in movies happens to be right now and then go and try and write that movie. Because by the time it gets made, the trend is over and there's something new. Try to start a new trend. The point is, don't be writing because you want to make a lot of money. That's the surest way to fail. Write because you love to write, because you love telling stories, because you love movies."

Why Do Certain Films Touch Us?

As human beings, we have access to a multitude of emotions that help to iden-tify who we are and that give meaning to the values we hold dear. The man-ner in which we choose to express these emotions helps to give us our uniqueness and colors the world in which we live.

For the characters who are telling us about their lives, their dreams, and their fears, it is much the same. There are many wonderful examples in which we are reminded that stories do not have to be complicated in order for us to be entertained, swept away, and mesmerized.

"I always look for the arc of the character, how at the very end, what les-son this character has learned," says Josefina Lopez. "Some of the films that I hate are the action-adventure kind. The bad guy kills the main character's wife, and he has to get revenge. And he does. So what did he learn at the end? Nothing. He learned that he was right, that he could kill the bad guy. That was a reaction, not a conscious choice. I would prefer to see how someone may have the same desire to go kill for revenge, but then maybe they don't do it. They've learned something different. They've learned compassion. And they learn something that gives them the freedom from that desire to get revenge or to react, and they actually make a choice not do that."

Numerous films have been made that did not receive awards nor achieve critical acclaim, yet were able to touch many people by conveying underlying messages through well-defined characters. *Patch Adams,* scripted by Steve Oedekerk, struck a nerve in audiences by virtue of its popular theme: the underdog against the establishment—in this case, the medical profession. Based on the life of the real Patch Adams, this film shows us a man who is not deterred when faced with having to choose between his personal values and compromising his beliefs for the sake of his career.

The story begins when Hunter Adams has suffered a nervous breakdown and has become suicidal. We learn, through his narration at the opening of the film, that his father had died when Hunter was just nine years old. He recounts a discussion in which his father told him that he had lost his soul in the Korean War. Not remembering this moment until now, Patch had always believed that he had been the reason why his father had died so suddenly. There is so much that he has forgotten and that has diminished his ability to relate to anyone. He voluntarily commits himself to a mental institution to be treated for the psychological pain he is experiencing. We learn more about him through his sessions with a psychiatrist, a doctor who is totally unable to relate to his patients.

During his stay at the mental hospital, he meets Arthur Mendelson, a brilliant scientist who is also a patient and who gives him the nickname "Patch." It is at this hospital that Patch discovers his greatest passion—to help people through their pain with laughter and respect. He feels tremendous joy while helping those patients who have given up. He knows that he has a gift—the ability to make people laugh—and he does all he can to share it with them. Nevertheless, Patch is faced with constant challenges as he interacts with the doctors who convey to their students that humanity has no place in a hospital. Patch goes beyond the dogma that is being preached, counteracting a set of complex moral issues. His determination to become a doctor, a healer of the sick, keeps him pushing forward. He defies those in charge and risks his career in the process.

In his opening monologue, he has given us a preview of what he will be called upon to do. He states, "All of life is a coming home . . . Finding a way home." He accomplishes his mission, for he never allows himself to succumb to the pressure of the establishment. His unwavering belief that laughter and humanness are antidotes to pain allows him to find his voice, and finally his "home."

Throughout this film, we witness a host of human behaviors, from the rigidity of some members of the medical profession who find Patch a threat to their old, worn-out beliefs and tenure, to the nursing staff who welcome Patch's determination to help suffering patients no matter the obstacles presented. There are moments when the film turns to melodrama for effect; however, moviegoers like to view films where the protagonist fights to beat the odds. They like to be reminded that there are, indeed, people who are willing to stand for the values they hold dear. In this story, they are reminded of how important the role of compassion is and how each of us yearns for respect and sensitivity when we are sick and dependent on strangers for our well-being. This is an uncomplicated film that evokes both laughter and tears. Although rather predictable, it has the power to reach us and to stay with us long after we have left the theater. Who has not experienced negative personal experiences with hospitals and bureaucracy? Who of us would not love to be under the care of a Patch Adams and be prescribed laughter as an antitoxic medication? Patch Adams is our conduit for attacking an establishment we often abhor. By standing for something bigger than ourselves, he also represents a tenaciousness that we admire and to which we aspire.

Writers have so much from which to choose when delving into the characters they will create and the stories they will tell. If you are having difficulty accessing your emotions, your characters will most likely have trouble accessing theirs. If you are opposed to using your own history, wisdom, and life experiences in developing your characters, your characters are more likely to become stereotypical, rigidly defined, and be people with whom your audience will have difficulty connecting.

In order to create believable characters, you must be willing to understand the psychology and motivation of each of your characters as you place them in your story. You must be able to access the emotions that often drive your own behavior. Your creativity will depend on how well you understand and accept your personal conflicts, fears, and motivations. You must dig deeply to find common threads between you and your characters. At times, you will have compassion for their plight, and at other times, you will find it difficult to relate to them. What is critical is not your like or dislike of the characters. What will stand out in your script is whether or not you have connected with them and taken your own life experiences to help give your characters powerful voices and valid reasons for belonging in your story. Do not give us gratuitous people who simply take up space in a film. Grab onto their visions, to their dreams, to their vulnerabilities, and be assured that your story will be all the more powerful and creative as a result.

When writing the Showtime Television movie *Free of Eden,* Delle Chatman was not afraid to put a lot of herself into the character of Nicole, a young girl from the projects seeking a better life. Delle and her Nicole share many common threads, such as striving for a good education. It has always been important for Delle to find her freedom through the use of words and language to search out the truth.

"Words are really my passion, and that's another place where I have something in common with Nicole," says Delle. "For me, it's the specifics of words and handling language and using words to get at the truth; for her it was new discoveries through education. She really became convinced, and I think rightly so, that education was her magic carpet. It could take her anywhere she wanted to go. If she didn't get it, she was going to be trapped. I think that I recognized very early on that words could build a bridge for me to get to the rest of the world, and they also built a sort of tunnel for me to sink into my deepest self. I like myself. I like what I have on my mind. I like getting to the bottom of what I'm feeling, and I always thought that writing is a way of celebrating my feelings, my own perspectives, and my ideas. I still feel that way."

Like Delle, screenwriter/director Paul Wei is not afraid to use himself in his stories. He draws from his Chinese roots to tell stories that he believes are meaningful.

"Chinese literature has always been toward more meaningful things," explains Paul. "When you tell a story, you want to tell a meaningful story. People in China, when they make a film, they are not thinking about making commercial films. They are thinking about making stories that will impress people with meaning. They are always talking about that—'it has meaning.' So that's why I think that when you tell a good story, it has to be a meaningful story."

Many scripts have been written with well-defined characters that have given power to the stories. Those screenwriters probably took copious notes about their observations of human behavior, attitudes, and the psychology that may be the guiding force in human beings. These writers may have solicited consultations from varied professionals with the hope that their characters would be credible to audiences. So, what happens when a story is sold and other creatives get their imaginations rolling on these scripts? Will the characters be presented as the original writers envisioned? Backstories are sometimes viewed as extraneous by the next set of writers hired for the rewrites. New visions of the script's messages might be introduced, and voilà, a new script is born!

It can become very discouraging to think of all the work entailed in constructing a good script and realize that once it leaves the writer's domain, everything in it can change. Is it worth all the effort to create memorable characters if someone else is going to determine their fate?

There is no question that these issues are terribly difficult to reconcile. They are perplexing and often anger-producing for any writer who takes pride in his creative vision. Perhaps the only solace to a bruised ego is that it is never a waste of time for screenwriters to write powerful stories with incredibly interesting and realistic characters. It is never a meaningless task to bring stories to their full potential, with the powerful voices of characters acting as emissaries of the writer's intended messages.

Ten Common Fears About Story and Character Development

1. I am embarrassed to be seen through my characters.
2. Once I write a story using myself, there will be no other stories to tell.
3. I'm afraid to divulge too much of myself in my characters for fear of what my friends/family will recognize.
4. I'm afraid to go beyond the script formula.
5. I'm afraid to show pain, because I won't do it well.
6. If I show a truthful ending instead of a happy one, audiences won't like it.
7. If I show too many emotional scenes, people will accuse me of writing a "tear-jerker."
8. If my characters are too serious, audiences will get bored.
9. If I create characters who show their fears, they will be considered weak.
10. I'm afraid to delve too much into the characters' emotions, because I will get lost in the process.

No matter what happens to the original script, all of the efforts made and all of the energy spent perfecting it will not have been for naught. We cannot determine what happens in the future, how the dream to create a winning script will become realized. What we do know is that in the scheme of things, our creative efforts are part of the screenwriter's journey. When stories mirror real life, we can come that much closer to honoring the fact that human beings are powerful because of the feelings that are in their hearts. The stories you will write will be everlasting if your characters provide links to our own traditions, themes, legacies, and humanity.

Will I Face the Fears?

In creating powerful stories and believable characters, writers must be willing to understand what stops them from writing what they know. What you have experienced in your own life is the key to your understanding of the inner workings of your unique characters. Being willing to explore their emotions in depth means that you will need to identify your sensitivities and the feelings you express, as well as those you keep hidden. If your characters shy away from showing their vulnerabilities, does that mean that you, as well, shy away from yours? If you are reticent to show your anger, sadness, rage, sorrow, frustration,

Ten Common Myths About Story and Character Development

1. It is not necessary to show "process" in film. Stories are more effective when they get to the point quickly, without pausing to get to know the characters.
2. Screenwriting formulas encourage quick-fix solutions because of structure constraints, so there's no other option.
3. Certain genres, such as comedy and action/adventure, don't require character depth, because audiences don't care about them; they only want to be entertained.
4. Agents are not interested in writers who are too "self-indulgent" and who use their own histories in scripts.
5. Writing believable characters and stories means that you have to present stereotypes with which audiences are familiar.
6. Because I'm young, I don't have the life experiences on which to draw material for my stories.
7. Putting oneself in the script is amateurish and the sign of an inexperienced writer.
8. There are too many time constraints to build in more than superficial backstories and character histories.
9. Agents and producers prefer clever scripts with quick resolutions and fast-paced character interaction.
10. No one pays attention to secondary characters, so you don't have to worry about giving them too much depth or emotion.

or loneliness, will your character be hesitant to do so as well? The following fears will encourage you to look into the mirror, which may shed some light and bring answers to the surface that will help clarify what the fears represent.

Will I Challenge the Myths?

Many myths can abound in the writer's imagination as a script begins its journey from start to finish. Fearing rejection, many writers listen to these myths, which often encourage them to write formulaic stories and those adhering to popular trends. It is crucial to combat these beliefs, which belong to the invisible voices that can rob the screenwriter of creative energy. The following myths are a few examples of the powerful messages that can stifle and inhibit the writer's true voice. When believed, these myths can only lead to disaster, for the creative process has been negated.

Will I Take the Risks?

Screenwriters are dependent on the knowledge of their craft in order to create meaningful stories with characters who will become memorable. If they strike a chord, it is because they have been created so that moviegoers can identify with the issues, as well as the feelings the characters are expressing. It may require that you take the time and effort to learn everything you can about your characters. It may involve hours of research with no assurances that your script will sell. If you decide to leave nothing to chance, then consider yourself a risk-taker, and continue writing the quality scripts you are dying to create.

How am I willing to . . .

1. Gain a deeper understanding of why I am writing this script and why I have chosen these specific characters and events for my story?
2. Draw upon my own history and life experiences in developing characters and story lines?
3. Explore the ways in which my characters should express themselves, and let them emerge fully and completely?
4. Use silence and nuance for character development whenever appropriate?
5. Ensure that my characters' evolvement is true to life?
6. Challenge worn-out myths and stereotypes that present negative or non–reality-based generalizations in film?
7. Experience what I want my characters to experience?
8. Commit to writing my story, instead of just fantasizing about it?
9. Prevent my own fears and hesitations from overriding my characters' behaviors and actions?
10. Explore my characters, their histories, their challenges, their secrets, and the ways in which they express emotions and inner feelings?

●

CHAPTER 10

Anne Rapp: Preserving the Heritage of Storytelling

*I'd rather touch ten people with a little short story than make a million
dollars with a Hollywood movie that doesn't touch anyone.*
Anne Rapp

The Journey Begins

*Although she would already be in her early forties before pursuing a writing career, Anne
Rapp had always enjoyed listening to and sharing stories. She was raised in the Texas
panhandle in a small town close enough to the Oklahoma border to consider herself part
Okie. She learned the art of storytelling from friends and families, who swapped yarns
on the front porch, something she now considers a lost art.*

Sitting around the porch and telling stories is what we used to do for entertainment. I was born in 1951, so it wasn't back in the covered wagon days. We
had television sets. But we lived in a small town that was very remote. Our
little town had three hundred people and was a hundred miles from any town
of any size. Saturday night, people came up to your house or you went down
to someone else's house, and somebody played the piano or people would sit
around and talk and tell stories of that time. I still think in terms of old-fash-
ioned storytelling as entertainment. It's much more interesting. As a screenwriter, as a fiction writer, and as a human being that goes to see movies and
reads books, I enjoy the kinds of stories that human beings can tell about
themselves and their particular aspects of life. I'm not into blowups and mon-
sters and all of that.

Taking Risks

As an adult, Anne lived in Dallas, then Los Angeles, spending sixteen years as a script supervisor for numerous well-known films, such as The Firm *and* The Accidental Tourist.

I've actually only been writing since about 1994, so five or six years at the most. Before that, I was a script supervisor, which is a craft job on the set. The script supervisor is basically in charge of continuity for a movie, because of the fact that a movie is shot completely out of sequence. You're like Girl Friday for the director, because you're keeping track of all the little details, so that all he or she has to concentrate on is the creative part.

I'd worked on all kinds of films, but had become bored with it. I thought, "It's not like some other director's going to come along and make it any more fun." I have to say that Robert Benton had a big impact on me initially. I used to tell him stories about things that happened to me while I was growing up. There was one story in particular that I told him, a high school story, that I had always loved. He had made the comment to me many times, You should write that story. So one summer, I had about three months off, and it was right before I was going to do *The Firm* in Memphis with Sydney Pollack. They pushed the movie back a little bit, so I ended up with about three months off, which I loved.

I decided to sit down and try to write some of my childhood memories. I didn't even know where to start, but I sat at the typewriter and started spitting stuff out. I realized very quickly, first of all, that I loved it. Instead of just writing down memories, I found myself trying to craft a little story. But I was all over the map, and I realized that the only way I was really going to learn something was to get into some kind of a structure where you have deadlines. No one can teach you to write, but if you commit yourself to a workshop or something, that's usually really just committing yourself to writing.

When I went to Memphis to do *The Firm,* I discovered Oxford, Mississippi, which is a wonderful town with a great literary history. Faulkner's home is there, and it has the best bookstore I've ever been to in my life, called Square Books. I was so inspired by that bookstore. I would go down there every Sunday that I had off, and I started reading a lot of Southern literature. I thought this might be the place I need to be, to give it a stab. I knew if I stayed in Hollywood, I'd get too distracted. The business is in your face constantly out here.

I'd been reading some of Barry Hannah's short stories, and he's a marvelous writer, and I found out he taught there in Oxford at the University of Mississippi. So I wrote him a letter and said, Can I get in your class? He saved a spot, and I saved every penny, so I could live in Oxford for a year. I went to this little town, where I really didn't know anybody. It's as far from Hollywood as you can get, which is exactly what I needed. To be honest, the best part about it was that nobody gave a hoot that I was from Hollywood. In fact, it was something I tried not to put emphasis on, because I wanted to see what I was made of without that. People say to me all the time, How courageous of you to do that. Quite honestly, I don't see it that way. The way I looked at it, I had nothing to lose. I had a great career. There's nothing that says that I'm supposed to be able to write, but I'm going to give it a shot, and if I do make it, that's great. If not, I haven't lost anything. I still have this great job, this great life, this great career, and I've given something a shot that, if nothing else, was a life-inspiring experience.

Cookie's Fortune

Living in Oxford provided inspiration for Anne's stories and characters. She believes that it is important to immerse yourself in the type of people and surroundings you want to write about.

I think as a writer, you can't always write about something from the outside. I think your best work is when you're truly on the inside. It all goes back to what they tell every starting writer—write what you know. That's a little cliché, but what it means is that, if you put yourself in an arena where you understand who the people are and exactly what they would do in situations that come up, half the battle's done for you. It gives you so much better opportunity for depth and for writing what's appropriate for every character with every turn of event, as opposed to writing about something from the outside. This is a whole different kind of writing. Just take adventure writing. I like to read about guys who climb glaciers and things, the kinds of articles you read in men's journals. And I guarantee you, you can tell the guys who are really in there and know it and the guys who did it from the outside. I think movies are that way too.

Anne typically starts the process by coming up with a general idea for a story line and central characters. Cookie's Fortune *was her first script to be made into a feature, directed by Robert Altman.*

Basically, I start with an event and characters that I know are going to be part of the story. In many ways, I let that event and those characters carry me. I'm not one of those writers who sits down and plots out an entire story on note cards to make sure it's all there. I'm not saying that a really strong plot line is not important. It's essential. But I have to find it through the characters and the events.

I'll use *Cookie's Fortune* as an example. It's very characteristic of the way I write. I had an idea of a woman who's very old and wants to join her dead husband, so she kills herself. A couple of her family members cover it up, because they consider it disgraceful, and it backfires on them. That was the idea. I showed Robert Altman the idea, and he really liked it and threw a couple of other things at me, too. He thought it would be a great movie idea if the backfire was that they covered it up to look like a robbery and murder, and somebody got implicated. Now, you've really got a conflict. So that was all we had to go with. I just started with the characters. You've got the old lady, and you've got the family members. We had talked about two nieces and the man who lived out back, the one who would be implicated. The first thing I did was try to figure out who these two people are and what their relationship is. Then all of a sudden, this character named Emma surfaced. A young girl who had a completely different point of view from the other two women. And this character just appeared uninvited. She eventually became one of the best characters in the movie.

I think what happens is this: If I'm writing and I've got a main character, for example, who goes to town to get groceries and goes into a store to buy catfish or something, there's got to be a *person* there that sells it instead of just "a catfish guy." From my experience growing up, everyone you run across is somehow in your life. It's not like going to a convenience store in L.A., and you'll never see that guy behind the counter again. He's almost not a real human being. He doesn't have anything to do with your life. But if you live in a small town, practically everybody you run into is an integral part of your life, and you know that you're going to see that person over and over again. They're going to somehow connect to you in some way. So as a writer, I can't create a bartender or someone who works in the dry cleaners without making them an integral part of the story and giving them a specific persona.

Never in my life, in the kinds of arenas I write in anyway, is there ever a gratuitous person. That's another thing that I love about small towns. That's why I don't write stories about Los Angeles.

Collaboration

Robert Altman would direct two other projects written by Anne Rapp—a one-hour episode for the ABC-TV series, Gun, *and a new feature called* Dr. T. *Anne believes she and Altman work so well together because they have a very similar sensibility.*

Our sense of humor is sort of the same. We're both huge risk-takers. We're both gamblers in our lives. We're both interested in people who are risk-takers and who step outside the line. We have a lot of similarities that way. And yet, the other side of the coin is that he's often very, very cynical, and I have a tendency to sway to the sweet and sappy. So we complement each other in that way. I've said this so many times in interviews, and I'm almost sick of hearing myself say it, but he hardened me when I needed it, and I softened him when he needed it. We're a circus net for each other, when we go overboard one way or another. But in general, we're always on the same train to the same place, and that's a great feeling, because I never sit down at that computer or print anything out on a piece of paper and hand it to him being afraid he's going to think I'm a bad writer. He has that amazing respect for writers.

Altman, contrary to a myth out there, is not arrogant at all. He's one of those guys who has complete respect for everybody that works on his films. My work, which I think is a masterpiece when I print that final draft out, is just a blueprint for Altman to do his work, for the actors to interpret the characters the way they want. They add a lot to every one of those characters. As a screenwriter, you have to know that going in. I think fifteen years as a script supervisor, watching the process from the front row seat, was invaluable in that way. I was the person who had a script in my lap every day, all day, watching actors change the lines, watching the scenes become something else, watching what good directors did with bad scripts, what bad directors did with good scripts. All that experience helped.

Parting Words

Anne believes that the modern age has taken things away from humanity, such as the ability to really listen to each other. As a storyteller, Anne's goal is to touch others by writing about the human condition.

It is important that we present something else out there besides the current sea of special effects and monster movies. Like small human stories. I try to stay up with the computer age, but quite honestly, it drives me crazy. I hate what we've lost in this high-tech world, what I've lost. Even if you're one of those people who'd like to ignore all those things, we're all caught up in it. There's no way out of it. We're so dependent on computers now. Several of the actors told me, when they read *Cookie's Fortune,* that one of the things they loved about it was that they were halfway through the script when someone pulled out a cell phone, and it was only at that moment that they realized this was a modern-day story. The script had taken them to a place that, with the exception of just a few little things, was almost like going back in time. I think there's a subconscious thing in me that never wants to let go of that. So, I almost capture it naturally in stories, because I'm just so desperate not to let go of the past, and the beauty of it, in my life.

The human condition, to me, is the only reason we're here and the only reason I want to write. Those are the kind of stories that have always appealed to me—the human stories, the family stories, about going day to day through life and making our lives as nice as we can possibly make them. That's what I like to read, that's the kind of movies I like to go see, and that's the only kind of stories I want to write.

●

CHAPTER 11

Will My Story, Characters, and Audience Connect?

We need movies that will uplift. We need to see
that maybe everything's going to be all right.
Betty Hager

What qualities do films have to have to be able to connect audiences to their stories and characters? Of course, we are each drawn to different types of themes and genres. Nevertheless, there are common threads that help to connect us. When a film can, even in a small way, achieve that connectedness, then something important has been realized.

In recent years, there have been a number of films that audiences enjoyed, spoke about, and loved to recount. One of the biggest blockbusters in recent years was *Titanic*, written and directed by James Cameron. What was it about that film that stirred our imagination? Was it the reality of the story, knowing that this tragedy had actually taken place? Was it the amazing special effects, the sweeping music, and elaborate sets and costumes? *Titanic* is an extraordinary example of the power of film and the impact it can have on an audience. It demonstrates an ability to alter the way in which we perceive monumental events that happen to innocent people. In this film, the characters' very private and personal story stayed with us much longer than our memories of the props, costumes, or special effects.

Like *Titanic*, the romantic comedy *Shakespeare in Love* was a big hit with audiences of all ages and won numerous Academy Awards, including Best

Original Screenplay for Mark Norman and Tom Stoppard. This undocumented account of William Shakespeare's love life begins with a young Will who is suffering from writer's block, as he attempts to write a new play titled *Romeo and Ethel, the Pirate's Daughter.* The main problem is that he has no inner spark from which to describe true feelings of love between his characters. As fate would have it, he soon meets Viola De Lesseps and falls madly in love with her. As Elizabethan social norms contrive to keep them apart, William is now inspired to turn his comedy into a great tragic romance.

Although the film transports us to a time when social norms were far more demanding, it modernizes age-old themes of love and passion, conveyed through poetry. Atop beautiful cinematography and top-notch acting and directing, the film triggers something more personal in its audience—a story of love, a love almost lost and, in the end, lost for the sake of social convention. Audiences responded to the power of this film, not only because of its exquisiteness, but because they recognized the pain, the passion, and the loss that knows no bounds and parallels—for many, the very same emotions they have endured. Could Shakespeare have imagined that a rendition of his poetic form would strike a chord with audiences in the twentieth century? The film demonstrates that across time, people have yearned to see reflections of their own humanness and appreciate spending a few moments in reverie, remembering their first introduction to love.

There are many films without traditional happy endings that are still able to impact audiences in powerful ways. One such example is the poignant and movingly-funny Oscar winner, *Life is Beautiful,* written and directed by Roberto Benigni, who also starred in the film. This Italian film explores the power of laughter to lift the human spirit, even when faced with incredible tragedy. The story begins in 1939 in the Tuscan town of Arezzo, where Guido falls in love, marries, and has a son with a beautiful teacher named Dora. Their fairytale marriage is marred by the dark shadow of Fascism. In 1945, the war is almost over, although Jewish-Italian families like Guido's are still being persecuted. One day, Guido's family is taken into police custody, then herded on a train to a concentration camp. Dora voluntarily joins her family and eventually becomes separated from them. Guido is determined to shield his son from the horrors and terrifying realities of life in a concentration camp. He uses his humor and imagination to spin a web of stories that help keep the boy's spirits from tumbling downward.

This powerful film demonstrates to what lengths a father, who fervently loves his son, will go to protect him. No parent can see this movie without reeling from the dread and pain it generates. It is a story of human tragedy, human survival, and the gift of love, portrayed with images that will not be forgotten. It would be hard to imagine how anyone could not be moved by Guido's courage, pure love, and the total sacrifice he displays to save his son. His passion for life, his gift of laughter, help us to grasp the very essence of what it means to love as only a parent can. The themes enable us to reflect on who we are, who we might become under certain conditions, and the creativity that can emerge under even the most horrendous moments.

There are films that may be less well-known with the general populace, yet which have also garnered audience approval. They often present us with subject matter that causes us to reflect on our own vulnerabilities. They remind us of the dire consequences to the human spirit when our lives are out of balance.

One such example is *What's Eating Gilbert Grape?* written by Peter Hedges and based on his novel, and directed by Lasse Hallstrom.

The story is about a young man, Gilbert Grape, who has taken on the role of father figure in caring for his obese mother, handicapped brother, and two younger sisters. His biological father is long dead, the victim of a suicide, and his five-hundred-pound mother barely moves from the sofa, where she has spent much of her adult life. Gilbert's gentle sweetness enables him to cope with one family crisis after another, although it is obvious that the trials of his days are beginning to suffocate him. It is only when he meets an extraordinary young woman, who arrives in his small town of Endora, Iowa, in an RV driven by her grandmother, that Gilbert finally begins to question his own desires and the dreams that he has put aside. His love for the girl creates a new tension and excitement that enables Gilbert to break free from his monotonous and difficult trappings. Those who yearn to escape exhausting responsibilities can appreciate how hard Gilbert worked to keep his family unit in tact. Those who battle weight can empathize with his mother's feelings of guilt, shame, and helplessness. It is another example of a story without a happy ending, and at the film's end, we sense that Gilbert has renewed hope and a better appreciation of life with which to continue his difficult journey.

Love stories have always drawn people into darkened theaters. Nora Ephron's *Sleepless in Seattle,* a remake of the classic *An Affair to Remember,* is about a widower, Sam, who has trouble coping with the swift and unexpected death of his wife. Concerned about his father's grief, Sam's son, Jonah, calls a nationally-broadcast radio talk show in search of a new wife for his father, who has become, literally, sleepless in Seattle. A young woman, Annie, hears the broadcast and, like thousands of other women across the country, is drawn to the young boy's plea. After Sam describes his feelings about his deceased wife to the on-air host, Annie becomes convinced that it is her destiny to meet Sam, despite her engagement to another man and despite the fact that Sam does not know that they are made for one another . . . at least not until Jonah intervenes.

Ten Common Fears About Your Audience

1. If I really expose my characters, audiences will be turned off.
2. Since I'm not a very deep person, showing emotions in my characters will come across as forced and pretentious.
3. Things that fascinate me about people will bore audiences.
4. No matter how hard I try, I won't be able to write a meaningful story with interesting characters.
5. I'm afraid to pick the genre I love best, rather than a genre that is popular at the moment.
6. I'm afraid to write a story without a happy ending, even if it's appropriate to do so.
7. If I get too involved with all my characters' histories and unique feelings, I'll get too overwhelmed and not be able to write clearly.
8. I'm afraid to show pain in any form other than anger without it seeming maudlin.
9. If I go beyond the accepted script formula, my story will falter and ramble, and I will get lost.
10. I have a powerful story to tell, but it might not be popular.

There are many themes presented in this film, from dealing with the loss of a loved one to the synchronicity of finding "true" love. Audiences long to believe in these messages and yearn for the happy endings that they want to experience in their own lives. They can identify with the impact of certain "accidental" meetings and wonder about the once-in-a-lifetime love affair that may happen to only a select few. As the success of this film demonstrated, conveying powerful emotions and universal themes will provide audiences with the much-needed moments of fantasizing that these films offer as gifts to our imagination. When films deliver characters and story lines that peak our interest, and when laughter is offered openly and convincingly, we can leave the theater refreshed and renewed. Over and over again, audiences express their appreciation to storytellers who have sought to create stories that not only entertain, but strike chords of recognition in our hearts.

Most screenwriters are committed to writing stories that fascinate and intrigue them. They seek to tell us stories that can elicit powerful emotions and trigger feelings that we may have "left behind" somewhere on our journey of life. As we sit in darkened theaters watching a story unfold, we are transported to other worlds and introduced to characters who may resemble us and share in our dreams.

Ten Common Myths About Your Audience

1. Audiences are comfortable with the Hollywood formula, and that's what they expect to see.
2. Audiences want to see "larger-than-life" characters, not people like themselves.
3. Audiences only want happy endings.
4. Writing stories that are important to me will not be exciting enough for the audience.
5. Audiences want to escape from everyday life and don't want to see films about painful and emotional issues.
6. Audiences want a lot of action and special effects, so they feel that they got their money's worth.
7. Scripts should either be character-driven or story-driven. If you try to do both, you'll confuse the audience.
8. Simple, human stories rarely get seen, because there isn't enough audience interest for them to make it to the big screen.
9. Audiences don't have the patience to sit through introspective stories. They want quick resolutions.
10. My role as a writer is not to tell audiences too much about the characters. Audiences like to figure that out for themselves.

When a story can penetrate our defenses, we must consider ourselves fortunate. We have been given an opportunity to connect with characters and a story worth remembering. When the writer has been successful in portraying characters as real human beings, complete with imperfections and vulnerabilities, we must applaud this experience and honor that we have witnessed the universal nature of the human condition.

Will I Face the Fears?

Screenwriters must be willing to ask a great deal of themselves, as they create the characters who will populate their stories. Putting yourself on the line and going against current trends can be scary. Writing your own original story means knowing why you are writing the story you have chosen in the first place. Are you willing to commit to this story, no matter what others recommend? The most powerful stories are those that often did not, in the very beginning, draw much attention. Write what you believe, and do not compromise when you create the characters of your imagination.

Will I Challenge the Myths?

If you believe that someone can predict what scripts will or will not sell, then you will be tempted to buy into false beliefs that will encourage you to write stories to which you are not truly committed. You will have to find the inner strength to be true to the stories and characters you know and understand, for those will bring you the most satisfaction and potential for success. Hollywood has the ability to deter you from your screenwriting experiences, if you allow yourself to believe common myths about the writing process. Challenging these myths will bring you closer to creating unforgettable stories and characters.

Will I Take the Risks?

What have you learned about the characters that you want to introduce in your script? Do you really know them? Writing what you know and what lies close to your heart may not fit the current trends. Are you willing to turn away from the seductions that seem to promise success and money, or will you write in a way that honors your own history and life experiences?

In what ways am I willing to . . .

1. Take the necessary risks in letting my characters really "be seen"?
2. Let the viewer get to know my characters, because they are reality-based and believable?
3. Use what I know in my writing and not succumb to popular trends?
4. Commit to researching the characters I have chosen for my story?
5. Avoid creating stereotypical characters and endings that reinforce clichés?
6. Make certain that I write from the heart and write what I love best?
7. Show my characters as real human beings with emotions, vulnerabilities, and imperfections?
8. Let my characters speak their own unique language, instead of pat, formulaic dialogue?
9. Avoid quick-fix solutions to complex problems?
10. Consult with people, when needed, who can give me the information I need to create believable characters?

●

CHAPTER 12

David Marconi: Digging for the Truth

*If you look for stumbling blocks, you will stumble. You have to
believe in your better judgment. You just have to go forward.*
David Marconi

The Journey Begins

*David Marconi first became interested in filmmaking at the age of ten, when he began mak-
ing home movies with his friends. Although he loved moviemaking, he abhorred the solitary process of writing and used his cinematic skills to get out of many writing assignments.*

I would make a story I wanted to tell, because I got tired of watching my
father's home movies. Every weekend, I would scrape together my pennies to
buy Super 8 cartridges and go off and make my little opuses—stories that were
important to me at the time. I put my friends in the movies, then I'd charge
them for seeing themselves, and I would charge their parents double. We would
have popcorn and make a night of it. We were ten- and twelve-year-olds at this
point. It's not like anyone had Hollywood in their eyes. I think today, the
younger generation is more savvy to that. But back then, it was all done in fun.

One thing led to the next, and I continued to make these movies in high
school. I continued to get better at it. In high school, I would get out of writing assignments by offering something different to my instructor. I'd say,
Listen, you're going to get five papers on Descartes. Why don't you just let me
take some of the theories and apply them to a little movie I'll make? So I'd
put together a story and shoot it with the drama department of the high

school, then march everybody down to the little theater. It was a fun way to get out of writing.

At the time, the idea of sitting in a room by myself writing wasn't appealing. I found more passion being with a bunch of friends and a camera and running around directing people. Some people are good in a room by themselves. I was an only child for eight years. I could certainly amuse myself, but any chance I got to hang out with my friends, I would do it. As an only child, you also retreat into a world of make-believe. I read a lot when I was a kid, especially about history. It was fascinating to me.

After high school, I was awarded an alumni merit scholarship for filmmaking, which sent me to the University of Southern California for film school. I packed my bags and entered their undergraduate film program. The people there making films were dedicated to it. It's a very intensive program, and there's not a lot of free time, so the insecurity and long hours was something you kind of fell into.

One of the things they did was force you to become a writer. They forced you to sit down and start crafting a story and then a script. They encouraged you to find your voice as a filmmaker. It was at that time that I started my first screenplay, which was based on an article I had read on terrorists in West Germany. I immediately dove into it, went to the library, and started researching. The more I delved into the story, the more the characters from the article started to come alive. I then sold my car, went to West Germany, and interviewed people about what was happening over there. I combined the trip with a summer course in Germany that USC offered at the time on the Nazi propaganda films made during the second World War. I came back and cowrote the script with a classmate. It was immediately optioned by my writing instructor, who gave us $250 and lunch at a restaurant called Maribelle on Sunset Boulevard. I thought, Wow, this is it, I'm on my way.

Despite the thrill of an option, David's passion still lay in filmmaking, rather than screenwriting. He gained invaluable production experience working on several Francis Ford Coppola features.

Directing was my passion. After getting out of college, I said, Hey, here I am, I'm ready to direct. They'd say, Well, where are your scripts? I realized I had to write the $1.5 million movie that someone would let me go out and do on my own. But I also had to survive. My girlfriend at the time was involved with Zoetrope, which is Francis Coppola's company. We volunteered our services to work on *The Outsiders* and *Rumble Fish*. We were in Tulsa for six or seven months working on those two movies. To me, that was my grad school. Francis is a man who knows how to tell great stories, as well as direct actors. I was able to apprentice directly under him for the better part of six months. After that, I wrote a script on my own, based on a short article that Francis had turned me onto. At the same time, I needed to survive, so my next job was doing craft service, setting out M&Ms and sodas for the crew. It was a bad "B" movie company. If people didn't get paid cash at the end of the day, they wouldn't show up for the next day's work. I thought there must be a better way to get into the film business.

Around this time, people started asking me if I wanted to be an art director. They asked me if I wanted to be a prop master. I was getting offers for these jobs, but it wasn't what I wanted to be doing. Because of the student films I had made and the previous scripts I had written, I got an agent, who was a friend of mine from film school. He hooked me up with a producer. I had this great idea for a script and pitched it to Warner Brothers. They responded, and boom, I got hired to write it.

David credits much of his early drive to succeed to his youth and to a belief that anything was possible, as evidenced by many USC alumni.

Well, I was a kid. When you're that age, you don't look at stumbling blocks. You just plow through, thinking that anything is possible. George Lucas had made it, Spielberg had made it, and there was a real energy at film school that said anybody could make it. None of us were going to be stopped. We looked at the other students who had graduated, and they were making it. They were taking over the industry. That filled our egos with a sense that we could do it. There was a real camaraderie and a good support group that helped us believe anything was possible. I imagine that if I'd spent my college career in Chicago in an unrelated field, I'd be looking at it through very different eyes. But because I spent my college career in Los Angeles and had a support system, I never saw the stumbling blocks.

You have to be willing to fall down and pick yourself up. You also have to be willing to know that the first script you write may not sell. The second script you write may not sell. But it's part of the learning process. The benefit I had was that when I was going through the learning process, I was in school. It wasn't like I had a family of five to support. I was able to take risks. To write a script requires a lot of energy. I think the most difficult thing is to find the time to sit down and write. If you're supporting a family and have a nine-to-five job, I would imagine it's hard to come home, spend time with your family, and still find two or three quiet hours in which to write the great American screenplay. It requires discipline and time management.

Mud, Sweat and Gears

David's first script for Warner Brothers was Mud, Sweat and Gears. *Although this would lead to other writing assignments, David began to feel increasingly frustrated when none of his stories were getting made.*

I had an original idea based on an incident that had happened to me in college. I developed the story with a producer, then we marched into Warner Brothers and told them the idea, and they said, Great, we want it. Here's a bunch of money. Go off and write it. So that was my first script. They hired Thomas Carter to direct it, which was great, because most of the time, they would read a script and say, Thank you very much, we'll get back to you. You'd get paid, but you would never hear from these people again. But in this case, they wanted to make it. Thomas Carter, at the time, had done several episodes of *Miami Vice* and was a hot director in town. But at the end of the day, he never stepped forward to make the movie, and the whole thing turned into an exercise in development, which to me was very disappointing. When you endeavor on a project for a year and a half and then it doesn't get made, it's frustrating. Scripts aren't the greatest written medium to read in the world. Unless the film is made, you don't feel a sense of gratification. You feel gratification in the sense you're paid to write and can say you're a working screenwriter, but eventually that's not enough. Eventually you want your films to get made, otherwise, what's the point of it all? So that's what happened there. After *Mud, Sweat and Gears*, I was hired to do another script for Warner Brothers. I wrote three movies back-to-back for them, but the movies weren't getting made. These were big-budget pictures, which require a lot of elements to get made, so again, I was feeling an incredible sense of frustration.

Eventually, one of the producers I'd worked for asked if I had any ideas of my own that I wanted to do. A friend of mine had told me this great idea, so I pitched it to the producer, and he liked it. He'd just worked with Morgan Mason, who produced *sex, lies, and videotape* and told the story to Morgan. Morgan took it to Columbia Tri-Star Home Video, and they said, Great, we love it, let's do it. The problem was, they had no development money, so I had to write the script without the big payday. They helped me with survival money, and that was it. I did three or four drafts and went broke during the process, but I was writing this one for me. I was going to direct it; it was my baby.

I had to move out of my apartment and into a friend's basement. There I was, sleeping on the couch in my late twenties. That was a difficult pill to swallow when I had friends who were starting to become attorneys and stuff. I still look back and remember those moments. They're days that certainly give one strength to weather the storms.

The Harvest

The Harvest was about a writer who believes he's uncovered an organ transplant scam. David knew he was taking a risk with this project, but it was a gamble that would pay off for him.

Eventually, after three or four drafts, I got the script to the point where the producers and actors and everybody said "great." It was a gamble. There are no sure things in the film business. Columbia Tri-Star finally got on board and "green-lit" the film. It was the big break in my career, because now I was a writer/director of a feature. We shot that down in Mexico, and they sold it to forty-four territories. It was a successful film for what it cost to make. It was a small action/adventure piece, but it caught the attention of the big action/adventure producers.

After *The Harvest* was complete, I was approached by Simpson/Brockheimer Productions. They wanted to do an action picture involving loss of personal freedom. As a kid, I grew up on the conspiracy films of the seventies—*The Parallax View, Marathon Man, Three Days of the Condor.* I loved conspiracy movies. I loved action movies. I grew up on the stuff. It was exciting to me. So I combined their idea with my interest in tech and started doing research. I went to the library and started reading and, like any good reporter, kept digging until a story started to appear. The movie would eventually become *Enemy of the State.* As far as the characters, I read books to find interesting character studies. I found a book called *Vendetta,* which is a story about what happened to Edmond Safra when Jim Robinson of American Express went after him in an attempt to discredit him and destroy his reputation. I used the basis of Safra's struggle to clear his name as a template for the Robert Dean character in *Enemy of the State.*

Living to Write

David believes it's difficult to write a great piece of work without having significant life experiences to draw from.

Great writers say that in order to have something to say, you need to live life. Look at Hemingway or Faulkner. These were people who lived their lives and ultimately had something to say. The problem with Hollywood is that it's an animal that eats its own entrails. People in Hollywood sit in their apartments and write about the last TV show they saw. And in that sense, it's a bad town to be in, because it doesn't generate any fresh ideas. It's also a town where they always want to see the other guy fail. It's one of the things that permeates Hollywood. It's unfortunate, but it's one of the reasons that I get out of that town a lot, to get away from the negativity. I'm constantly trying to put myself out there to find the stories and places I've never been before, to be inspired.

What motivates me are films with characters that I can relate to, or when someone is put into an extraordinary situation. That's what really pulls my strings as far as stories go. I really enjoy movies that, at the end of the day, give me something to go home with. Movies that try to communicate some kind of message without bludgeoning you over the head. Filmmaking is a fantastic medium. Films are still one of the few places that you can still communicate in a way that's more meaningful than what's packaged for the six o'clock news. You can watch CNN or read *Time* magazine and feel well-informed, but that's not really the case. There are many points of view out there from many different sources. They always say that truth has three sides: his version and her version and the truth. To really explore issues, you have to get beneath what people say or understand why a particular thing happened. You have to examine and understand the issues from many angles.

Now, I'm fortunate in that I can live basically anywhere I want. I go to Europe to write for about four or five months of the year. It refreshes my brain. It's refreshing to meet people who are what they do. In Los Angeles, you're in the city of make-believe. Everyone is one thing, but they're trying to be something else. There's nothing wrong with that, but as far as feeding your creativity and getting a good down-to-earth story, it's not really the place to be. You want to come in fresh with something that hasn't been recycled. The moment an interesting story comes out in the *Los Angeles Times,* by eight o'clock in the morning, it's on the desk of fifty producers. Once an article comes out in *Time* magazine or *Vanity Fair,* it's optioned by the time you read it. The studios have already pored over all the books that come out in galley form before they ever hit the publishers. So, to be a writer and come up with something fresh, you need to explore the smaller nooks we live in—the stories that the big producers in town won't have access to, whether it's an interpersonal story or something that you and your buddy have made up, like *The Blair Witch Project.* There are millions of stories out there. You have to go into your inner self and find what motivates you as a person. Hang your hat on that, because ultimately, whatever you do has to pull you through the process, which could be anywhere from a year to three years.

Ultimately, everybody has their own path. I believe that in order to write well, you have to be happy. You have to be in a good environment. You just have to allow the creative juices to flow, as they say. The best way to do that is to be in a stress-free world, if that's possible, whether it's in a basement in Iowa or in an apartment in Rome.

Despite his success with films such as Enemy of the State, *the* Mission Impossible *sequel and* wwIII.com, *David has a very grounded view about where his screenwriting journey has been and where it's taking him.*

My success didn't happen overnight. I worked twelve years on writing before my movies started getting made. It was a long, hard struggle. I don't look at my success as something that happened instantly, nor do I take it for granted. It's something that happened very incrementally. And it was something that I worked very long and hard on.

I've been happy with the way things have gone. The studio usually pays a lot more than the independent world. You're also able to do bigger-budget action pictures, which I tend to write. The fact that I've written big-action studio pictures makes me a more interesting commodity for an independent company. I'm also able to parlay my success as a studio writer into writer/director deals at the independent level. For example, I'm now being offered writing/directing deals because of the success of *Enemy of the State.*

Ideally, I would like to do one project I care about per year. I don't want to get too spread out. I don't want a big production company. I want to be find a balance between my work and my personal life. Again, I believe you need to live life in order to have something to say.

Parting Words

Look at the stories around you. There's room for all types of movies. They can be about a family in a small town or about Uncle Fester who went a little crazy and was taken away one night. It can be anything from *Ordinary People* to *Terminator II.* What's most important is that the characters you create are real for you and that they have a resonance for you. If you can tell the truth and be honest with yourself about the characters that you're creating, then people will always be able to relate to that honesty and, ultimately, your story.

Summary

Creating meaningful stories and believable characters requires you to be willing to truly know about the people you are creating. It is not enough to skim the surface and present superficialities if you want audiences to connect with your stories. If you intend to bring audiences the stories that honor universal themes and that will impact them for years to come, you must be willing to use yourself in your writing and challenge the many myths that encourage you to write for popular trends.

Audiences today yearn for films that have the ability to parallel their own lives; to connect with characters who can portray real human emotions, ranging from laughter to tears. They want to be entertained, but more than that, they want to share a common identity. Writers who portray realistic characters have a great deal from which to choose if they allow themselves to tap into their own sense of being. Are you willing to explore what lies deep inside of you and motivates your behavior for the sake of getting to know your characters? Are you willing to learn about honest expression and avoid stereotypical character representation? In doing so, you will be called upon to challenge your own fears and take risks that you may never before have considered.

Meaningful stories are best told by believable characters. To be believable, characters must be able to demonstrate the great array of emotions that humans have the ability to access. The truly-everlasting stories are those in which the characters are links to our own traditions. They will remind us of who we are, of the voice of truth inside of us that we may have stilled, of the creativity that has been left untapped, and of the sacrifices to our own identity that were made out of unconsciousness. Screenwriters who wish to be remembered have only to realize that nothing can surpass writing what you know. It is those stories and characters that have been created from the writer's own personal experiences that will carry the messages audiences yearn to hear.

●

Creating Meaningful Stories and Believable Characters: Questionnaire for Self-Evaluation

The following questions are meant for introspection and affirmation. They are proposed for the benefit of clarity and a better understanding of how to proceed when approaching the "stuck" places and those moments when reevaluation is needed.

1. Why is this story important for me to write? Am I writing it because I think Hollywood will like it or because I feel it's a story I must tell?
2. How real are the characters that I'm creating?
3. How well do I know these characters, their histories, problems, thoughts, secrets, and emotions? How do I want these characters to act and sound?
4. What is the nature of the relationships being developed, and how do the characters interrelate and connect?
5. What influences from my experiences have I brought to my characters? Are they appropriate for the characters I am developing?
6. Do words override the behavior/actions of the characters?
7. How do the characters' actions and emotional evolvement add to the plot?
8. Are my characters one-dimensional due to stereotyping?
9. Am I using reality-based subtleties of behavior and feelings in developing my characters and the human condition they portray?
10. Do my characters change in the course of the script, and how effectively are these transformations brought about?
11. What specific emotions do I want the viewer to experience?
12. Am I portraying my characters' inner struggles accurately?
13. Do my script's theme and plot lead to a new awareness?
14. Have I hesitated doing the research on my story or characters because of the time commitment, which may not pay off in the long run?
15. What cinematic myths or stereotypes am I attempting to dispel or encourage in this script?

PART III

Writer's Block and the Myths That Bind

DONNA FLINT

Memoir of a Screenwriter—Act II

My dog-eared notebook provided inspiration for a few decent screenplays. Nevertheless, there was always a good reason to put off my creative writing. I had a business to run, kids who needed attention, the usual chores on my ever-growing To-Do list. Besides, I knew that "making it" as a screenwriter was still a long shot. I figured I'd more likely step on the moon than get the kind of miraculous break intended for the select few. Years passed. Then one day, I flew to Los Angeles for a popular screenwriting workshop called "Selling to Hollywood." I felt terribly guilty about going, since it cost me more than a month's rent, between registration fees, hotel expenses, and round-trip airfare from Chicago.

Once there, someone said something I'll never forget—that screenwriting could not be a hobby if you wanted to succeed. You had to be 100 percent committed to it. When I returned home, refreshed and encouraged, I committed myself. I rewrote my business plan so that screenwriting was a priority, the most important part of my work day. I became more aggressive in learning about the industry and disregarding worn-out myths that had prevented me from moving forward. I didn't have to walk on the moon to realize my dreams. I could make them happen in my own way, by my own rules. And thus, I was able to break free from the guilt that had bound my creativity to do what I loved best—conjure up a good story.

Part of my commitment was the decision to move to Hollywood, mecca of the entertainment industry. My family and I rumbled down old Route 66 in a battered Dodge van and settled into a cramped apartment on the north edge of Los Angeles county. Once unpacked, I devoted myself to writing and networking, with a new sense of legitimacy.

I followed every contact and lead I had. Each new person I met lifted my spirits with a strong sense of hope. All sorts of production companies seemed interested in my scripts and in me as a potential writer for other projects. Friends and family waited in anticipation for me to clinch a deal. I was confident that I was finally close to realizing my dreams.

At least six months passed before I began to see a trend. All too often, I was hearing statements like "It's gone to the next level" and "We love the writing; send us something else." A few projects were optioned and sank into a murk called "development"—nothing's actually developing, but we've been given just enough permission to say things like, "My script's being considered by "XYZ" or "XYZ has put my script on their development pile" or "The producer who optioned my script is giving it to XYZ to read." This fuzzy state of ambiguity can go on for years, its sprinkling of fodder just enough for our hardened egos to live on.

After a year, friends and family stopped asking about my projects. Despite many small gains, they seemed to seriously lack luster, and I was feeling "stuck." I was writing and networking less and less, while spending more and more time slopping around the apartment in my jammies, as feelings of failure and despair took over.

I tried to force myself to write at least a little every day, though I easily found more "urgent" chores to fill up my schedule. When I'd finally sit down at my computer and look at the jumbled smattering of my next masterpiece, my mind would start to wander. Pretty soon, I'd be neatening my cuticles or picking every letter off my keyboard to give its innards a good cleaning. Once, I baked enough lasagna to feed an infantry, paying particular attention to how I diced the garlic and onions so the sauce wouldn't be too chunky.

Friends in Hollywood began badgering me to get "out there," telling me I'd never get anywhere if I wasn't doing at least one pitch session a week. I'd never actually pitched a project in person, though I knew it was something screenwriters were supposed to do. The thought of it paralyzed me. Who was I to think I could have done this in the first place? Suddenly, that old log cabin in the holler started to look pretty good—a sanctuary I could hide in for the rest of my life. I could grow a vegetable garden and make my own not-too-chunky homemade pasta sauce. That's enough for most people, isn't it?

●

CHAPTER 13

Writer's Block and Its Role in the Creative Process

I don't think writer's block is a magical thing. It means that there's actually something wrong. You can find it and fix it. It's not a situation where you're just mystically blocked.

Ed Bernero

A ll writers at various points in their careers will experience moments of feeling a terrible blankness, an emptiness, and a creative void. This can be a frightening time—a time of feeling lost, helpless, and even hopeless. Commonly referred to as "writer's block," this experience has a way of knocking self-esteem to the far reaches of our universe. It offers you no solace to know that many writers may experience this block of energy, when your greatest desire is to complete a script, sell it, and get on with writing more fabulous stories.

The creative energy that was so apparent one moment can disappear within seconds, leaving the writer perplexed and walking around in a daze. The ideas that had flowed in abundance have now evaporated. The creative silence has triggered all of the self-doubts that had previously been nicely tucked away, leaving only a sense of confusion and dismay. There seems to be no clear understanding of what has transpired, and the lack of control the writer may be feeling could not make things any worse.

Writer's block has been described as something writers develop, like a disease, which, when caught, has almost no chance of being cured. It is regarded as something negative and something to be avoided at all costs. There is no question that experiencing a block of creativity is frightening, especially when the writer is banking everything on the ability to be productive and success-ful. Is it really fair, however, to expect that these moments will never occur as writers move from one level of their development to another? It is important to accept that as writers pursue their careers, writer's block will become a familiar presence throughout their journey.

What is it about experiencing this unexpected pause that can bring about a new way of evaluating the writing process? Is there something to be gained from having had to stop and rethink what was being written? Is there a benefit to having had to stop, albeit abruptly, that can offer the writer advantages rather than seeing this moment only in terms of the disadvantages it represents?

There is a great deal of information that can be obtained if the writer allows the moment to exist, rather than attempt to deny it. Going through the darkness, even when it may seem untenable, may offer rewards yet unseen.

It is a common fact that as human beings, we tend to learn the most about ourselves through the difficult moments and struggles we experience. The blocks that often appear, and which writers are called upon to face, can offer such moments of clarity. It can be a time when old beliefs are challenged, and it can offer a time for renewal. These somewhat precarious experiences can aid in the replenishing of creative ideas and can introduce the writer to a part of his creative nature never before experienced.

Rather than shying away from these moments, it would definitely be more advantageous to accept that writer's block is a natural part of the screenwrit-ing process. Screenwriters will not always experience great moments of lucid-ity. They will not always spend hours enjoying the writing process. Their finished scripts will not necessarily provide them with great inner fulfillment. There will be times, perhaps many of them, when the hours spent writing will have been for naught.

When a writer is forced to stop a writing project, when the ideas are no longer flowing easily and with the intended momentum, all reason fails. Any attempt to be logical about such moments meets with further resistance. The more the attempt to rationalize and figure out what is happening, the more it leads to continued frustration. It becomes a tug-of-war that produces no win-ner. It most certainly is disconcerting, and probably more negatively viewed, because of the belief that creative people are never supposed to feel this way.

It is amazing how many expectations we put on ourselves that have an overpowering influence on how we view our capabilities. Human beings are never supposed to admit that they are unknowing or uncertain. They are required, no matter what, to propel themselves forward, try harder, be assertive, ambitious, and never stop. Productivity is the mission, and any hint of this not emerging from the hours spent writing stories is a moment of pure disaster!

There are no remedies for curing writer's block, for there need be none. Rather, writers need to accept that there will be times when the writing of the script will have to be altered. They must accept that there will also be times when fatigue rules, when fear and being on overload come crashing together, and no creative ideas are able to emerge. It is a time that deserves complete understanding and gentleness, not reproach and criticism.

The key to really understanding the role of writer's block is for you to accept your own humanness. Human beings are not machines that can forever produce grand ideas and operate on relentless energy.

In order to fulfill your mission of telling stories, you need to take time out to ponder, to stop long enough to regroup, and to take the breaks necessary to regenerate your creativity. If your wisdom does not allow for these moments of pausing, there is a good chance that the blocks will occur in just such a way as to force you to do what you may have been fighting—rest, allow time for the ideas to emerge, gather the support you need, then go forward.

Even when screenwriters love what they are doing and would choose nothing else, it is important to understand that pressure and stress can exist and impact the writing process in significant ways. Sometimes, within the writer's hidden wisdom, opportunities will emerge that will allow for reevaluation, regrouping, and for getting back on the track that was momentarily interrupted.

Writer's block is not something to be avoided, nor a condition that needs to be "fixed" or "cured." It is not permanent; it does not mean that you are doomed from ever again being able to write meaningful stories. Quite the contrary—it can serve as a tremendous opportunity in which to learn more about yourself, as well as the stories and characters you want to create. It can be the catalyst that brings about new ways of writing and offers opportunities for positive change.

Fear, self-criticism, an abundance of unreasonable expectations, and a lack of confidence are but a few of the reasons why writer's block is given its power. By viewing it as a natural component to the creative process, you will have a greater opportunity to use these moments in a positive way rather than to let them become destructive to your mission.

As long as screenwriting is your dream, you must be willing to accept the quiet moments when innovative ideas are at a standstill and know that they will pass. The dream will not dissipate, unless you wish to negate it. Unique stories and characters will still be born through your imagination, and the wonderful world of screenwriting can continue to be yours indefinitely.

Fear and Its Power to Inhibit

There can be no discussion of writer's block without addressing the role that fear plays in inhibiting the creative process. These moments can be propitious in moving the writer forward and offer new awarenesses that can enhance the process. It is also essential to honor fear's role in influencing your decision to push forward, stop momentarily, or end the dream permanently.

Writer's block refers to a specific time in a writer's life when a powerful force of fear has interrupted the creative flow that previously existed. Sometimes, these moments can occur suddenly and with no warning. Other times its onset is slow, causing an increased inner discomfort that becomes more painful as the creative juices can no longer be accessed. Either way, there seems to be no immediate reason to adequately explain what has happened.

Perhaps the wisest perspective is to accept the fact that when we make "big" decisions, we sometimes try to override our intuition and spend hours ruminating. To any writer who has been willing to take the risk, writer's block has the appearance of venturing into the unknown. Fear generates feelings that can both confuse and fascinate us. It can make us question our ability to be creative writers and complete something worthwhile.

If we looked at writer's block in slow motion, what would we actually see happening? What has the writer just ingested that has made him stop in his tracks? What was the sudden realization? Was his goal to complete the script's first draft not accomplished within the assigned timeframe? Was he suddenly hearing a critical voice from the past that interrupted the energy flow? Had thoughts of failure and the fact that he may be disappointing others suddenly become significant stressors? Was the story losing its focus? Were the characters too one-dimensional? What "rules" were interfering with the joy of writing? Who were the people creating these rules, and who claimed to know the truth about how you should write a script that would sell?

When you are forced to stop abruptly, it usually means that fear has taken over and been allowed into the driver's seat. Unless you are willing to use this time to better understand what has happened and to accept that it is necessary to take time out to get renewed, more confusion will ensue. Without pausing to take the necessary breath, more fearful moments will most probably appear.

Unfortunately, in our Western culture, the tendency is to view "taking time out" as being undisciplined or succumbing to feelings of failure in some way— we are being unproductive and should try harder to accomplish our goals. As long as we buy into this philosophy of success, pushing harder to assert our will no matter what, the consciousness we need in order to move forward with clarity and purpose will not be available to us. We will continue to define our-selves as lacking in imagination, and the grip around our creative throats will eventually choke us.

"I have never written a script without, at some point, having a severe anx-iety attack," admits Anne Rapp. "I call it 'fire ants,' because it feels like the inside of my whole body is full of fire ants. It's nothing but fear."

Writers who believe that there will never be such moments are the ones who tend to view writer's block as a terminal illness to be avoided and dreaded. How each writer interprets and accepts these experiences will deter-mine how prepared he is to face certain obstacles or how easily he will decide to give up. This can be a moment of pure negativity from which you will not recover, or it can serve as an advantage. Taking the time to scrutinize the story premise to see if it has evolved in the manner you intended is one way in which to use writer's block productively. Developing new ideas that have been waiting patiently in the background to emerge can help to reaffirm your mis-sion of storytelling and aid in bringing back the balance. As with everything else you may choose regarding your screenwriting journey, it will take courage to stop and reflect, rather than unmercifully pushing forward. It is important to accept the fact that every creative person experiences moments when cre-ative endeavors do not flow easily. If you explore these anxious moments, you may discover insights into your own creative process that will help you to redefine your voice as a writer.

"I learned as a cop that one of the things you fight is your gut," says Ed Bernero. "I learned to trust my gut. I think it's helped me in my writing. Instead of just plodding through when I'm stuck, I need to trust that some-thing is wrong. I need to step back and try to figure out what it is. Once I figure out what it is, it's unbelievably easy to keep going."

Ed's ability to listen to his intuition when the fear prods him is a gift that he has learned to appreciate and honor. As a result, it provides him with new information that resets his course of action.

"There may be some self-destructive behavior happening, which is very common in any venture," suggests Ken Mader. "Whether it's writing for Hollywood or the general business world, going after the gold is scary. I think in anything you do that involves risk, there's always that opportunity to hold yourself back."

Ken has experienced the inner trepidations that occur when reaching for a dream, and he is willing to take the necessary risks rather than let the fear win out. As he knows so well, there are many reasons why writers may find themselves on the edge of a rocky precipice.

"I once started a script with the idea that I was doing something more commercial," says Noah Baumbach. "I ended up abandoning it in the process, because I realized I wasn't interested in it, I was writing completely out of myself."

In this instance, Noah found his creative voice was muddled by expectations that he should write something marketable. He soon discovered that simply trying to please others, and making that the preferred goal, can have a negative impact on the creative process. Even if you believe it to be the secret to your success, it will not provide you with the conviction to go further on your own journey. Whether the people you are trying to please are family members, friends, colleagues, agents, or industry professionals, the result will be the same—a loss of your own identity, a loss of your own unique voice as a creative storyteller. What could be a greater block than that!

Each of the writers who have shared their journeys in this book have recognized that the self-questioning that occurs during the creative process is a natural aspect of their chosen career. Noah's experience is just one example of what can happen when a writer's expectations overwhelm the writing process. When a writer launches into projects that occupy hours upon hours of thinking and musing, the pressure to then sell that work, win contests, or build a career upon it can seem monumental. If you lose sight of why you love writing and become preoccupied with future expectations and listening to exterior voices for acceptance and approval, then you undoubtedly will be headed for that scary experience called writer's block. This pressure can continue with the additional stress of needing to justify to yourself and others why so much time is being spent on this unprofitable pursuit.

We have all experienced the impact that fear can have on our willingness to pursue our creative dreams. We have been witness to the power it holds over us and how it can obliterate our desire to go forward. For some, the fear can be so tenacious that all ability to become disentangled seems like an impossible feat. It has the power to erode everything we have worked hard to accomplish. It can even create such paranoia that we will no longer allow ourselves to trust those around us. What has made us halt and put aside the very dreams that we had so ardently claimed we wanted?

The expectations we have set in front of us can be monumental in scope. These expectations can run the gamut from small, surmountable ones to those that virtually stifle every move we make. Fears are tied to the tremendous expectations we feel must be met, no matter what the cost personally and professionally. Screenwriters want their stories to be accepted. They want their efforts to pay off and can forget that becoming a storyteller is a process that can have moments of both exhilaration and disappointment. When fear takes over, we can feel as if we have lost our creativity forever. In extreme cases, these feelings of anxiety can even convince us to give up writing. The writer will feel a lack of direction and struggle to find the structure that has been suddenly lost. Feeling a loss of control can become overwhelming and make it very difficult to access the adult part of ourselves, leaving us feeling very small and vulnerable. It can make us angry and confused, and sometimes even despairing. In the moment, we may not know what to do or where to turn. The more that these feelings take hold, the more the grip tightens.

"The biggest challenge for me," says Josefina Lopez about her initial screenwriting success, "was getting past feelings like, Who do I think I am? I don't deserve this."

Human beings have a great need to feel accepted, loved, appreciated, and made to feel important. Much energy can be spent in the pursuit of these goals. When you begin to express yourself and allow yourself to be visible to the world, you can easily begin to feel all of the voices humming their critical and judgmental mantras, until you no longer recognize to whose voice you are listening. Therefore, it is imperative that you are able to challenge the voices that promote fear, and that you have the courage to acknowledge and understand them for what they have represented as part of your past. This means that you must make an effort to consciously choose to listen to your own voice, rather than to be seduced to listening to others. Protecting your intuitive function will be required as long as you strive for the creativity that is the bedrock of your fulfillment. You must make absolutely certain that your personal voice wins out and is the vehicle that guides you forward, no matter how often writer's block makes its way into your creative space.

"If I have a vision for this story, I know it's eventually going to work, even though I momentarily feel discouraged," says Paul Wei. "In my heart, I believe it's going to be finished and it will be a good story. So that will keep me going, will get me to sit at the desk, turn on the computer, and write again. I keep asking questions and getting answers, and then I will find something really good."

Questioning the Pause

Writer's block is not a condition that only affects new or undiscovered writers. Writers like Anne Rapp and Ed Bernero still experience moments of fear that end up blocking them and creating feelings of self-doubt.

"It's not a cakewalk to sit down and write," explains Anne Rapp. "There's always a point about halfway through a script that it becomes agonizing, because you're not sure you're on the right track. So out of fear, you get totally scared. You're like, God, I've already written sixty pages, it could all be trash. I don't know if I'm ever going to see that light at the end of the tunnel."

Ed had similar feelings when writing the second episode of his television series, *Third Watch*.

"About halfway through, I went completely blank. The second episode of a show is very important. The pilot will get watched, because it will be promoted for months. I believe that at some point in the second episode, people will decide if they're going to watch this every week or not. So I had this in my head and knew all along I'd be writing the second episode. I thought that was my problem, and I just needed to get away from it. I printed what I had, put it aside, and went shopping with my wife. Then, I went back and looked at it and realized there was something wrong with the story."

Stopping, putting the project aside, and taking that magical breath can act as a wonderful alternative when all reason has failed. The important point is to accept that a pause is needed before being able to move forward with energy and creativity.

All the writers interviewed in this book expressed wonderful and unique ways in which to deal with the "pauses." All of them found it necessary to ride the fear rather than try to fight it. Stepping away from their work, taking time to sort out and discover what elements in their current projects might be stifling them, made it possible to go on and complete their scripts.

"I used to fight that kind of thing. Now I just get up and do the laundry," says Ed Bernero. "My wife loves when I'm writing at home, because I get all the laundry done. Before, I would sit there in front of the computer doing nothing except thinking about doing laundry and getting mad at myself for thinking about doing laundry. Where now, if I feel like going to Starbucks to get a cup of coffee when I'm working at home—like I couldn't make coffee in my own kitchen—I don't fight it. I get up and go get coffee. It gives me time away from the computer to think about what I'm going to do next."

Tony Bui has an equally clean house when he gets "stuck" in the writing process.

"I wash the dishes, I do the laundry, I organize things. I'll clean the floors once in a while. When I have writing blocks, the house is spotless."

Being willing to stop is the kindest thing you can do for yourself when you get stuck. For many writers, giving themselves permission to stop is extremely difficult. Nevertheless, it can prove to be the exact intervention they need for those moments when the brain is tired and the creative pores are clogged. As Ed and Tony have found out, writing pauses can also contribute to clean and orderly surroundings!

All too often, we expect to remedy our concerns, anxieties, and frustrations on our own. Writers often get into the mindset that the writing experience is meant to be a solitary exercise. They try to convince themselves that since they chose this profession, they have to take the good with the bad, promoting a kind of all-or-nothing attitude. Sometimes, getting unstuck means gaining the support of others, from words of encouragement to new perspectives on our work. Sometimes a small recommendation or observation can get us moving again. When we receive the affirmation from those we admire and respect, it can be a gift that comes at a time when it is the most needed.

Pausing to reflect never means something negative. You are being called upon to listen to a message that comes from your own wisdom. In order to fully accept your role as a creative agent, you need to embrace all aspects of this role. Stopping, allowing the lull so that you can catch your breath, learning to give yourself the permission you need, all represent valuable aspects of your unique screenwriting journey that must not be avoided. The manner in which you will eventually give birth to your story will depend on your ability to accept all facets of the screenwriting profession.

If you experience a time when you are running out of ideas and find yourself going in circles with no tangible results, there are questions following this chapter that you can ask yourself that may help to dislodge you from the stuck places. These questions may simply help you to understand that you can begin to stimulate answers and learn from this momentary pause by looking inward. It is crucial to know that you have gotten yourself out of frightening places in the past, and using this knowledge of how you accomplished this before will help you now. Asking yourself what you did the last time you felt like this may very well be the key to opening the door. When you pause and look inward, you may once again gain your grounding and be able to ask yourself, "What can I learn from my fear? What is it teaching me that is crucial to understanding the characters and stories I want to create?"

Writer's block can and will act as a catalyst if you permit it. If you allow yourself to recognize your needs and give up fighting unnecessary battles, you will acquire the tools with which to move through these frightening moments.

Will I Face the Fears?

Anytime that we are stopped in our tracks, immobilized and seemingly unable to move forward, we are given an opportunity to gain a new respect for our vulnerabilities. Putting ourselves in the public eye, gaining visibility and recognition for our talents can create moments of great stress. When we have deadlines to meet and creative stories to provide, blocks in our imagination can occur. Writer's block can be intimidating, because it feels as though it will last forever. Learning to accept it as a momentary pause can help to put it into a normal framework. Creative people who are willing to honor their imagina-

Ten Common Fears About Writer's Block

1. I'm afraid I won't be able to get beyond the "stuck" places and I will lose my creative ideas.
2. I'm afraid of disappointing myself, my family, and my friends when the writing process seems to have stopped indefinitely.
3. I feel an immense pressure to always have to write great scripts.
4. I'm afraid I won't succeed in writing what I want to say.
5. I'm afraid to reach out to others for help.
6. I'm afraid I won't know what to do when the energy stops.
7. I'm afraid of disappointing colleagues and writing partners who are counting on me.
8. I'm afraid I won't be able to complete the scripts I want to write.
9. I'm afraid that I won't meet the expectations others have of me.
10. I don't think I know enough about the craft of screenwriting.

tion will be introduced to many pauses throughout their lives. Accepting these moments, rather than spending vital energy resisting them, is the key.

Will I Challenge the Myths?

Creative storytellers often do not expect to experience many moments of being blocked as they write their scripts. They have done everything humanly possible to avoid those moments and are stunned when they appear. The error is to think of writer's block as a unique and unusual event in the writer's life. It is part of any creative endeavor, and if accepted as such, can offer positive moments for reflection, change, and renewed inspiration. Challenging the myth that blocks should not exist for the talented writer will be an ongoing task.

Will I Take the Risks?

As you continue your screenwriting journey, you will encounter doubts, fears, and many moments of uncertainty. The risks you will take will require that you accept that all of these frightening moments are to be expected and are a very natural part of the journey. Writer's block will need to assume its natural place in your life and will demand your attention and gentle acceptance. The biggest risk will be in your ability to move through these precarious moments, rather than attempting to escape them.

Ten Common Myths About Writer's Block

1. If I get blocked, I must not be a very good writer.
2. Writer's block is a weakness, one that must be overcome to succeed.
3. The best way to deal with writer's block is to ignore it.
4. Writer's block is synonymous with not knowing how to write a good script.
5. Writer's block is an internal problem and has nothing to do with what is going on around me.
6. No one else can help you get "unstuck" when you have writer's block.
7. If there are days when I don't feel like writing, then I should not be pursuing the craft.
8. If fears are stopping me from writing, I certainly won't be able to cope with the bigger fears that I face once the script is done.
9. Writer's block only happens to beginning or unsuccessful writers.
10. Once I sell my first screenplay, I'll never experience writer's block again.

Am I willing to ask myself . . .

1. What is stopping me now from being able to move forward?
2. What comments have been made regarding my work that have discouraged me?
3. Have I lost the focus of why I wanted to write the story in the first place?
4. Am I afraid to finish the work because of what I will have to do when it is done?
5. Is this a form of writing that I really want to do?
6. Have I told someone else that this is what I would accomplish and now I realize that it is not something I really love doing?
7. What does this fear remind me of?
8. What have I done in the past to help myself when I have felt this pause?
9. Will I give myself permission to stop writing when I feel stuck, rather than pushing forward unmercifully?
10. Why I have stopped listening to my own voice instead of listening to others?

CHAPTER 14

Adam Rifkin: Laughing in the Face of the Odds

I think the biggest myth is that it's impossible to direct a movie in
Hollywood. I just laughed in the face of it. I thought, How absurd,
the idea of second-guessing one's ability to do what one wants because
someone else says the odds are against you.

Adam Rifkin

The Journey Begins

*Adam Rifkin began his screenwriting journey in Chicago. Like Tony Bui, Adam knew
from a very young age that he wanted to be a filmmaker. He attended the Academy for
the Visual and Performing Arts High School of Chicago, where he was able to access
film equipment and begin learning filmmaking techniques with a Super 8 camera. As
a child, he was a big fan of the Abbot and Costello comedies, as well as of horror and
monster films.*

I loved Abbot and Costello, so *Abbot and Costello Meet Frankenstein* was the perfect collaboration of scary and funny. I thought that was really cool. As I got
older, I started to appreciate all kinds of movies, like *One Flew Over the Cuckoo's
Nest*. It was one of the first movies that made me appreciate film as an art form.

*Adam was fortunate to have a strong, liberated support system. All the films he was
allowed to see only fuelled his passion to become a filmmaker.*

My parents never censored anything from me. I was always able to see anything I wanted. I saw *The Exorcist* when it came out, and I loved it. None of

my friends were allowed to see it, so when I got to go to school, I would tell them all about it. Same thing with the movie *Ten*. I'd go to school and tell everybody what you did or didn't get to see in the film. I think the lack of censorship helped a lot. My parents always trusted that anything I would see, I would be able to process.

So I'm getting older, and I'm just a movie fanatic at this point. I love old movies. I love new movies. I start to get into specific filmmakers, like Woody Allen and Ingmar Bergman. And I learned about Ingmar Bergman, because I'd read that Woody Allen was influenced by him. I loved Martin Scorcese movies. I'd read about Martin Scorcese and learned that he really dug Fellini movies and film noir movies, so then I'd go check out those movies. So I really tried to be a student of film. The more I saw and the more I was inspired, the more hungry I became to go to Hollywood and try to crack the Hollywood nut.

The Move West

At seventeen, I moved to Hollywood to go to college. I used college as an excuse to get to California. When I got to California, I dropped out of college, because I had decided that I wanted to be a filmmaker, and I asked, What is the only thing keeping me from making a movie? I didn't believe there was anything keeping me from making a movie other than the money I needed to finance it. I was convinced that anybody could make a film if you just had the money to do so. It's just that simple. So I decided I was going to find money to make a film.

I had been reading a lot about independent filmmaking and a lot about independent filmmakers—all these books about David Lynch and John Waters and all these sort of cult filmmakers who made these indie movies that were really low-budget, but had made a splash because they were really unique films. So I thought, the only way I'm going to be able to get the money to make a film is if I write something that's really unique. It's the only way I'm going to be able to stand out in town, because everyone else is writing movies that crack the studio system. I'm going to write something that's so outrageous that I'm going to stand alone, and that's how I'll get attention. I was about nineteen when I wrote my first script. It was called *The Dark Backward*. My initial intention was to make it on 16mm in black and white for $100,000. Now, I never saw myself as a screenwriter per se. I wanted to be a film director. But I needed to have something to direct, so I figured I needed to write something if I was going to direct it. So that's why I sat down and wrote a screenplay.

Never On Tuesday

*Although an astute film buff, Adam was naïve to the workings of the Hollywood indus-
try. Nevertheless, he views this naïveté as an asset, since it helped give him the courage
to pursue getting his projects from script to screen.*

Naïveté was a big asset in that I didn't know about the odds. I didn't care about
the odds. I didn't know how to write a screenplay. I'd never written one
before. But I knew that I loved movies, and I felt confident that I knew how
to make a movie. So I read a couple of screenplays just to get the format in
my mind. After I wrote *The Dark Backward,* I very naïvely went about trying
to find money to get it financed. I was going to big lawyers and doctors, rich
people that I thought would just give me money. It was the wrong way to go
about it, but I didn't really know better. At the time, in the mid-eighties, a ton
of movies were being made to go straight to video, so there were a million
little companies that were financing small movies. I submitted my script to a
bunch of those little companies, and nobody wanted to make it. But one of
the readers at one of the companies was friends with Brad Weiman, who
turned out to be both my partner and my manager.

Anyway, Brad Weiman was twenty-two at the time, and he'd just produced
his first feature. The reader told Brad Weiman that here's a movie that will
never be made, but you should read it, because it's a good read. So Brad read
it and sought me out. We had a meeting, and he said, Why don't we try to
finance it together? Why don't we run around town and try to make this
movie? I turned him down flat, because I thought, what do I need him for? I
can do this myself. So I ran around a little bit with still no success. A few
months later, I called him back and I said, Hey, does that offer still stand? He
said, Sure. I said, Okay, let's run around together then. Maybe you know something I don't know. So we ran around together and had no success. But in the
meantime, I'd written several other screenplays that I just put on a shelf, since
I didn't know what to do with them. *The Dark Backward* was the movie I really
wanted to make.

At the time, Brad was working for an old-time producer named Elliot
Castner, who had produced billions of big movies throughout the fifties and
sixties and seventies, like *Where Eagles Dare* and *Missourri Break,* starring Brando.
In the eighties, he produced *Angel Heart,* with DeNiro. He had his own company, and Brad was working for him. So we presented my script to him to see
if he would finance it through his company. He said, Absolutely not. But he
said teen movies make a lot of money. Write me a teen movie, and maybe I'll
finance it. He said, Make it real cheap, so we can do it for nothing and shoot

it in a really short amount of time. He wanted us to make it all in one location and give it like three characters. A sort of teen *Waiting for Godot*.

I was very charged on adrenaline, thinking, here's my chance. I wrote a screenplay in about six days called *Never on Tuesday*. I thought it was very cutting-edge in my nineteen-year-old mind. It's about two libidinous teenage boys on a road trip from Ohio to California. They want fun in the sun and girls. And they get into a car accident in the middle of the desert, where they meet this very beautiful woman. They think, Hey, we're stuck out in the middle of nowhere with this great-looking girl, and if it's just us and her, we might get lucky. It turns out that she's gay. I thought that I was being really controversial with the subject matter. Anyway, Elliot said, Great, let's make it. So, of course, I was elated. So we very quickly put together *Never on Tuesday,* which we shot for a very little money. Brad Weiman was, at the time, in with the biggest young movie stars of the day, which were the Brat Pack. Because he was so close to them, we got a few of them to do cameos in the movie. Charlie Sheen did a cameo right after *Wall Street,* as well as Nicholas Cage, Emilio Esteves, and Judd Nelson. For my first film, I think it turned out okay, though it sort of was my film school, and it really was an educational experience.

Conceiving a Mouse Hunt

Adam would eventually make his cult classic, The Dark Backward, *starring Bill Paxton, Judd Nelson, and James Caan, as well as a comedy called* The Chase, *with Charlie Sheen, for Twentieth Century Fox. One of his most successful scripts was* Mouse Hunt, *which was purchased by DreamWorks.*

I had written twenty-nine screenplays prior to *Mouse Hunt* that didn't sell. *Mouse Hunt* was the thirtieth one that I wrote, and it sold. If after not having sold twenty-nine screenplays I'd said, Ah, screw this, it's not working so I'm going back to Chicago, I wouldn't have written the thirtieth script, which did sell.

I hope it doesn't sound disenchanting, but I have a very nuts and bolts approach to the way I write, in that I rely more on my intuition than on a formula or process. And to me, writing is all about the end result. When I write a script, I want to get it done as quickly as possible, so I'll have another piece of material to try to get made. This was the process with Mouse Hunt.

I'm sort of an amateur cartoonist, and I get some of my ideas just by doodling. I doodled a doodle that gave me the idea for *Mouse Hunt.* It was of two guys coming back from a hunt. Imagine two guys coming through the brush with a pole slung over both their shoulders, and instead of hanging from the

pole being something like a wild boar, it's just a mouse. I labelled the doodle
Mouse Hunt. And I thought, Well, maybe there's a movie idea in this somewhere. Then, I harkened back to all the hours of *Tom and Jerry* cartoons I had
watched when I was a kid, and I thought, Alright, maybe two grown men chasing a mouse around for a whole movie could be funny. Maybe it could be really
stupid, too. I wasn't sure. I told Brad Weiman my idea. I said I don't know if it's
the dumbest idea I've ever had or if it's a good idea, but it's sort of like a live-
action cartoon about two brothers who inherit a house, and they learn the
house is very valuable, so they're going to fix it up and sell it. But during the
process, there's a very pesky mouse that lives in the house that's not going to
give it up, because it's his house. Basically, at that point, it's two grown men
waging war on a very smart mouse, and everything goes wrong for these guys.
Brad said, It's just so stupid, it'll sell for a million dollars. Write it immediately.

When writing Mouse Hunt, *Adam reached into his past to draw on styles from
favorite classics he grew up with.*

In my mind, I thought of Laurel and Hardy, with the cantankerous fat one and
the sweet skinny one. I think that's as deep as I got. I made them brothers that
don't get along at the beginning, and you know through whatever adventures
they go through, they're going to come together in the end and learn that
brotherly love is the most important thing. If you do it right, it'll work on
some heartstring kind of level. So I thought, Okay, brothers who don't get
along at the beginning—it'll pay off at the end, and hopefully warm some
hearts.

Then I had to set up the brothers' lives and show why they're down on
their luck and why they've been forced together. I tried to think of what could
be funny about why these guys are down on their luck. So I made the fat guy
a chef, and at the opening of his big restaurant, the mayor eats a cockroach,
has a heart attack, and dies. He's ostracized from the chef's world, so he's down
on his luck. The skinny one is the one who's loyal to the dead father and is
going to take over the dying string factory. His wife is so upset that he didn't
sell to a big corporation that would have actually given him some money, so
she kicks him out of the house. So now he's down on his luck. He's sweet and
believes in his father's dying wish of saving the string factory, so you love him,
hopefully, because of that.

Okay, cut to the brothers, and it's Christmas. It's worse when you're down
on your luck and it's Christmas time. They meet up in a diner, and they're
down on their luck. And they remember that in Dad's will, they were left this
old, shabby house. They've got nowhere to live, so they go to the house. They

learn, quite by accident, that the house is worth a lot of money. So now, they've got dollar signs in their eyes and want to fix up the house and make a lot of money. Now, we've got two brothers who don't get along, but they'll deal with each other, because they've now got a plan. And they've also got a Ralph Cramden and Ed Norton thing about it—the get-rich-quick scheme. These are things that inspired me from when I was a kid. I watched *The Honeymooners* all the time. I loved *The Three Stooges,* I loved *Laurel and Hardy,* I loved *The Little Rascals.* All the things that I loved as a kid, watching hours and hours of television, actually helped me with *Mouse Hunt,* because they were references for me.

Story and Character

As a screenwriter, Adam strives to make his stories flow smoothly and make logical sense.

I want to make sure that it feels like an organic progression from beginning to end, that everything moves forward. Let's say, for the sake of argument, I'm doing a movie about five guys who rob a bank. I'm going to want to make sure that I know who they are at the beginning and why they want to rob the bank by the end of act one. I want to know who they are, what makes them feel that they need to turn to a life of desperation, and at the end of act one, okay, we are robbing that bank. I want to make sure it's a logical progression to that point.

Then, in act two, I want to see how they rob this bank and how do the personalities, conflicting with one another, make planning robbing a bank a funny thing or a scary thing or an intense thing. Hopefully, everything is escalating on several levels. Plotwise, it's escalating, because they're getting closer to robbing the bank. Characterwise it's escalating, because we learn that one is sleeping with the other one's wife, and he finds out on the way to the bank. So you create all the little complications that, hopefully, organically interweave everything, so that when they pull up to the bank and they're about to run in there to rob it, somehow, it's really interesting and has reached a fever pitch.

Then, you've got the bank robbery scene, which I would make really different from every other bank robbery scene you've ever seen. Let's say the bank robbery goes all wrong. How can I show how these characters that I've established deal with the fact that this bank robbery has gone all wrong? What is going to make it funny or scary about these people robbing this bank that makes a difference? And how am I going to continually keep the story moving forward, so it doesn't seem like it's going off on tangents? Like, I don't care about the bank teller's conversation with his wife on the phone for three pages. All I care about is what's moving the story forward. Then, hopefully, I could think of some really interesting resolve for our characters, whether they all die at the end or whether they get caught or whether they all get away with it. So just from the beginning to the end, it has a flow to it and feels organic and entertaining.

Adam's credits include both commercial and independent-style projects. He takes a realistic approach about how one discipline can help him achieve the other.

I look at different scripts different ways. I write some scripts because I have to write them, because I have a story I must tell. When I write a script like that, I just write it for me. Someday, I hope to make it, and if it doesn't ever get made, that's okay, because I have a script that I know could someday make a great movie. Then, some scripts I write because I think this movie could sell and make a lot of money, like *Mouse Hunt*. Then, there's the kind of script that's like, hey, Adam, here's a ton of money for you to write this movie. Now, would I have ever chosen to write that type of movie on my own? Probably not. But I'll do it. I can do it pretty quickly, and I'll be able to have some money in the bank and not have to worry about paying my rent for a while, which gives me the freedom to write something that I really want to write. So I look at some of these writing jobs-for-hire as a means of supporting myself and having the freedom to do the things that I love to do. But I wouldn't take a job to write a movie that I hated. I would have to find something fun or neat or exciting about it.

Parting Words

I've been really lucky up to now. I feel that I do work hard. I can admit that without feeling guilty about saying it. And I've been lucky, and so far so good. But tomorrow, it could all go to shit, so I always want to remember that and never take anything for granted.

●

CHAPTER 15

Redefining Creative Success

Living in L.A. will never discourage me, because this is what I want
to do. Although there are so many things you can do in this world,
I don't want to do anything else. Filmmaking is my only choice.
Paul Wei

T he fears associated with writer's block often stem from the myths that we have integrated regarding our creative abilities and the profession of screenwriting. There are very few people who do not want to feel inspired and who do not want to feel that they have contributed, in some way, to the betterment of the world. Some writers begin their journeys with the belief that their written word can change and impact others. They dream about their stories and characters, which will become the vehicles through which their messages will infiltrate the lives of those who will see their films. They begin their screenwriting journeys with optimism and with a great desire to reach audiences, so that they will be remembered forever.

There are still hundreds of others who remain hesitant and will actually allow their stories to be unwritten. They are cautious and afraid to claim their creative voice. They have become frightened of going forward and have held onto outdated beliefs, which have encouraged their immobility. They have allowed certain myths to guide their every decision, and have become confused as to why life has begun to lose its luster and why they have not been able to propel themselves into the world of professional screenwriting. They have been witness to others who have launched themselves successfully. Why has this not happened to them? What is stopping them, and can they alter their destiny?

Myths are the culprits that have the power to bring about stagnation, worry, and obsessive thinking and can prevent us from expressing our individuality and originality. They often surface as "the voices of reason." Perhaps the greatest harm they can elicit, if we listen, is to prevent our inner creative voice from emerging.

"You wonder whether or not it will be any good," says Ken Mader, "or are my ideas full of crap? Is it too close to something else that's been done already? I think I go down that list of fears every day."

Buying into our own personal myths has a way of negatively infiltrating the writing process more quickly and with more toxicity than anything else. It becomes rather insidious, because it is a very slow process. The writer begins with an initial enthusiasm and inner joy at the prospect of actually doing what he loves best. As the days pass, he recognizes more and more that he has discovered that writing brings real excitement and meaning to his life.

Sit back for a moment and think about a time when you thought about a wonderful story you wanted to write. You had the characters formed in your mind and the story was moving exactly as you had imagined it. You had the courage to write from your own experiences, and you were not feeling awkward about using aspects of your own life within the story's context. You knew that you were on the right track, because your energy was flowing and you could hardly slow the ideas down to capture them. All of a sudden, something tremendously powerful attacks your very being. You step back and realize that those famous voices of "reason" have come looming in front of you, making you ask yourself questions like, Am I writing the kind of story an agent would want? Has this idea been done before? Is it clever enough? I like it, but will they? Do I really know what I'm doing?

Out fly your exciting thoughts, passion, hope, and bountiful energy. Your mission of writing wonderful screenplays is about to be aborted. You thought you had prepared for such frightening moments, but the nightmare seems to just be starting. You had really believed that you could make it, and now, in an instant, all the confidence is gone. What you had allowed yourself to believe has suddenly slipped away, thanks to strong messages from those invisible "myth-givers." When we give our power to experts who claim to know the truth about the screenwriting industry, we may unconsciously buy into beliefs that are projected onto us. These myths gain their power because they are initiated by others who claim to know "the truth." In the process, we have unconsciously moved within their line of fire, giving our own power away.

These moments can last only seconds, but can pack a wallop that will remain with us for a long, long time.

There are millions of books, journals, seminars, and workshops led by gurus who have "made it" in the film and television industry. Each claims to know what is best for you, how to get your script sold, the right way to get an agent, write a query letter, structure a character and plot, and the secrets you must know to be in the "winner's circle." After awhile, if you buy into all of these myths about success that the filmmaking books and experts may be promoting, you may feel as if you are in a hierarchy in which there is only one right way up the ladder to achieve your goals. If the myths have really taken hold, it becomes evident that a hierarchy is slowly being established and maintained, and your task is to keep attempting to climb the ladder to the top. Hierarchies help to maintain the myths that have been created. They are extremely debilitating, regressive, and destructive to any person who is striving to experience his own creativity. They lead to uncertainty, to disempowerment, and are flamed by fear. The tragedy is that, if the writer continues to believe that this is the only path toward attaining success, he will eventually become invisible and lose the gift of storytelling that is in his blood.

"I always felt that some of the people who run those workshops and seminars are just trying to make money off other people's dreams," says Ed Bernero. "I'm not suggesting that there aren't people with valuable things to say at these seminars. It's just that I find most writers are procrastinators, and if there's another seminar to take, they'll feel like if they attend it, they'll be able to write their script. I think those people would be much better served to spend their time writing than looking for another seminar or another quick fix, because you really aren't going to learn the craft until you do it. If not, there's a whole bunch of people who'd be very happy to take your $225."

There are endless myths that have circulated within the film and television industry. It is impossible to challenge them all. What is critical, however, is to be cognizant of those myths that are taking a hold of your creative voice and be willing to fight hard not to buy into them.

Anne Rapp never pursued a formal education in writing. She took her first screenwriting class at the age of forty-three. If she had listened to the myths regarding what it takes to be a successful screenwriter, we would have been cheated out of her wonderful and powerful story, *Cookie's Fortune*. Fortunately, she had not forced herself to believe that in order to make it as a writer, she had to obtain a degree from a prestigious film school, or that she would have been shunned because she was too old or too inexperienced.

"I didn't come from a real academic background," says Anne. "I wasn't one of those kids who had a book on her nose growing up. I was into sports. I was a jock. So sometimes I get intimidated by that academic thing. When I went into Barry Hannah's class at forty-three years old in Oxford, Mississippi, I was scared to death. I knew that all the twenty-year-olds sitting next to me had read ten times more than I had."

Harold Ramis puts the myth about needing a film school degree in an interesting perspective.

"Many more people will go to film school than will be successful, and a lot of people will be successful who have not gone to film school. Film school is not a guarantee of anything. I went to see a great John Singer Sergeant exhibition in Boston. I saw a brilliant splash of light on one of the paintings. I walked up to it so I could more closely see the small, yellow brush stroke. As a painter, you wouldn't need to go to school to see that you can evoke light with just a small dab of paint. If you're a careful observer, you don't need a teacher to tell you how something is done."

Anne Rapp will soon be sitting on the other side of the desk, passing on her knowledge as a visiting professor in the Michener Center for Writers at the University of Texas in Austin.

"The best thing I'll be able to tell the students is that no one can teach you to write, and you don't learn to write screenplays by going out to Hollywood and trying to copy somebody else's work or watching a jillion movies," says Anne. "As hard as it is, what you want to say to these kids is, Go out and have your heart broken about three times in a row. Go out and lose something you really want in life. Go out and fall on your face a dozen times and get back up. And then go write."

Anne mentioned another big myth surrounding the screenwriting industry—that you have to live in Hollywood to sell a screenplay. Those who have experienced the reality of spending time or living in Hollywood often have different perspectives.

"If you're going to write a script, you don't have to move to Hollywood," says David Marconi. "You write a few scripts, put them under your arm, and get a couple of people to read them. Make sure they make sense. Then, go out to Los Angeles for a couple weeks, take some meetings, show your scripts. You can write from anywhere in the world. Believe me, if you come up with a great script, people will buy it. You can be in a basement in Iowa, going to your 9-to-5 job, and writing just fine. You can be in a toll booth in the night shift writing a screenplay in that toll booth about a truck driver who drove by."

"When you're in Los Angeles, it can feel like everyone else is doing well except you," says Noah Baumbach, who resides in New York and makes frequent trips to the West Coast. "Everyone's reading *Variety,* and there's this feeling like everyone's getting deals for millions of dollars. A really well-established actor who I knew once told me he hadn't read *Variety* in fifteen years, because he didn't like to find out how much better everyone else was doing. So I think that tends to motivate people in the wrong direction. It becomes more about making the big deal. More than any city I've ever been in, everyone has something to do with the film industry. I suppose, on one hand, it can be sort of nice to have all those people with the same interest, but I think it can also be a little crazy-making."

Paul Wei is one of millions of aspiring writers who ventured to Los Angeles in pursuit of a dream.

"I did experience the doubt," he admits. "There are so many talented people in the industry, I wondered, How can I succeed in Hollywood? There are so many people wanting to be writers, so many people wanting to be directors. I had been here for six years without making a film. I was lost as to what to do or how to go about realizing my dream. It took me a long time to figure out, I just had to go in and do it."

No one knows exactly what "realistic" means for you or where your creative journey will take you. No one knows when your stories will attract attention or when the time will present itself for you to gain the recognition you need to propel you to the next step. Only you can know the truth that resides inside of you. By giving your knowledge away, believing that someone else knows your time lines, your realities, your wisdom and intuition, you have entered into collusion with the myths that you have allowed to distort your truth—this is deadly to the human spirit. That is not to say that you should not use consultants, attend film school, workshops, and seminars, or read useful material on writing. The key is to be selective in choosing the information that fits you best at a given time, and not to rush to fulfill someone else's definition of when, where, and how you should claim your dream.

In order to work through the blocks that will appear throughout your career, you must be willing to risk challenging the myths that the film and television industry encourage. Remember that in buying into someone else's belief system, you will be giving up your voice, and you will potentially feel a paralysis that attacks the creative process. Myths have no place in your life. They have no validity, and their power lies in their ability to intimidate and restrict your personal journey.

"If writing movies is your passion, you're going to have ups, you're going to have downs, you're going to have low periods," says Adam Rifkin. "But you're doing what you love, so in that, you'll always be successful."

Fortunately, Adam and the other writers throughout this book were able to challenge and eventually ignore the myths that could have stifled their creativity. Instead, they were able to find their own unique ways to move through the maze and bring us their wonderful stories and characters.

Josefina Lopez has always tried to challenge one of the most common myths about writing for the big screen—that the hero, especially in action/adventure films, has to be a white male.

"You constantly see stories about the white guy saving the world, so everybody else doesn't get to tell their point of view. It's almost like we don't have a say in the matter, like history is written by the winner or the victor. Coming from a very underrepresented, marginalized community like mine, we have no voice. That's the biggest myth we have to challenge. Everything around you tells you that. That's why you have to tell yourself, No, I have a heart, and I am a human being, so I get to have a say in the matter."

Like Josefina, claiming our own truths means that we must continuously be willing to question and evaluate whose truth we accept, to whose voice we will listen, and to determine to what lengths we will go to unburden ourselves from the fears, blocks, and negative assumptions that have the power to keep our creativity in shackles.

Language That Binds

It is amazing how powerful words and expressions can be and how easily they can taint the picture you paint of yourself.

With very little effort, the language you use to define yourself can become a mantra that, more often than not, will denigrate, confuse, and cancel your true value. Writers not only have to become sensitive to the role of writer's block, myths, fears, and expectations and how they impact the process of screenwriting, but they also have to become aware of the language they impose on themselves.

Often the words are innocent enough and acceptable to many. However, they have a tendency to reinforce negativity and judgment. Their impact disempowers and puts down the positive qualities inherent in all of us. If something is repeated often enough, it will be believed. When discussing writer's block and the pause that binds, writers often refer to their "procrastination." They talk about being "unfocused" or say they are "undisciplined" and "unproductive."

Writers rarely speak to themselves about their fears, as they write their scripts and send them out for public approval. They rarely discuss their stuck places and how they felt when their stories and characters refused to cooperate. They are reluctant to admit that they feel scared about what will happen if the story does not sell—anxiety that is amplified as friends and family wait on the sidelines to witness the event.

All too often, negative expressions become the catchphrases for fear. How often have you heard or said things like, I have to get a real job where I have security and benefits? Or, writing is a luxury I cannot afford.

In each of these expressions, there lies a powerful seed of negativity that can slowly erode the creative spirit. Each carries the ability to squash any feelings of excitement and aspiration. This language has its roots in fear, the same kind that blocks our creative process. The language of self-criticism is insidious, for it can travel the length of the screenwriter's journey.

Unfortunately, there is no easy way out of the labyrinth, nor easy ways to discredit the language that has become so popular and familiar to our own ears. The language that is used with such ease has become commonplace and will necessitate renewed sensitivity and awareness in order to change it. The challenge will be to find new ways of describing who you are and the feelings you experience.

Examples of Language that Binds

Foolish, futile, impractical, incapable, lack of concentration, lazy, lethargic, not good enough, pointless, procrastination, too busy, unmotivated, undisciplined, unfocused, uninspired, arrogant, unproductive, unrealistic, untalented, worthless, too bold, stupid, crazy

The common denominator of all these words lies in its root of fear. This language is, of course, not unique to the screenwriter. It is the voice of criticism and judgment, which causes tremendous confusion and ends the ability required to access the strength we need in order to move forward. Any time that we take risks to claim what we want, the negative voices can appear almost instantly. Pay attention to what happens when you begin a new script or are about to submit the finished one. What happens as you are about to put yourself on the line and you feel that your success lies in the hands of others? The language that binds can magically become the force that keeps you from going forward. It has the potential of reinforcing your worst beliefs about yourself—that you are not worthy to be the professional screenwriter you dream of being.

Without getting much deeper into all the layers of the psychological influences that place us in double binds and dark places, suffice it to say that it was not an overnight process that gave the fear and the negative and critical thoughts their power. The negative words and phrases, with which we identify, are the result of a much deeper state of mind. We often base our present-day experiences and belief systems on history and exposure to early influences. Perhaps it all lies dormant until the day we decide to release ourselves from the shackles and challenge what has kept us silent and invisible. Breaking free is no easy task, and requires tremendous determination and a true commitment to releasing our creative spirit. The good news is that change is possible. Redefining how we refer to ourselves, how we walk on this earth, and the respect we give to our inner voice are goals worthy of our every effort.

In undertaking as difficult a journey as screenwriting, writers can easily use negative labels that end up convincing them of their inadequacies and inferiority. To get past this self-inflicted state of mind, you must learn to disengage from this language and challenge the words you may have used all too often in describing yourself. When you listen and do not confront the destructive self-talk, your ability to share your ideas is compromised. In pursuing our personal dreams, there is no room for the toxicity that cancels our self-worth. In any creative pursuit, there must be room to experience everything we need in order to better understand our humanness. There must be time allowed to regroup whenever necessary, without the critical shadows looking over our shoulders. Perhaps more than any other moment during the creative process, you must be willing to seek support, understanding, and encouragement and not allow your spirit to be numbed.

We all need to give ourselves permission to seek help, no matter how advanced we are in our professions. You must give yourself time in which to find new and creative ways to fight the solitude and discouragement that often reinforce disparaging language. You must be able to reevaluate your expectations and choose new options, so that your mission of storytelling does not get deterred. You need to approach a problem with a new language and expressions, which you may not have been able to do in the past.

From a psychological perspective, there is nothing more debilitating than a voice that echoes disapproval and condemnation. It is the prison from which we can barely escape, which stifles us and makes us feel paralyzed and mute. It depletes us of hope and joy and drives us to choose paths that lack creativity and fulfillment.

"You have to be able to handle criticism about what you're trying to do," warns Ken Mader. "That's a big one, because everyone's going to give it to you. You kind of have to psych yourself out and continue to forge ahead in spite of the naysayers."

"It's a hard thing to get anybody to read your script, to get anybody to finance your movie, and to get your movies made," says Adam Rifkin. "But it's hard to do a lot of things. It's hard to climb mountains, but people can do it. So you just have to keep trying. Most people don't succeed at these things,

---

Ten Common Fears That Bind

1. If I start to get in touch with my feelings, I'm afraid that I'll just sink into a big hole and won't be able to write.
2. I'm afraid to ask for help because of what others will think.
3. I'm afraid that once I lose my focus, I won't be able to get it back.
4. I'm afraid that I will need to abandon a script on which I have worked so hard.
5. I'm afraid that getting blocked will imply that something is wrong with me or that I'm being lazy or unproductive.
6. I really want to listen to my own ideas, but I'm afraid that others will criticize me and I won't be strong enough to ignore their words.
7. I know that I am talented as a writer, but I'm afraid that others will be jealous of me, so I put myself down so that they won't have to compete with me.
8. I freeze when I think about someone else evaluating my writing.
9. I know what I want to write, but am afraid to start, because it won't sound right.
10. If I really push to get what I want, others will think I'm too aggressive.

---

and they're going to want to make sure that if they don't succeed, you won't either. It's, Hey, I haven't made it, and you won't either. I think a lot of people listen to them. You can't listen. You have to ignore anybody who says you'll never make it, because they're wrong. You know you'll make it. You just have to keep working hard."

Only one person in the whole world can speak in terms of your truth. Only one person can speak to the fears, myths, language, and blocks that bind and prevent forward motion on the journey you have chosen. Only one person knows about the creativity, passion, and destiny that lies inside of you—the truth of the what, where, and how of your life. No journey is free of struggles. No journey can be completely crisis-free. You will present us with characters and stories involving turmoil, conflict, and struggles. Your ability to accept these in yourself will enable you to write strong, meaningful scripts, with believable characters who will speak their truths in ways that will touch all of us.

Will I Face the Fears?

Writer's block is the moment when fear has struck. It is also a moment when you can gain a clearer perspective of what has stopped the creativity from

Ten Common Myths That Bind

1. If I have any fears about screenwriting process, then I'm not ready to write for the industry.
2. I can't make screenwriting a priority until I make money from it.
3. I don't deserve to be a successful screenwriter.
4. I need to pay heed to other people's criticisms to improve my craft.
5. I'm wasting my time trying to be a screenwriter if I don't live in Hollywood.
6. The story I really want to write won't be commercial enough to sell.
7. I haven't had enough formal education in writing to be taken seriously.
8. I don't have a chance of breaking into the industry if I'm over thirty.
9. In Hollywood, you can only be viewed as a commodity, not as an individual.
10. If I become a television writer, I will never be taken seriously as a feature writer.

flowing. Each of us has experienced these frightening moments, and we have, for the most part, benefitted from the experience. Allow yourself to accept that these blocks will happen, and take the opportunity to discover more about your uniqueness and the fears that visit you from time to time.

Will I Challenge the Myths?

There have always been myths surrounding the concept of writer's block. This blocking of energy is a natural phenomenon in any profession that involves the use of creative energy for its success. When we put ourselves in the spotlight with a profession that is based on a great deal of subjectivity and evaluation, a set of fears can certainly appear without warning. Fears are based on myths that writers will have to fight hard to reject. Your ongoing task is to recognize what these myths represent and to challenge what does not fit your unique journey.

Will I Take the Risks?

As you continue on your screenwriting journey, you will encounter doubts, fears, and many moments of uncertainty. The risks you will take will require that you accept that all of those frightening moments are a very normal part of the journey. You will need to become more aware of the words and expressions you use to describe your progress. Will you constantly put yourself down, devaluing your efforts? Will you see your abilities only in what you are not accomplishing, or will you allow yourself to acknowledge the small victories along the way?

Am I willing to . . .

1. Understand that fear is a natural part of the screenwriting process?
2. Accept that I will experience fear throughout my screenwriting career, no matter how successful I become?
3. Make screenwriting a priority, no matter what else is going on in my life?
4. Allow myself to enjoy what I love to do without guilt?
5. Pursue my dreams in the location that best suits me, not in the one in where I feel I should have to live?
6. Write stories I love, rather than stories I believe will sell?
7. Study my craft in my own unique way, not in the manner in which others may recommend?
8. Stop using negative and disrespectful terminology to define who I am?
9. Be sensitive to not create hierarchies, which have the tendency to regress me and leave me feeling worthless?
10. Allow myself to believe that there isn't just one way to become a successful screenwriter?

●

CHAPTER 16

Josefina Lopez:
Embracing Humanity

One of the things that's made me a very powerful and resilient person
is that I've walked away from so many things that seemed logical to do,
but my gut said, No, don't do it. I don't know why I walked away, but
I knew that if I didn't, I'd be selling out my soul.

Josefina Lopez

The Journey Begins

*Screenwriter-playwright-performer Josefina Lopez was born on March 19, 1969, in
San Luis Potosi, Mexico. When she was five, her family moved to Los Angeles, where
they lived for almost thirteen years as undocumented immigrants. Despite the hardships
of growing up in East L.A., Josefina managed to find her own unique voice at a very
young age, through poetry, stories, and plays. Josefina credits her initial interest in stories to an argument she overheard at the age of five.*

My brother was telling my mother that he had read in a school book that the
world was going to end, because man was going to destroy it. My mother told
him that that was not so, because in the Bible, it said that God was going to
destroy the world with fire. I remember them arguing about how the world
was going to end. I was so scared. I went to bed and covered myself up with
a blanket, hoping that I wouldn't hear it anymore. I had this vision that I was
the last person on earth, and I was with all these characters from Hanna and
Barbera, like Yogi Bear, and we were driving throughout the world. There was
nothing but rubble and little remains of the buildings. There was no one
except me and these cartoon characters. It was a really scary thought, and I
think from that moment on, I looked at the world differently. From that

moment on, I became an activist. I thought, Why do we have to destroy ourselves, or why does God have to destroy us? I was already asking those questions when I was that young, because I was that kind of kid. All of a sudden,
I started thinking, Well, if we're all going to die, then what's the point of living? Well, maybe it is to celebrate the fact that we are alive. Then I started
looking at people differently, and I appreciated a lot of things. I started to
appreciate people that as a little kid, not knowing any better, I would have
made fun of. So after that, I knew I couldn't make fun of someone else,
because their life was also a celebration. In my young way, I thought of this
differently, but now I can articulate what I was feeling. I think that's what got
me started.

The other big influence was that my mother was such a wonderful storyteller. One of the things that I've learned about Chicano literature, through
teaching the course, is that so much of Chicano literature isn't written yet. So
much of it is oral. It comes from an old tradition, like my mother telling me
stories or gossiping. The way she gossiped was a gift she had, because she had
no formal education. She couldn't put it down on paper. When I was growing up, the biggest treat for me was to listen to my mother tell us ghost stories. It wasn't like she was just telling these stories; it was like she was forming
them. So as a little kid I thought, God, what a gift to be able to captivate an
audience. Not to do anything except just say something, and for people to go,
Ah! or Oh! Growing up as a middle child in a large family of, like, eight kids,
I thought, What a great way to get attention. So I started by telling jokes and
little stories. Whenever someone would have a story, I would memorize it and
learn it and then repeat it.

*Family problems also gave Josefina a sense of activism, of wanting to help women like
her mother, who she was incapable of rescuing as a child.*

I saw how much my mother suffered. I remember wanting to rescue her. So
being unable to rescue her from my father in many senses, I felt like I had to
become a superhero as a writer, as an activist. I could liberate women in this
way. Growing up, I remember thinking that if I came across a woman in a similar situation and she didn't know she had power, that somehow I had to get
it across, as an opportunity to save my mother, which is an issue I still have to
work on, because sometimes it's such a burden.

*As a child, Josefina began to realize that there were no Latino voices in the media.
Coupled with the fact that she was an undocumented immigrant, Josefina felt increasingly invisible to the world around her.*

Howard Rosenberg of the *Los Angeles Times* mentioned how there are no minorities in the 1999 fall shows for television. When I was a child in the seventies, I don't remember one single Latino star. I remember thinking that we really must be from another planet. I really believed with all my heart that we were not legal people, that somehow we were inhabiting this Los Angeles planet, and no one knew we existed, because we were really aliens. It was a very painful thing to grow up with. I felt invisible for the longest time, until I started writing, until I started making myself real with my words and playing my humanity into my words. Instead of saying, Well, every story is about white girls and white guys, they were stories about this Latina, who happens to be a human being and who happens to want to go to college.

Josefina went on to attend the Los Angeles County High School for the Arts, where she majored in theater.

I started to write plays. Little by little, I started making myself the protagonist of the stories. It took encouragement from my writing teacher to say, Why don't you write about your life? Because I was like, No, nobody wants to hear about my life. It was wonderful to have her say, Write about what you know. And go as far as you can. I had this image of this young Mexican girl who was getting squashed by a giant tortilla, because when I was six years old, my parents always said, Go heat the tortillas, go heat the tortillas. I remember being so upset, because it felt like the tortillas were ruling my life. So I had an image of this young woman running around with this giant tortilla with a plastic emblem that read "Seventeen Years of Oppression" squashing her. I asked my teacher, Is this too much? If she would have said, Yes, that's ridiculous, I probably would have held back and just written dramas. But instead she said, No, go as far as you want. You can edit later. And I did. I remember having been given that permission to write what I feel and what I think is valid.

At seventeen years old, Josefina was a member of the Young Playwrights Lab at the Los Angeles Theater Center when she wrote her first play, the Emmy-winning Simply Maria or the American Dream. *The first production in 1990 of her most-produced play,* Real Women Have Curves, *earned her a six-week Playwrights Fellowship for the Izadora Aguirre Playwriting Lab. It was a play in which Josefina learned how important it was to write about what she knew.*

At the beginning, it was very difficult to write about my life. I remember writing a scene about this girl and how she discovered her sexuality. She kept touching herself. When it was on stage, it was very subtle, yet I was so embarrassed. I thought, Oh my God, people will think I masturbated as a kid. Then I thought, You know what? That's what it means to be human, and if they can't see that, then they have the problem, not you. If I can embrace my humanity, maybe this will allow other people to do so as well. In *Real Women Have Curves,* there are five women of different sizes that make dresses for Bloomingdale's. These women in the play, like the ones I knew in real life, were making these beautiful gowns for women who would wear them to the opera or to a beautiful ballroom dance. Yet none of them could experience that, because they couldn't afford it or they weren't in that life. I remember the tragedy of being there and thinking, these women who would sew were sometimes wearing mismatched clothes, because they couldn't afford to buy new things, and there they were making these beautiful sequinned gowns. They were like surrogate mothers. They labored over these dresses, they created them, and then the dresses would be taken away for the women who would get to wear them.

The most powerful scene in the play is when these women are suffering from the heat, but they're working all night trying to finish an order to save the factory. My character takes off her shirt, because she's sweating. All the other women start criticizing her body, but she has no problem with it. When the other women start criticizing her again, she takes off her pants. She doesn't care what they think. She's burning up after steam ironing all day. The other women start examining their bodies and saying things like, I've got the biggest stretch marks, or I've got the biggest ass. They compare body parts, until they're all undressed. Then, finally, they stop and look at themselves and embrace their humanity and their bodies. The most powerful thing they could do in that oppressive environment is to take off their clothes. What happens to people in the audience when they see this is, they get so uncomfortable. But after they get used to seeing real bodies on real women on stage, they slowly start to feel comfortable in their own skin. Then, they start laughing with the women and getting beyond that. Then, everybody has fun. It's like the audience is also liberated.

Broken Dreams

Josefina's life as a writer suddenly seemed full of possibilities. Little did she know that she was about to be thrust into a series of promising opportunities that would all lead to disappointment and frustration.

When I was twenty-one, I heard this young writer tell me, I can't wait until I get a deal. I said, Be careful what you ask for, because you might get it, and you might not be ready for it. It's worse if you get it and you're not ready. It was very painful, because initially, it was like a dream come true for me. I didn't go seeking it; it found me. I had a movie deal at twenty-one, and I was like, Wow! Then, I thought, can I do it? At the time, I was sure they were not going to end up doing it. Even though I'm now thirty and working with New Line Cinema, there's still a voice that says, No. They keep telling you they're going to do Latino stories, then somehow they pull the plug and don't keep their word. So finally, when I started believing that it was going to happen, it didn't. It was a very awful experience.

I had a producer who was really excited about the project, so I wrote the first draft for the screenplay. There were rumors that the producer was going to be in our studio. My agent told me that she was planning to leave and to get the producer attached to my project, or it would go into development hell. He kept telling me this, but I did not know anything about anything, and it was a scary time. It was like, Wow, I got this deal, but I don't know anything about what comes next. I turned in the first draft, and then the producer left. I never got any feedback. At that time, at twenty-one, I thought she had left and nothing happened because I was an awful writer. I thought, God, I did a terrible job. I had been paid all this money, because it was in my contract to do a rewrite, and I didn't even do a rewrite. So I felt cheap. Then, I heard from a producer who was in the business that part of the reason that they had picked this project is because a study had been done by an agency that showed that Disney, Warner Brothers, and a number of other studios had not hired any minority writers, or at least did not show that they'd hired any. Part of the reason that my project might have gotten chosen was the fact that they could show that they hired a minority. I don't know if this is true or not, but I just felt so awful. So I decided to stop, and I went off to college in Chicago to study filmmaking. I got my B.A., and when I graduated, I got a job writing on a sitcom.

Things were good again, because I was making a good salary. I thought, Wow, it's so great. I'm working with all these amazing people. But then, it became so frustrating, because none of my writing was getting produced, so again, I was getting paid all this money to do nothing. It was awful. I felt like it was a waste of time, and I couldn't live up to the challenge, and I was such a failure. So after I did the sitcom, I immediately got another job for another comedy show, working with a Latino group. Again, it was very exciting at the beginning, but also got very frustrating. Again, none of my stuff was getting done. I was writing about Latina women, because that's what I thought I'd been hired to do, since I was the only female in the writing pool. The rest were all male producers and male writers. I welcomed the challenge, because I've always been in that situation where I'm the only Latina, the youngest person, or the only woman. It was also very adventurous, and I was getting paid good money. But none of my material was getting made. At the time, in my crazy way, it felt like I was being bought. I would speak up, and they'd think that they'd want my ideas, but then they would say, No, we don't want to hear it.

After that, I started doing a play. I get so much satisfaction out of doing theater and performing. I think that theater is my way of rejuvenating myself. When I give up and get frustrated, I go into theater. I was really satisfied, because I got so much great feedback from the audience, and I felt like I made an impact with the plays. Then, I started writing for *A Different World*. It was about immigrants' experiences, so it was perfect. I wrote the draft. The producer left that studio, and then I didn't get any feedback, and I got paid all this money. So that happened, but in a way, I was lucky, because that year, I was working with a manager who became my writing partner.

Giving Up and Coming Back

Having a new writing partner brought new hope for Josefina, especially when they managed to get three simultaneous television deals with Norman Lear, ABC Productions and UPN.

For a whole year, I worked on these three pilots. They had so much promise, like, God, one of them has to hit. It's inevitable. And then the same thing happened—nothing. I had all this money from doing these three pilots, and nothing happened. After that, I just couldn't take it anymore. It was too painful. You give so much of your soul. I had imagined these shows on TV and that they would represent something from my heart. It was so devastating, because there was no explanation for it, except that the sitcom we did for Normal Lear got passed over because ABC had commissioned three pilots about Latinos and had picked a show about "two fat Mexican DJs." It was like, I couldn't believe a Norman Lear show got passed over for that. It was awful.

My writing partner's wife was dying of cancer, and it had been really painful trying to write a sitcom with him while his wife was dying. And then, the man that I loved was supposed to come from Japan and we were supposed to get married, and he didn't come. It was all supposed to lead to something amazing, and then nothing happened. I just couldn't take it anymore. I went to Mexico to visit my grandmother. I was only there for four days, but it saved my life. I went there, because I heard she might be dying. My mother had to go and be with her in case she was going to die. I wanted to see her, because I wanted to take a picture with her and my mother. I went, and luckily, she didn't die. It was Mother's Day, and I remember giving her a card in which I had written all these wonderful things about her. She looked at it, and she closed it, then she sniffed the flowers. I told my mother, she didn't read it. My mother said, She doesn't know how to read. Then, it occurred to me that I knew very little about my grandmother. I took all these things for granted, like, of course, she knows how to read. The fact that I've gotten an education and do all the things I do is amazing, because a couple generations down, no one had an education. It made me realize, there's so much I don't know.

I decided to give up writing. It takes courage to do that. I remember when I first told my writing partner, he said, Don't be ridiculous. Don't be an idiot. How could you do that? You're at the top. Even if none of these things happen, you still have a name. If you leave now, you can never come back. Or it can take you years to get back. I said, You know what? I don't have a desire anymore. When I was sixteen, seventeen years old, no one had to tell me to write, because I wanted to write. Now, the fact that you have to push me all the time is telling me that I'm not having fun. That I have to go find more stories and live the kind of life I want. It sounds ridiculous, but my gut was telling me to do this.

So I decided take a flower designing course, and I opened a shop in East L.A. That didn't work out. I also dated a lot of men who were psycho-sociopaths. At that time, I began to realize how much of my writing had been to get back at my father. It was a way to humiliate him. Inside, I saw how much my mother was hurting, so publicly I wanted to get him back, since I couldn't do it to his face. Finally, I had to say, Stop doing that. Let him go. Give up that hate. So I thought, Why do I write? I was really going to give it all up, and I then I thought, No, I have to continue writing, and now, I have a choice about what I want to write about. I became a poet. I started doing self-publishing. I wrote a self-help book for Latinas. Eventually, I started getting back into writing and got a manager. I still think about giving up all the time. What you have to do if you feel like giving up and there's nothing left, instead of forcing it and saying it's not there, you kind of own it. And I thank God I went on that journey for three years, because now I have all this material to write the screenplays.

Although Josefina had initially resisted a formal education, she is now completing her masters degree in screenwriting at UCLA. Little could she have predicted that one day she would be teaching students herself.

For the longest time, I resisted, because most of the education I've gotten in writing is from things I did outside of the classroom, like in theater. So for me, it's kind of strange to be going to UCLA to get a masters. Some of the students there are very accomplished, and others are very good writers who are just starting out. Sometimes, I feel kind of odd, because when they're mentioning the studio system or giving L.A. executives what they want, a lot of times, I already know it, because I started in the Hollywood system at twenty-one, when I optioned *Real Women Have Curves*. So sometimes, I sit there and go, Wow, there are a lot of things I already know. But there are a lot of things I don't know.

A few years ago, I wanted to walk away from Hollywood. I thought, What else can I do? I had this dream that I was with hundreds of people at a colosseum, and I was a great teacher. So that semester, I had a friend who told me about a position teaching contemporary Chicano literature, and they gave me the job. I had such a wonderful time teaching Chicano literature as an experience, and not as something that's dead that you have to study. I realized that most of my students were Chicana. I said, I'm going to make you responsible for the future of Chicano literature. There are so few Chicanas who are writing that, instead of observing the path of what someone else has done, it will come from your experience. It's something that you helped create, that you're a part of, that you're responsible for. The students were very empowered.

Today, Josefina is busy writing a new project for New Line Cinema that is based—as are all the stories she cares about—on her personal experiences.

I'm so happy that New Line Cinema is the first studio to make the commitment to start a Latino division. When I got the deal, I just couldn't believe it. It's a studio that finally recognizes the market value, and they're going to make a commitment to Latino films, whether they make millions or not. But eventually, just like African-American films, I know they're going to succeed. So the biggest challenge for me was getting past the feeling that I didn't deserve it or wouldn't write something they wanted. Luckily, I have been working with wonderful executives and a great producer, and slowly, but surely, this script is coming along. I really do feel that, and I really hope that it gets made. It's a story of my Mom—rather, my fantasy of my Mom leaving my Dad. It's done through comedy. I'm working with two executives who are not Latino, but they are very conscious of the fact that they don't know that much about being Latino, though they know how to write screenplays. Sometimes, the challenge is how to tell a story in the way I want and not alienate people who are not Latino to make it acceptable for them, too. The first thing they always say is that it's got too much Spanish in it. The reality would be that these people would be speaking in Spanish. So I have to figure out a way to show that a person doesn't speak English while speaking English, and you have to get that across somehow. Little things like that, so that it's accessible to everyone. Part of me sometimes asks, Why? What do we have to do that for? Why do we have to carry the burden of always having to explain ourselves? And then, there's a part of me that says, Wouldn't it be wonderful to have a story that's universal, which everybody could identify with?

Josefina also recently opened Rascuachi Rep, a new theater company in Boyle Heights. This theater company is her chance to give something back her community.

I always had this commitment to go back to the neighborhood, the barrio, and giving something back. So many of my stories are about the people I met growing up, so that I felt like I can't just succeed and get ahead by representing Chicano people without giving something back. We started a theater company and have been having a lot of fun. I found it so empowering, because I took my image back.

Parting Words

I'm a writer. That's what I love to do, and I'll never stop being a writer, whether I make money or not. For me, it's that vision of being a little Latino kid feeling so neglected on television. Every time I think about giving up and I want to give up or I have given up and then come back, I tell myself that these stories need to be told. It's not because of my ego. At the very beginning, maybe, I started out wanting to be rich and famous and getting the love that I didn't get as a child. A lot of people start out with that need, and I think it's very detrimental, because that love that you didn't get when you were a kid, you're not going to get it if you make millions and people love you. It's still not going to come. It does not fill the void. I'm doing this because these stories need to be told. In a way, I feel like I'm a humanitarian for Latinos. I'm making people aware of our humanity. And the fact that we're not acknowledged as human beings is a reflection of the humanity that has not been embraced by the general public.

Summary

In order for you to honor and respect your role as a storyteller, it will demand that you accept the moments of fear and self-doubt that may travel by your side.

Struggling does not mean that you are not meant for the destiny you have chosen. Experiencing painful emotions and frustrations does not mean that you are too weak for the job. Being scared does not infer that you are incapable of pursuing your dream.

You may still be tempted to believe that others are more talented, more knowledgeable, better equipped to meet industry demands, and more creative in the art of storytelling. You may also be tempted to buy into the belief that only a chosen few get what they want in their lives.

There will be many moments along the journey when your hesitations will scare you and cause you to question everything you have dreamed about and worked hard to accomplish. You may find that facing the blocks head-on is not enough. You may also need to change many of the beliefs you have held about your creativity and your determination to be able to make things happen as you have envisioned.

Getting unstuck will require a great deal of focus and energy directed to the goals you wish to pursue. It will require you to face your own truths and be willing to turn away from the projections that have been placed on you by others who do not understand your mission. When the pauses demand that you regroup and take the time to clear your mind, you will have to do so with as little resistance as possible.

To fully accept your role as a creative agent, you will need to embrace all of the ups and downs, the roller-coaster rides, and the moments when only stillness exists. Pausing, reevaluating, breathing past the stuck moments, even agonizing over a character's role or plot line will become important aspects of your journey. As you give birth to your story, you will need to respect your own process and pursue the support systems that will enrich you. It will become clear that there will be no room for the creation of hierarchies, for you will be reminded of their destructive qualities.

The pausing that may appear unannounced will act as a catalyst, if you permit yourself not to fight it, but rather to move through it as if it were a dark tunnel with light just visible at the end of it.

You may experience the dread that seeps in when all of your creativity seems to have dried up. If writer's block takes a momentary hold, you will need to challenge the beliefs that negate who you are and what your essence represents. You have but to look to the past to become aware of how you were able to move yourself forward when it seemed impossible to do so.

When you have lost your footing, remember that within you lie all of the tools you need to succeed in unlocking the door to your creativity. Ask yourself what you can learn from the fear and what it is teaching you that may be crucial to understanding the characters and stories you wish to create.

Accept your vulnerabilities, your fears, your hesitations, and your willingness to be human. Remember that your success lies in your ability to listen to your own voice, to follow the dream you have claimed, and to remain faithful to the stories and characters that you will bring to life. No matter how hard the journey has been, no matter how long it has taken you to arrive where you now reside, when you have honored your own spirit and claimed the storyteller's dream, nothing will be more inwardly rewarding nor fill your heart with such immense joy.

●

Writer's Block and the Myths That Bind: Questionnaire for Self-Evaluation

The following questions are meant for introspection and affirmation. They are proposed for the benefit of clarity and a better understanding of how to proceed when approaching the "stuck" places and those moments when reevaluation is needed.

1. What will I do if I encounter a block of energy that stops me from writing?
2. What do I know about writer's block and its role in any creative process?
3. What are the ways in which I stop myself and sabotage my writing efforts?
4. How may I have prevented myself from feeling the natural anxieties that arise when one is willing to take risks?
5. How have I refused to get the help and support I need as a result of stubbornness, rigidity, and pride?
6. If I have stopped myself from seeking support systems, what am I willing to do about it?
7. When did I last become aware of the language I use to describe myself and whether it really represents my true self?
8. What is the caution, anxiety, or fear that is causing me to use the "what ifs" in my language?
9. What was happening in my life during the times that I wanted quick financial rewards and resorted to writing trendy scripts, rather than honoring my own voice?
10. Why am I sometimes critical about the Hollywood scene, when secretly I would love to be included in it?
11. In what ways am I considering all the options that may be available to me when I run out of creative ideas?
12. If I have kept myself in isolation, what has been hindering me from connecting and working with other writers?
13. What stops me from acknowledging that an underlying fear may be making me feel helpless and confused?
14. In what ways would I be willing to explore my emotions when I feel incapacitated and stuck?
15. What are the ramifications of thinking more highly of others' opinions and putting my own validity on hold?

16. When I think about writer's block, why is it so hard to believe that I might experience these stuck moments?

17. How do I let my ego stop me from admitting that I don't always know how to fill the creative voids I sometimes experience?

18. What are some of the changes in my belief systems that I may need to make in order to prevent negative thoughts from setting in and causing me to become blocked?

19. When I've created overwhelming and stifling expectations for myself, what will it take for me to reevaluate my goals?

20. Why do I have difficulty accepting my inner strength and the knowledge that I have the ability to survive disappointments?

21. When I feel empty and lose my creative energy, how does my thinking have to shift to accept those moments?

PART IV

The Power of Collaboration

DONNA FLINT

Memoir of a Screenwriter—Act III

I decided that making my own not-too-chunky homemade pasta sauce was not going to be enough. So I stepped back and took a look at my life. Here I was, a mother of two, running a business out of my apartment. Outside of my children's school activities, getting out a few nights a month, and struggling to keep my business afloat, I basically had no life and was still a galaxy away from realizing my dreams. What had been the point of moving to Los Angeles? What had happened to all of my aspirations? And what had made me backpedal my way into this isolated corner?

A number of thoughts ran through my mind: I couldn't cut the mustard, because things like pitch sessions and cold calls absolutely petrified me; I lacked the pizazz that got producers' attention; I didn't hustle enough; twenty-something grads out of UCLA made me look as fresh and exciting as leftover mashed potatoes. My friends back in Chicago couldn't relate to my dilemma. Some of them encouraged me to "come home" and pick up where I'd left off. I'd had a good life there, even if it wasn't lassoing the moon.

Throughout my life, I've been stubborn to a fault, even when it might have been in my best interest to quietly tiptoe away from certain situations. When I was five, my aunt rented a bicycle on a promenade so I could practice riding without training wheels. The more I fell and scraped my knees, the more I screamed at, threw, and kicked the mechanical ass. The bike rental manager tried to retrieve the beast, so I kicked and screamed at him as well. All my poor aunt could do was laugh with embarrassment, which only intensified my fury. My aunt and the bike rental guy ended up in a tug-of-war, one pulling my shrieking, writhing body and the other, the mangled bike, as my indignant howls drew a crowd.

Because of my stubborn traits, I knew I'd go down kicking and screaming before I'd ever hang my screenwriter's hat on the peg. But before getting ugly about it, I decided to embark on a more dignified crusade.

Many friends in the industry had told me about a workshop that I might benefit from. It piqued my interest, because unlike other workshops I had attended, it wasn't exclusive to screenwriters. It brought all facets of the industry—writers, actors, producers, directors, editors, cinematographers, etc.—into the same environment. The focus of the workshop also intrigued me. It wasn't on how to improve your craft, but on how to achieve your dream. I entered the session cautiously, worried that I was wasting my money or would find myself in the nightmare situation of pitching my scripts to strangers. Luckily, the pendulum didn't swing in either of those directions, and I finally came to understand a simple yet valuable grain of wisdom from the experience—you don't have to go it all alone. There's a comfort in meeting others who are also reaching for the stars. And as I would soon discover, our combined energies could lead to something quite amazing.

Six months later, I found myself as the producer/writer on the set of my first independent film, which involved many people I had met in the workshop. The craft person didn't show up, so I decided to take on the role myself. I knew if I didn't feed the crew, I would have a mutiny on my hands, considering what I was (or rather was not) paying them. As I weaved my way through the house with a tray of Chinese dumplings and spring rolls, I noticed the gaffers dangling lights from the ceiling and crossed my fingers that we wouldn't need to use the workman's comp. The assistant director paced with nervous energy, shaking his head every time he looked at his watch. When I made it to the makeup room, I discovered that one of the actors had disappeared and was being tracked down by a P.A. in the neighboring woods. Within the first few hours, we were way behind schedule. It was the sort of stuff that made me uptight on day one, but by day six, not having slept a wink and functioning purely on adrenaline, I would just shrug my shoulders if someone told me the set was on fire.

As I cruised through Hollywood on my way to the last dailies drop-off, I couldn't believe that we had pulled off the unimaginable. We had made a film. We had landed on the moon. When one feels like this, there is only one thing to do—scream like a maniac. I'm sure anyone driving past me on the 101 thought I was a deranged lunatic, as I drove with my mouth agape like a happy version of an Edward Munch painting.

For the last three years, I still get together every month with four friends from that workshop. We meet at Lulu's Alibi off Santa Monica Boulevard and talk about our goals and dreams. We commiserate over our disappointments and rejections. Perhaps we do this because we all need the same thing from each other. We need support and encouragement, but most importantly, we need to know that our dreams are worth kicking and screaming for.

●

CHAPTER 17

The Role of Collaboration in Screenwriting

Collaboration takes a very special relationship and a sense of shared
destiny. For a long time, you really have to shape your life around
working with that other person.

Harold Ramis

One of the most powerful questions that screenwriters will find
themselves asking is, "What will
it take for me to become successful?" As each phase of a screenwriter's journey is addressed, new answers to this question will determine what steps will
need to be taken in order to propel the process forward.

Whether or not the writer initially takes the path alone, at some critical
point in the writing and development of the script, the issue of collaboration
will surface. Perhaps in the very beginning of the journey, there may not be
the need, nor the desire, to view the process of screenwriting in its totality, for
this can prove to be overwhelming. However, as the script unfolds and the
desire for visibility increases, it can become a necessary issue to be contemplated.

Collaboration is an inherent part of the screenwriting process. It is a complex issue that is often viewed in terms of an all-or-nothing option. Entering
into a writing partnership requires a certain level of self-understanding. There
are many ways in which writers can find themselves involved in a collaborative relationship, from scripting with a cowriter, consulting with an expert, or
working with a director and producer as a script goes into production.

It is often difficult for beginning screenwriters to view their work as part of a collaborative filmmaking process. It is an ongoing challenge to recognize that even when their work gets sold, it may be revised multiple times before it is actually made into a film. As discouraging as it may sound, the writer who has originated the script is often left out of the loop, as studio and network writers are brought onto the project for their creative input, as well as any additional writers who are striving for their place on this script. It is a strong probability that the cinematic interpretation of the original story will be continuously revised. What was once a single idea, brought about by one creative voice, will be either enhanced or diluted by the input of others and influenced by the director's vision, the D.P.'s eye, and the editor's sense of rhythm and visual coherence. The critical concern should not be whether or not to collaborate, but rather for the writer to accept that collaboration is the cornerstone of the filmmaking and television industry.

There is a caveat, however. The initial stages of writing a script is the time in which you will have the opportunity to discern if writing with someone else will prove to be beneficial. It is up to you to know if doing so can provide the positive force you may need to push the project to the next level. When will turning to collaboration be appropriate, and with whom will you choose to share your story? Once the script is sold, it will be out of your hands, and you will need to accept that other creative voices will be involved.

For many writers, a new way of thinking will be required. Writing in solitude may no longer be energizing. Perhaps the genre selected will require a team effort in order to generate the ideas necessary to bring the story to its conclusion. For others who have thought of working together on a project, there may have been a tendency to shy away from the idea of collaboration, as there appear to be no ready answers to the questions: How can this realistically work? What dynamics are involved in creating a cowriting team? How can I maintain my integrity and individual style with a writing partner? How do we divide the work fairly? What if we do not agree on characters or plot points? What if my partner tries to take over the project? How do I protect my own personal vision?

There is great pride in completing a project alone, of knowing that the challenge will be to discipline yourself to translate an idea into a one-hundred-and-twenty-page story. Many writers find a great sense of fulfillment and enjoyment in striking their keyboards in solitude.

"I'm the type of person that loves to work alone," says Chicago writer Carmen Brown. "If I'm running with a story, I don't want to stop and say, You read it and tell me what's wrong. You may not even get to the next scene, because you're trying to show the other person your vision, which is usually impossible to do. On the other hand, at times you may get stuck, and you need to have someone else look at it. Another person can see it a different way and let you know what works and what doesn't. So, I'm not totally against working with someone if we shared the same vision. It could definitely work."

Although many writers like Carmen prefer to work alone, collaboration is a process that is often crucial in bringing projects to fruition. Unfortunately, many writers fear that if they avail themselves of working within the framework of a partnership, it means that they were not talented enough to bring the project to completion alone. They often walk away with a less-than-quality experience about their work and about collaboration, and are left without this vital tool, which has the potential of bringing the story a new and enriched perspective.

Noah Baumbach reminds us that writing can never be a truly isolated process.

"If a writer has an inclination to write by himself, I think he should do that. But making a movie is ultimately about collaboration. Collaboration with a producer, with actors, with a crew, the restraints of a budget, etc. I had a good lesson making *Kicking and Screaming.* The financing fell through twice, and ultimately I had to write Eric Stoltz a part to get the movie made. Up until then, I'd felt the script was this precious document, but suddenly, I had to write in an entirely new character to get the money. I wrote the part in a way that I knew I could cut it out if it didn't work, but it ended up making the movie better."

Collaboration is not a luxury, nor simply a vehicle to be used when stuck. It is a basic component of the screenwriting journey that, when it is embraced without resistance, can offer the tools to move from a model of isolation to a shared effort, bringing tremendous satisfaction and unforeseen rewards. Although used to working primarily on his own, Noah decided to collaborate on several projects, including a television pilot and a film script with Carlos Jacott, a Los Angeles actor, who appeared in both of Noah's films. Noah decided to collaborate with Carlos when he realized that his first draft needed renewed energy.

"I had written a draft that wasn't working, so I sent it to Carlos," says Noah. "I'd collaborated with him as actor twice, and he's a great improvisor, so I thought maybe we could start the collaboration earlier in the process this time. He ended up coming on the project as a cowriter, and it was a rewarding experience."

There is something quite special when people come together for the purpose of sharing a dream. There is something quite amazing that can take place when a story's message can be given amplification because of the combined energies it has received. What could be more rewarding than an idea that was once but a speck, now developing into a strong and fantastic story because of dedicated creative partners who shared a similar vision?

How Does the Collaborative Process Work?

For many writers who prefer to collaborate, the thought of writing alone presents a picture of tremendous loneliness and solitude, where ideas become stymied rather than being allowed the freedom to emerge without restraint. Others prefer writing alone and availing themselves of readers, consultants, friends, and other colleagues at moments when they feel that the input they are soliciting can benefit the progress of their scripts. There are no set rules to the collaborative process, nor are there black-or-white situations that dictate when or how to best utilize this tool, since there are so many variables to be considered. The most effective use of collaboration is when writers choose to come together for the goal of propelling a story forward. When this happens, real benefits can occur from their combined energies, which makes the collaborative effort a very special and unique relationship.

"The biggest challenge in any collaboration is having the right collaborator," says Harold Ramis. "Sometimes, we want to work with people we like, but it doesn't necessarily lead to the best work. We're less likely to collaborate with someone we don't like, but ideally you find someone who you can be in a room with for weeks and months and who you feel is at least your equal, if not of superior talent."

It is a misconception to believe that partners will always see eye to eye on a story's messages and mission. Is it really realistic to believe that the collaborative process will always run smoothly and without a hitch? Sometimes moments of conflict can bring about fruitful results, expansive visions, and a script filled with bountiful images and characters. Even when everyone shares the same vision, it does not preclude the fact that disagreements will occur. The goal should not be to try to avoid the differences, rather to ascertain that the partners are capable of resolving them for the good of the screenplay process. There may be heated discussions, battles over a character's history and purpose, and differing views on how a story should end. This may cause consternation and ongoing tugs-of-war, but this does not mean that the collaboration will not become a positive one. Partnerships become negative when battles are fought on personal ground, putting the mission of the screenplay at risk.

One screenwriter shared with us his collaborative experiences on both ends of the continuum. He described two such episodes as his "partnership in heaven" and "collaboration from hell." The partnership in heaven was not free from disagreements, yet both writers were positioned from a place of mutual respect. Arguments and debates did not involve knocking down ideas in a cruel or demeaning manner. When major differences appeared, both partners were able to work through issues by spending the time necessary to talk about the conflicts and were able to discover new ways of problem solving for the benefit of both parties. The goal continued to be the integrity of the story, not who would need to be right at any cost. Clearly, the collaborative relationship had become valuable, as each person had been willing to listen to the other and had met their differences without resorting to power struggles.

In the collaboration from hell, the fulfillment of ego superseded any feelings of respect or caring about the relationship. Our screenwriter described the horror of what happened whenever he attempted to make changes or offer recommendations to his partner. The story lost its focus, the characters became a secondary consideration, and the process soon became a battle of wills. The disagreements turned into fights with personal attacks, leaving no possibility for moving forward. He surprised himself by having entered into such a relationship, and it took a lot of soul searching before he could extricate himself from the project. It had become a no-win situation, and the script was becoming bogged down by the negative energy. In fact, there was no true partnership and, as a result, no ability to share ideas.

There may be many such examples of writers who initiated a collaboration with the idea that a wonderful and exciting screenplay would emerge. When one of the partners begins to value a "right-or-wrong" mentality, with the determination to win, it is clearly a situation that will negate positive results. There is a big difference between two people who come together for the benefit of the script, versus a person whose ego is so frail and vulnerable that the script takes a back seat to the fulfillment of the psychological and emotional needs being sought. It is for this reason that a potential collaboration must be carefully evaluated and considered from many different vantage points. Be very certain to clarify why you are choosing this person with whom to share the project and what level of trust you have in your ability to problem-solve together. Pay attention to the cues and clues your partner may be sharing, as you clarify your tasks and the goals ahead, and most importantly, listen to your intuition. Do not override your initial response to what you are experiencing, and give yourself the time to sort out your thoughts. In the long run, reevaluating your choice of partner will save you days, weeks, and even months of potential frustration and discouragement.

There will be opportunities to reevaluate whether the partnership is meeting with success. Writers will often question whether they made a mistake collaborating on their project and whether the effort was really worth it. The bottom line for the screenwriter, however, entails going back to the original questions—what will it take for me to meet with success, and what do I need to do to bring this project to completion?

Forming Successful Collaborations

Critics of the collaborative process may contend that it is impossible for more than one person to actually share in the development of a creative vision.

Is it really possible for two or more writers to come together and formulate a story's mission in a manner that will leave the story intact and not fragmented? Can more than one voice be heard, so that each individual does not feel sacrificed in the process? Can differing styles be blended in a unified way? Are two (or more) heads really better than one?

When writers are prepared for the process and when viewed with enthusiasm, more often than not, two heads can provide amazing insights into a story's purpose. The key to forming a successful partnership is to discuss the process in as much detail as is needed, so that assumptions are kept to a minimum. As in any successful team effort, there must be an understanding by all parties of what the process will entail. Most collaborative disasters occur when there is not a clear concept of each person's role or the intricacies of that particular team dynamic prior to the agreement to work together.

The when, where, and how of the relationship must be considered and not be taken for granted. Leaving doors open for frequent communication is crucial, even when it appears that everything is working smoothly. When partners do not allow ample time for the clarification of issues, it will not take long for the first assumptions to be made and, shortly thereafter, for the writers to experience the tremendous friction they have caused. The misunderstandings take time to be addressed, yet can offer opportunities for a new setting of goals and direction that can be incorporated into the writing process.

Even in relationships where an effort is made to keep the lines of communication open, there will not always be harmonious interactions. The important factor is to remember what value the collaboration brings to the project. When writers are willing to discuss their differences, when assumptions and perceptions are checked, there is a much better chance for the collaboration to be successful. It can lead to incredible results in bringing a story to its next arena, without sacrificing the partnership.

How a collaboration contributes to positive outcomes will depend on each partner's strengths and weaknesses, as well as how they directly deal with their personal writing preferences and desires. There are numerous variations on a theme, and no one way of working together will always be appropriate for each assignment that is undertaken. Some writers pride themselves on initiating creative concepts, while others are masterful in nailing the dialogue. Combining the strongest qualities of each person, rather than attempting to divide the work with a fifty-fifty mentality, will most probably yield the positive results desired by both partners. In the long run, the gift to the script will be the ability for each writer to be flexible and spontaneous. They will need to allow for open communication and ongoing dialogue in order to deal with the disagreements that will occur along the way.

The writing environment that the partners choose, plus the general logistical considerations, will play a major consideration in establishing how the goals and deadlines will be attained. Where will the writing actually take place? How often will you meet? Who will do the actual typing and incorporate updates? How will responsibilities be divided? These details should not be taken for granted, for in doing so, a positive working relationship is potentially incapacitated.

If there are personality conflicts or strong differences of opinion and they are left to fester, the partnership will suffer, as well as the well-being of the project. Each collaborative relationship you develop will require establishing its own parameters in order to be successful. To be effective, you should not expect the collaborative process to be predictable, static, or routine. No creative endeavor flourishes when the process of communication is left unattended. Misunderstandings require attention when they occur, and if not addressed will potentially lead to the dissolution of the partnership and a project left unfinished.

Productive collaboration involves working as a team, bouncing ideas back and forth, with one partner often acting as the devil's advocate, as the essence of each character's history and personality is uncovered and the story line is strengthened. There is never a right or wrong in the process of collaboration, for a writer's vision cannot and should not be evaluated according to the predictability of the success value of that vision. What needs to be stressed is the ability of the collaborative process to solicit new insights and possibilities for the development of the script, which will, in turn, bring it the recognition it deserves.

David Marconi's experience with the collaborative process has given him a firsthand look at what is required in making the process beneficial for both the team and the story.

"Maybe something you wrote that was perfectly clear in your mind, other people really don't understand," says David. "You have to accept that and say, Alright, maybe there is a problem here. Maybe something that's absolutely crystal clear in my mind is not clear in other people's minds. Just because they don't understand it doesn't necessarily mean they're idiots. You have to accept that maybe you did not communicate something clearly. Or your message was misunderstood. That's why you have to be very open about the process and not take things personally."

When conflict occurs and the assumptions that were made have led to confusion, it is critical that the partners take the time necessary to rectify the problems, and that they have the courage to confront the issues when they believe that creativity is being inhibited and the sharing of ideas restricted.

Sharing a Common Goal

Screenwriters who have given some thought to collaborating on a project often change their minds after asking themselves if it can realistically work—and if it can really be successful in increasing their productivity. Before engaging in a collaboration, writers need to ask themselves questions, including:

- How do I maintain my integrity and individual style with a writing partner?
- Will my ideas be sacrificed?
- Will I have to concede my position on the story and characters even when I do not feel it is appropriate to do so?
- Will I lose my individuality?
- How will the writing tasks be divided fairly?

One of the key elements to consider before entering into a collaborative relationship is whether everyone involved shares in the same vision. It is a given that differences will arise as the process evolves, and more often than not, these differences can actually prove to be beneficial to the story's outcome. However, no story will be empowered if each individual writer perceives the core message of the project differently. There must be a shared commitment to the story's mission, or the partnership will more than likely become ineffective. If there is little agreement, the story will risk becoming fragmented, rather than sounding like one voice.

"I've read scripts by friends that felt like they were written by two different people," explains Noah Baumbach. "That's the problem with many collaborations. You may have two very good writers, but half the script feels like one person and the other half, the other person."

Even writers who believe that stories can be born completely in solitude will eventually need to reach out to others to promote their script. Some writers are threatened by the notion that they will eventually have to share their ideas with others. They would prefer to struggle on their own, no matter what the cost. They may even go as far as letting an idea die rather than bringing in a fresh perspective.

What has been so terrifying about the collaborative process that a writer would choose to abandon a story rather than meet the challenges of getting a script completed? What has caused him to dismiss any opportunity to bring the story to new heights and open the door to possible success? Writers who abhor the thought of writing partners often experience feelings of fear—fear that someone will steal their ideas; fear that they will not be considered "legitimate" if they are dependent on a writing partner; fear of sharing credits, lest they should lose out somehow.

In sharing a common goal, fear can become the enemy that can stop all progress. Partners must learn how to protect the shared vision, as they move to bring the project to its finale. Anxieties can prevail, and concerns about the process can interrupt the dialogues that had been working quite well. Successfully sharing a common goal requires that each partner be sensitive to the concerns that may crop up suddenly. They should explore what has triggered the doubts and what can be done to alleviate them.

The most important question to consider as you seek a collaborative relationship is whether or not you trust the person with whom you will be sharing this project.

"I have a small group of people whose opinions I respect," says Adam Rifkin.

"When I'm done with a project, I let them read it. If they have opinions or ideas that are good, I'll incorporate them. You should use any idea that makes your script better. Who cares who came up with the idea if it makes it a better script? You only have something to gain from that."

Without the element of trust, a script will not benefit from the use of writing partnerships. Many questions will arise as writers evaluate when, with whom, and how they will use collaboration to bring their scripts to completion. Writers who are struggling with this decision may benefit from asking questions that can bring them the answers needed to help them resolve the hesitations:

- Is my project in need of help?
- What kind of help do I need?
- Would I benefit from having a writing partner?
- With whom would I trust sharing my vision and goals?
- What options must I consider if the story is to go forward and be made visible?

The screenwriting journey is fraught with many moments when hard decisions will need to be tackled, questioned, evaluated, and resolved. Choosing to enter into a writing partnership or team effort may feel precarious, yet may prove to be the best decision, not only for the writers involved, but for the stories and writing projects they yearn to create.

Sharing a common goal requires choosing the appropriate partner or team who can be trusted to help bring the desired results. It demands a willingness to address the fears and hesitations together and to use the ingenuity required to honor the story's purpose.

Collaboration as a Process

The screenwriting journey is a fluid one, which should not become static, rigid, or lacking in creative energy. Even though there may be moments when writers get stuck, the way in which they choose to work through those moments will determine the next steps of the journey.

Collaboration, because of its ability to change a writer's precepts about how the project will proceed, can be an ever-present influence throughout every aspect of a story's development. Many writers believe that the use of writing partners or other collaborative partners is an all-or-nothing decision— you either work well alone or you work well with others. They believe you cannot have it both ways. Others who have had a negative experience or possibly even two in the past may decide that all collaborative partnerships will not work for them. Again, the bottom line is, how will your script get made? Collaboration is an ongoing process, because for each story conceived, for every project in development, the same considerations will need attention— what will it take to make my dream happen? How will I bring attention to this project, and what is the best way to bring it the success it deserves?

Every writer who has collaborated with others has undoubtedly experienced both the positive and negative aspects of creative partnerships. Although each team effort may not produce the desired results, each partnership has the potential of contributing to a greater self-awareness of who you are as a screenwriter and what you need in order to move forward on your journey.

Collaborations that have gone awry are not failures. They are opportunities to become more sophisticated about what you may need to honor your vision and what elements are required for you to form strong and positive writing partnerships.

Josefina Lopez collaborated with a writer who she believed would add a new perspective to the writing process. Unfortunately, it was a partnership in which her own voice would become silenced.

"It sounded like a good idea at first, but then it was not a very good idea, because this partner was male and almost twice as old as me," explains Josefina.

"At the beginning, I thought, Wow, how wonderful to have male and female points of view. But it didn't work out. I come from a culture where you respect your elders. Even though I'm modern and I'm aware of those things, it's something hard to change. Whenever he spoke, I wanted to challenge him, but a part of me said, No, he's older so he must know better. Yet, my instinct knew that he was not always right. I was fighting myself. I was being quiet, so on the page, my voice was silent. I felt helpless and like I was sixteen again. What would come out was his reflection on life. I ended up not working with him anymore. It was a very painful breakup. I'm very happy, though, because otherwise, I would have written something that wasn't me."

Depending on the personalities, each collaborative effort will have a different tone. You may find that in one situation, you can be very open about sharing ideas and opinions and you do not have to set any limits on how you work together, since you are both striving for the "good of the project."

Los Angeles writer Betty Hager had a positive collaborative experience with another writer. The partnership involved the blending of two very different styles.

"The last time I collaborated was with a woman in my book club, who is about fifteen years younger than me," says Betty about the experience. "I went over to her and I said, I want you to write a screenplay with me. She fainted. She'd never written anything in her life. But she's an unusually brilliant woman. So she started doing the research. If we had any problems working together, it was because she was very organized and was doing charts and using colors and all kinds of things that weren't my way. I said, You do your thing and I'll do mine, and we'll just blend it together. We did have a wonderful time together. I've never found a story so exhilarating or exciting. I couldn't wait for her to get here, so we could get on that computer working together. We finally did get the script written. It took us about a year. It's out there now, so we'll see what happens. The nice thing about my particular collaboration is that this woman is now planning to write. I'm delighted."

As in everything else that is important in our lives, the timing of the decisions we make is crucial to how we will bring the success to the projects we want to accomplish. There is a wonderful adage that states, "The right thing at the wrong time is the wrong thing." The timing for if and when to collaborate will depend on the project, as well as the writer's ability or inability to move the story forward on his own.

When the writer feels unable to continue alone, the collaborative process may offer new ways of evaluating characters and story lines. Most importantly, it offers writers a moment when they can actually see "something happen" within the story and appreciate the contribution that different perspectives have brought to the project. When the struggles and solitude can be kept to a minimum, there need no longer be the negative shadows that can hinder the writing experience.

There are tremendous advantages to working with other creative partners as you travel on your unique path. The positive energy, more often than not, will outweigh the momentary setbacks you may experience. The following list offers but a few of the most obvious advantages you will receive as you create your own writing environment.

Advantages of Collaboration

- Immediate feedback from another person
- A team effort is often more efficient than writing an entire script alone
- Collaborators help us feel credible
- Collaborators can offer us encouragement when we are discouraged
- Collaborators broaden our network base of industry contacts
- Collaborators have a vested interest in seeing the project succeed; two people promoting a project can be better than one
- Brainstorming with collaborators can help us to "unblock" when we're suffering from writer's block
- Collaborators help make us accountable, and we are less likely to put off the writing
- Collaborators can draw on each other's strengths, knowledge, and experience
- Collaborators can play the role of the devil's advocate by questioning and probing the work to bring out new ideas that would ordinarily not be there
- Collaboration is more fun than going it alone and a lot less scary

Ken Mader has experienced the pros and cons of writing partnerships and has found his own way of evaluating when he will or will not use the process of collaboration.

"There's a certain creative energy that happens when collaborating," says Ken. "I think things can get done a lot faster. If you can find someone that you get along with really well, collaboration can be a great thing. The downside is that one person can end up doing most of the work. That can be a little distracting. You also have to make compromises. There's a certain give and take in any collaboration. Your ideas are not always going to be the best or not always going to win out. You just have to accept that."

When collaboration is seen as an ongoing process, it can offer limitless opportunities throughout a writer's entire screenwriting career. It can offer great solace to those writers who believe that they have to ponder every word they write alone, rewriting and rewriting, yet never finding the perfect scenario, dialogue, or character interaction. They may have convinced themselves that they have a fabulous story, yet sitting alone in the quiet, nothing evolves but more silence.

Somewhere along the line, the wisdom will be to reach out to others for input, support, affirmation, and encouragement. Each project will be defined by its own set of requirements, for collaboration will not always offer what the script or writer may need. Knowing when your story needs the additional energy and reorganizing, when your wisest course of action will require a collaborative relationship, will always lie within your intuition. Listening to your own voice when a decision is to be made as to how to proceed will bring you the partners and the writing experiences most advantageous for your script's mission.

Whether or not to collaborate, and at what point such a partnership might take place, are very personal decisions. There is no right or wrong answer in any situation. What really makes the difference is how successful a project can become with or without a partner. Writers who can put their fears aside and remain open to working within a different modality will experience more fulfilling rewards and a greater satisfaction with the writing process. Remember, your story left untold changes nothing. A story that you have written, no matter how it was brought to completion, has the power to impact, influence, and provide audiences with the gift of connection.

Will I Face the Fears?

The thought of collaborating can fill many writers with trepidation. They may have many questions about how the process can realistically work or may be frightened by horror stories from other writers who have had negative experiences in collaborative partnerships. It certainly can be an unproductive experience for writers who choose this option solely out of desperation, because they fear venturing into the unknown alone. Collaborations chosen for the benefit of the project, in whatever configuration such partnerships will be formed, have a far more likely chance of producing a positive and challenging experience, beyond what you may even have imagined.

Will I Challenge the Myths?

Some writers believe that collaboration can only be successful if everyone on the team agrees on all aspects of the project. This myth suggests that successful partnerships are devoid of conflict, confrontations, and misunderstandings.

Ten Common Fears about Collaboration

1. I'm afraid that I will lose control of the project.
2. I'm afraid that I'll end up in a power struggle with another person.
3. I'm afraid to depend on someone who will probably let me down in the end.
4. If I share my ideas with someone else and things don't work out, he or she might steal them.
5. If I collaborate and things go wrong, it will have been a waste of time.
6. I'm afraid that my voice won't be heard if another writer is involved.
7. I'm afraid that I'll end up doing most of the work, but we'll still have to share the credit.
8. I'm concerned that my partner will expect too much from me.
9. I'm afraid to lose a friendship if the collaboration goes amok.
10. People will give my writing partner recognition for contributions that I have made.

Of course, successful partnerships, like successful marriages, rarely completely escape these moments. The point is not to try to determine the reasons whether or not to collaborate based on myths you may have heard. Rather, the key is to understand the timing of when to choose collaboration and whether it will, indeed, benefit the project.

Will I Take the Risks?

Any time we rely on others for support, encouragement, affirmation and to help bring a project to fruition, we are relinquishing a level of control, which can be frightening. Can we, however, go through the process of creating meaningful stories without ever turning to others to help propel those stories to visibility? Being a screenwriter means accepting the role that collaboration will play throughout your journey. You will have to risk sharing your ideas, asking for consult, writing with partners of differing minds, and doing whatever it takes for you to bring your story to the appropriate arena. There will be no ready solution or easy compromises. There will be, however, fabulous opportunities to learn with others and to be given the creative energy that collaboration can offer.

Ten Common Myths about Collaboration

1. If I don't write my script alone, it won't be as worthy or valuable.
2. I will lose control of my story and ideas.
3. It will be too difficult to rely on someone else's schedule.
4. A partner will slow down the writing process.
5. A script needs to have a single vision, not two people's individual views of the project.
6. Collaborations always end up in conflict.
7. Writing is a solitary process. A partner would cause too many distractions.
8. The only way to collaborate is for the partners to be in the same room taking turns typing.
9. One writer is going to be better than another, so there can't ever be an equal partnership.
10. You can only collaborate successfully with a good friend.

Am I willing to ask myself . . .

1. Why do I or don't I want to collaborate on a particular project?
2. When I collaborated in the past (not necessarily on a script), what was that experience like?
3. Who do I know with whom I would want to collaborate on a project? What strengths and weaknesses would they bring to the project?
4. How can I supply all the knowledge I need for my script idea on my own?
5. What within me stops me from seeking help, advice, or support?
6. What compromises would I be willing to make?
7. Is the person I'm considering as a writing partner someone I really admire and respect, and with whom I would feel comfortable working?
8. Am I too afraid to give up control of my project?
9. Would I prefer to relinquish my story rather than get help through partnerships that can propel it forward?
10. Why is sharing a writing credit unacceptable to me?

●

CHAPTER 18

Sharon Y. Cobb:
Celebrating the Victories

Never lose sight of your humanity. Don't sacrifice your soul to the
Hollywood devil. If you lose your soul, you lose your writing.
Sharon Y. Cobb

The Journey Begins

Award-winning writer Sharon Y. Cobb never aspired to be a writer as a young person growing up in Florida. Nevertheless, throughout her early life, she was laying the foundation for a long and often difficult screenwriting journey. Whenever Sharon would reach a crossroad, she knew to let her own instincts guide her in the right direction.

I had no idea I would be a writer or anything to do with the movies. I wanted to be an artist all my life. I was always drawing pictures from age four and was very influenced by my uncle, Richard Lyons, who was a commercial artist. I loved writing little stories when I was young as well. So if you put the writing and the visual art together, then it's screenwriting. As an adult, I became a graphic designer and then opened an advertising agency. I had to write all the copy. I had to write all the news releases, all the nonfiction material. When I moved to Key West, I became very influenced to write fiction by meeting Tennessee Williams. I ended up becoming a publisher. Oddly enough, my writing, publishing, and journalistic career started out backwards. Normally, you would start out as a freelance journalist and then get on staff and then become an editor and then a publisher. Mine was totally backwards. I started as a publisher, became an editor, wrote for the magazine, and then became a freelance journalist.

I was writing fiction since I moved to Key West. Mostly short stories. I thought, Okay, I'd really like to be a fiction writer. I went to the library and did some research and found out that short story writers make no living at all. I think in the United States, the top salary was $12,000. I thought, Okay, how about a novelist or a screenwriter? But at that point, I really didn't know anything about screenwriting. I had my publishing company at the time, and one of my employees brought a brochure back from a convention that said, "Screenwriting Seminar This Weekend."

As soon as I saw it, an alarm went off. I've been very, very blessed to have this all my life—when I see something that's the right next step for me, it's like alarms go off. Dee-dee, dee-dee. I don't know how to describe it, except that I knew I had to do that. So I called, and they had one space left in the seminar. I took off for Fort Lauderdale. Within the first hour of the class, I knew this was it. The book I'd been working on became a screenplay. I'd been having too much trouble with it in the novel form, and I knew right then that I was going to be a screenwriter.

Sharon's background in advertising, marketing, and publishing gave her confidence in her writing abilities, though she knew there was still a lot to learn about the screenwriting craft before making the move to Los Angeles.

I was very confident about my nonfiction and fiction writing by the time I journeyed into screenwriting. There's a lot to learn about screenwriting. The craft is totally different than any other form of fiction writing. But I had a real solid base. I'd been writing for several years before I came to L.A. It gave me the foundation I needed to build the house on, so to speak. Once I came to L.A., my background in marketing assisted me, needless to say, as well as my networking skills from doing public relations. Networking is everything out here, especially in the beginning. That's really where the key to my success has been. Not only do I love the writing, and I write fast and I write well, but the networking was so, so important.

What most writers don't understand is, once they get the script finished, what do they do? Now, that's where the brick wall comes. They're running up the Hollywood hill toward the fortress, and once they get there, they find out that all the doors are closed and the walls are really high and the walls are really thick. And they're not getting in. If you don't understand the business here, it looks like a fortress. If you don't understand it, how do you negotiate it? How do you make your path through the doorway? You don't know. That's why I tell new writers that outside the Hollywood fortress, there are these little camps of independent producers. You just need to go in there. They're a lot easier to approach. If you can get these independent producers interested in your project, sell a few projects, and then get the attention of the smaller agent who will represent you, then things start developing. So, many writers think that what they should do is finish their script and send it to the studio. What they need to do is understand how the process works. There's a huge gap of knowledge that needs to be addressed, because of what happens when writers finish their first script or third or fourth and have no idea of what to do with it afterward.

I recently completed teaching two private workshops on How to Sell Your Script Without an Agent. They were four-week classes, and I had twelve people in the first one, sixteen in the next. Now, these writers had all won competitions, they had written five to ten or fifteen scripts. Many had optioned scripts. But I was shocked at what they didn't know about how the business works and how to work with producers. I was shocked. But I don't know of a place to learn about this. There are a couple of exceptions, but most successful writers who have made the leap into the Hollywood system either don't have time or just aren't interested in giving back this kind of information.

Fearless Rider

Sharon believes that many writers could benefit from facing more physical challenges in their lives. Although she has taken many risks in her life, Sharon says she has never experienced fear herself, except maybe behind the wheel of a race car while revving the engine up to five thousand rpms.

The majority of screenwriters I meet are very much in their heads. Very cerebral people. They're not people who choose to face the physical challenges that include fear or danger. I've always been exactly the opposite. As a kid, I was a tomboy. I was always climbing the highest tree. I was always falling out of the tree. I just needed to do that. I also used to race Go-Karts. That translated into racing SCCA, the Sports Car Club of America. I raced SCCA for several years, including formula cars. Was there any fear when I was racing? Fear. Maybe that's when my heart's racing fast. I remember that when I would get to the start line, there would be this huge rush of adrenaline, and my heart would pump and my breathing would be rapid, because I was revving the engine up to like five thousand rpms. But yet, even though I spun the car out, I never wrecked or anything like that. I never really hurt myself physically, though I always knew there was a chance of doing that. Every time you went out on the track, there was a chance of doing that. But yet, I always chose to pop that clutch at five thousand rpms and see if I could do the fastest time of day. I also play paint ball. I love paint ball. It's a thrill. I'm really sorry more women don't do it, because there is a confidence—a body confidence, a self-confidence—that comes from playing paint ball. I feel that it would be great for more writers to get out there and play paint ball as well. I think it would help them to overcome other sorts of fears.

Sharon admits she did come close to feelings of fear when she first moved to Los Angeles.

If you can say I was ever facing fear, I guess that would be probably the closest. I was very anxious about it, mainly because I had never lived in a city this large. I don't like to be surrounded by these huge tall buildings and all these people and this traffic. In a way, it has hurt me by being here. I've become much more cynical. The cynicism is an alteration in how my thinking processes work, and I don't like that. For example, I'll take a new script, and when I first open the first page, I say, What's wrong with this, what's wrong with that script. That's a very bad thing. I don't like that. Normally, I'm a positive thinker. So moving to L.A., not knowing anyone out here, and then dealing with the whole searching and the hostility that comes out in the traffic and waiting in lines and so on was very difficult. The best thing I did when I came out here was join workshops and support groups. It's essential. There are a lot of writers in L.A. who can share information. The bad thing is that the competition is fierce. I've known many who have come out here with the money to stay for a couple of years, and then they ended up totally discouraged and left.

Finding a Balance

Sharon worked tenaciously during her early years in Los Angeles. She sold a number of scripts to independent producers and directors and became a coproducer of many of her own projects. She rewrote and polished the script for Just Write, *starring JoBeth Williams. Sharon also cowrote* The River and the Knife *with Academy Award winner William Kelley (*Witness*). She wrote a novelization of two episodes of* Touched by an Angel *for CBS that sold over 170,000 copies in bookstores nationwide. Her work was featured in the 1996 Women in Film Post Oscar Showcase, and she began lecturing on screenwriting at UCLA and the Directors' Guild of America (DGA). Despite these many successes, something was missing in Sharon's life—a sense of balance.*

I had zero balance. I'm very aware that I had none. I knew it would take this kind of dedication, literally working from nine until noon, one to five, and then again seven to ten to do what I've done. For five years, this is what it's taken—extremely intense dedication to work. Sacrificing everything. I had no personal life. Any time I went out, it was with business associates or to a screening. It took that kind of dedication to be able to make it work. My next step is having balance in my life, and I'm delighted to say I met an amazing man. We're perfect for each other. We're now married, and we're having a real life outside our careers.

I'm not sure that men, as far as screenwriters are concerned, want a balance. I'm a lot like men in that way. Total dedication to career with sacrifice to a personal life. Especially the successful male screenwriters are still doing exactly what I had been doing the last five years. Fortunately, when you get to a certain level, which is basically the studio writing level, the income is dramatically more than writing for the independent producers. That has allowed a lot more leeway as far as my time is concerned. I could enjoy life a lot more now. My husband, Robert Ward, is an international journalist who covers Hollywood for newspapers in New Zealand, Britain, and Australia. He's in the business in a different sort of way, yet we're both freelancers, so to speak, so we can take three days in the middle of the week to go to Joshua Tree.

Collaboration

One of Sharon's recent projects includes a feature for Fox 2000, starring Danny Glover, and a movie of the week for TBS. She is also writing and directing two short films. She has collaborated on many projects throughout her career and has experienced the pros and cons of working with others.

In the project for Fox 2000 (*Return of the Sweet Birds*), I have an equal writing partner, Carolyn McDonald. She's Danny Glover's producing partner, which is how the whole project got started. We pitched our idea to Danny, and he said "yes." Then we brought in Baby Face Edmonds' company (Edmonds Entertainment), because they know the music and have produced several films. The actual process of working with Carolyn has been wonderful. We're both very intuitive. We generated the characters together, and I will say that through writing 116 pages, there were only two places where we disagreed on what should happen. A line of dialogue or something like that. You know what we did? We came up with a third alternative that we both agreed on. If you say you are not willing to compromise, that means things have to be done your way. But there is no "your way" in Hollywood. Even if you don't have a writing partner, the process is collaborative. Besides that, what the writer must totally understand is that even if they sell a spec script to a production company, that spec script no longer belongs to them. Sometimes, they are allowed to be brought on to actually do another pass on the script. Usually, they're dumped off the project. If they are allowed to come in, then they have to come in with the mind-set that this is no longer their script, no longer their characters.

The Journey Continues

I am going to be directing a couple of short films. I'm delighted with that. I love working with the actors. It's helping to complete the process. I'm very visual, and I love shooting. I'm actually going to shoot a project myself on digital video, and I'm really excited about that. Yet, the interesting thing is, working on these short films, I realize how incredibly demanding a feature film would be for a director, and I'm not sure if I'll go down that path or not. I know that at least I've gotten to where I'm directing short films, and that's cool and I love the process, so we'll see. I think I would really enjoy it, yet I also realize that it takes a lot of time, and I couldn't be writing five screenplays a year if I did that. Maybe I would like to direct one independent film a year and then write three or four other studio films. The interesting thing is that the directing allows a communication with the actor and the character. The writer/director is the bridge between the character that was created by the writer and the director who's directing the actor. It's just a phenomenal process. It's a very intuitive process. And it's also very collaborative, because even off-screen characters may see a specific thing. They may see it differently, and then the job is to try to transfer that energy back and forth.

Parting Words

Celebrate your small victories. This business is weird. So when do you celebrate? Do you celebrate when someone says "yes"? Do you celebrate when you hear from an agent or a producer who's interested? Or do you celebrate when you've signed the deal? It's a never-ending process. So you know what? You celebrate them all.

●

CHAPTER 19

Noah Baumbach: Honoring the Muse Within

You have to be resilient, and you can't take rejection personally,
because it's a business. You need to feel like you tried everything
shy of getting a digital camera and shooting it yourself.

Noah Baumbach

The Journey Begins

*As the son of a New York City novelist with a passion for movies, Noah Baumbach
was raised with an appreciation for a wide variety of film styles and genres. Although
he never separated writing and directing in his mind, he knew at a very young age that
filmmaking was his destiny.*

Growing up, I always looked at the world in terms of movies. I'd figure out
how I could make a particular situation or experience into a movie. *Lancelot
du Lac* was the first film I ever saw in the theater. I also wrote comic books.
Obviously, none of this was professional, but I think I realized that some of
my strength as a writer was in dialogue. And at a young age, I just got it into
my head that I was going to make movies. So it seemed like a natural progression, even though ultimately, as I got older and set out to actually getting
a movie made, I didn't know what I was doing.

As a teenager, I loved movies with Bill Murray and Steve Martin, but my
parents made me aware of many of the classic American and European films.
I never really considered the formal structure of a screenplay until I was in
college. In college, we didn't have the equipment to shoot any sound film, so

I wrote plays. After graduation, I wrote my first screenplay, and that turned out to be *Kicking and Screaming*.

When you're starting out, it's great to be both naïve and ambitious. I think the difference now versus when I was starting out is that in the beginning, I didn't know what the risks were.

I just had a script that I was submitting, with the confidence that I could direct it. Anything seemed possible. Having gone through it now, I almost miss that kind of ignorance. At the time I was writing the script, I wasn't thinking about whether it fit in the marketplace. I was just writing the story I wanted to tell. Now that I get paid in advance to write something, I have to worry about whether the studio's actually going make this movie, is it what the studio's looking for, and so on. It was great not to know how hard what I was trying to do really was.

Collaboration

Noah's first film, which he wrote and directed, was based on many experiences he and his friends had shared in college. Kicking and Screaming, starring Eric Stoltz, is a story about four recent college graduates trying to adjust to the harsh realities of life after college.

I came up with the characters and the story for *Kicking and Screaming* with a friend. This was done very informally, right out of college. He's a very funny and very good friend who I'd known all of my life. I told him I wanted to write a story about a group of friends. We started by sitting around a table laughing about stuff we'd remember and thinking, Wouldn't it be funny if such-and-such happened. Then, I went ahead and wrote the script. I've rarely written with somebody else in the room with me. I like the quiet process of writing alone.

This was the process for Noah with Mr. Jealousy, *his second film, again starring Eric Stoltz.*

When I wrote *Mr. Jealousy*, I never felt I needed a collaborator. However, I'm now with an actor friend of mine, Carlos Jacott, who was in both *Kicking and Screaming* and *Mr. Jealousy*. He's a great improvisor and the funniest person I know. I've always felt comfortable having him improvise off my dialogue, because we're on the same wavelength and he usually comes up with something better than what I had anyway. I was having trouble figuring out my most recent script, so I enlisted Carlos, because I thought he'd have insight into what I originally thought was good about the story. We collaborated through e-mail. This makes writing more entertaining, because I look forward to what he's sending next.

The other major collaboration I've had was on a TV pilot with Steve Martin, which is the only time that I've written something that was someone else's idea. It was thrilling for me, because I've always idolized Steve Martin. But it was also really challenging. I contributed to the characters, but I was writing within certain boundaries that he'd created.

What's Next

The movies I've made so far have been very low-budget. For all my criticism of Hollywood and the studio system, I think it's very hard to exist for a long time on the fringe. If my sensibility was more obscure, I wouldn't have any choice, but my sensibility rides the line of both the studio and the independent worlds. It's figuring out a way to meet them somewhere in the middle, without compromising what I want to do. That's the next challenge for me. I could go out and make another movie for a million dollars, but I'd rather try to work in a system with a more solid foundation. Ultimately, it's too much work for the movie not to be seen by as many people as you want to see it.

Parting Words

The further you get along in the process, the higher the bar keeps raising. At first, you might think, "If I could only get so and so to read it. If I could only get an agent. If only a producer would want to make it." Then, once you achieve those things, it becomes, "If I could just get the movie made." And then, once the movie's made, you want a good distributor, then you want it in more theaters. Ultimately, you have to do work you believe in, because so much effort is spent from the time you write "FADE IN" to the time the movie comes out in theaters. And that's assuming you're lucky enough to get that far. And you have to suffer many rejections. Lots of people I know get that one rejection and then put the script in a drawer, and that's that. If you really want to write for film and you really want to be successful at it, you have to keep putting yourself out there. Keep sending your work out. And try to enjoy it, because it's an exciting business, as maddening as it is.

Summary

A great deal of introspection has to take place before deciding whether or not collaboration on a project will be appropriate for you. To enter into a creative partnership is, indeed, a great opportunity to share in a common vision. There is truth in the saying, "The whole is greater than the sum of its parts." The vision is everything, and it is what keeps most creative spirits awake at night wondering about the execution of something wonderful that they have imagined. Can we really succeed without the help of others? Is there not a certain level of arrogance in holding on to the belief that we are capable of doing it all alone? Is there not something rather foolish about our stubbornness in struggling and suffering in silence, rather than seeking the consult or support we need? What stops us from reaching out to the resources that can bring relief, support, and fresh perspectives? Help is just a call away, if we have the courage to admit that none of us can always pull our successes out of our own ingenuity.

The creative process can be enhanced by the energy of others who believe in our dreams and in the purpose of our storytelling mission. It is energy you can use to fuel the fires when your own energy may not be able to sustain a project from beginning to end. If you listen to your own intuitive voice, you will know when a collaborative effort is needed to nourish a story. If you trust the moment, there is a good chance of propelling the project to new levels.

Some screenwriters will rarely enter into partnerships more than once, others will work with the same people on many, many projects. Some writers will choose to collaborate on most of their projects, others rarely in their careers. Whether a story is told by one or many writers or by first-time or long-term writing teams is not what is important. Rather, you must ask yourself if you can truly finish your project alone, or if a collaborative partnership will enhance it in a way needed to bring it the attention required to find its success.

Filmmaking is a profession that is dependent on collaborative energy for its survival. The script is just one component of what is literally the "big picture." Although a writer may have given birth to a story and its characters, there are many others—directors, producers, cinematographers, and distributors, to name a few—who will take it in new directions with their own personal vision, creativity, and wisdom.

Whatever the destiny, there is no doubt that the process of completing a script is a demanding task. In many cases, many months and even years have been spent on a single script. It is an investment in a dream that carries no guarantee of success. As is often the case, it is not until the rigors are over that screenwriters can truly appreciate the risks that they have taken and the challenges that they were demanded to face. Many writers experience the fears and difficulties alone in the darkness, for it is not always possible or even appropriate to share such feelings with others. At other times, unique stories and characters may not present themselves to the writer's imagination, which can lead to continued feelings of frustration and self-doubt. Was this the journey that would really bring the inner fulfillment they so desired and were longing to experience?

The road to success is a demanding one and requires a deep commitment to one's creative self. The paths are not smooth, and sometimes the peaks of success are all too infrequently felt. The screenwriting journey is not for everyone, yet for those who have claimed it as their own, there can be tremendous satisfaction.

Throughout this book, questions have been presented that you will be called upon to answer at various times on your journey. The questions serve as a catalyst; they do not require immediate answers, for at times, pauses will be necessary in order to provide guidance along the way. Allow yourself to honor your courage and to accept that claiming your voice takes personal commitment. Do not forget to celebrate every victory, no matter how small, for each moment of success deserves your respect, as you bring us the stories and the characters that have the power to entertain, amaze, heal, mirror, amuse, and bring audiences to their feet.

●

The Power of Collaboration: Questionnaire for Self-Evaluation

The following questions are meant for introspection and affirmation. They are proposed for the benefit of clarity and for gaining a better understanding of when, where, how, and with whom to form collaborative relationships, as well as to become knowledgeable about how they can propel your project forward.

1. Am I aware of the multitude of ways in which a collaboration could help me in developing my script?
2. Do I have a closed mind about the pros and cons of partnerships?
3. Is my ego too frail to include others in my project?
4. Would I be too protective of sharing my story ideas with another person?
5. Am I ready to concede that writing alone may not be working for me?
6. Will I be negatively viewed if I decide to use the services of another writer when I get stuck on my own story?
7. Do I judge others who enter into collaborations because it seems more legitimate to write alone?
8. Am I making excuses when I say that I would not collaborate with another writer because I do not believe I am talented enough?
9. When other writers get together to work on a project, do I feel left out and isolated?
10. Have I told myself that my stories do not lend themselves to the collaborative process?
11. Am I too ego-centered to use the recommendations of others to help me move my script to its next level?
12. Am I really knowledgeable about the various consulting services that could lend a positive hand when my screenplay needs new energy?
13. Am I holding back from collaborative opportunities because I am worried that my ideas will be stolen?
14. Am I afraid to work with friends on a project because our relationship may change?
15. Have I made up my mind that my writing style is too unique and to incorporate another person's style of writing would not be possible?
16. Have I made myself so busy that my schedule would never allow collaborating with another writer?
17. Would I be able to contribute enough to the project if more than one writer was working on the same story?
18. Would my fierce goal-setting style get in the way of collaborating with someone whose style is more laid back?

About the Authors

Writer and producer **Sara Caldwell** founded Amphion Productions (*www.amphionpro.com*) in 1991 and has since generated more than 130 film, television, video, CD-ROM, and satellite teleconference projects for national and international clients. She has written numerous articles on the screenwriting process and is co-author of *Write Here,* a regular column for *Scr(i)pt* magazine online. Sara has been hired to write feature and television scripts for various production companies in Los Angeles and Chicago and is currently a freelance writer/producer for a Discovery Health Channel documentary series. Prior to forming her own company, Sara wrote and produced commercial, corporate, and educational videos for Motion Masters in Charleston, West Virginia. Before that, she was a writer/producer with Worldnet Television in Washington, D.C., working on live video teleconferences on a variety of topics for audiences in Africa, the Near East, and East Asia. Sara received her Bachelors degree in Communications from the University of Iowa, where she was a member of the Iowa Writer's Workshop. In addition to spending time with her two children, Sara loves traveling, volunteer work, painting, and running. She is represented by the Quillco Agency of Los Angeles.

Marie-Eve Kielson, a licensed marriage and family therapist in private practice, created Kielson Media Consulting in 1991 to provide psychological script consultation for screenwriters and film/video production companies throughout the United States. The formation of her firm was inspired by her innate fascination with human nature, a love for the cinema, and a recognition that even major-studio movies often miss the boat when it comes to plausible psychology of character. Marie-Eve has led several workshops and seminars on psychological character and plot development in scripts, including "Getting to Know Your Character's Psychology" (Chicago), "Bringing Your Script to the Shrink—Expanding Realities" (New York), and "The Psychology of Character and Plot—Amplifying the Creative Process" (Winnetka, Illinois). She is the creator of the television pilot, *Journey to Success* and co-creator of *Cinema Romance: A Review.* Marie-Eve has written numerous articles on the screenwriting process for *Scr(i)pt, Creative Screenwriting, Insider, The Writer's Aide,* and *Hollywood Scriptwriter,* and was featured in *The New York Screenwriter Monthly.* She is co-author of the regular column *Write Here* for *Scr(i)pt* magazine online. Marie-Eve received her Masters degree in Guidance and Counseling from Northeastern Illinois University. She resides in Winnetka, Illinois, and is currently collaborating with Sara Caldwell on their second book entitled *Are We Really So Different: A Primer of Parallel Lives.*

The authors are contributing a percentage of their royalties from the sale of this book to Cabrini Connections, a nonprofit tutor/mentor organization serving educationally disadvantaged youth in Chicago. For more information on Cabrini Connections, please visit www.tutormentorconnection.org.

●

About the Contributors

Carla L. Hacken is Executive Vice President of Fox 2000 Pictures, a division of Twentieth Century Fox Filmed Entertainment. She has been an executive with the studio since January 1997. Her responsibilities as creative and production executive include finding material from all sources, developing the screenplays, and overseeing these films during production. Prior to joining Fox, she was a motion picture talent and literary agent for nine years at International Creative Management (ICM), one of the preeminent talent agencies worldwide. She is a graduate of UCLA, with a major in Dramatic Creative Writing and English Literature.

Noah Baumbach was born and raised in Brooklyn, New York, a city that mirrors his energy and enthusiasm for filmmaking. He made his writing and directing debut at the age of twenty-four with the art house hit *Kicking and Screaming,* the story of four young men who graduate from college and refuse to move on with their lives. The film premiered in 1995 at the prestigious New York Film Festival to tremendous critical acclaim. Noah was chosen as one of *Newsweek*'s "Ten New Faces of 1996." The film appeared on numerous "Top Ten" lists. The issues that men often face as they reach adulthood continued to be a theme in Noah's second film, *Mr. Jealousy,* which he also wrote and directed. This film brought us in contact with the inner turmoil one man experiences when he feels replaced and abandoned in a love relationship. *Mr. Jealousy* premiered at the Toronto Film Festival and was released by Lions Gate Films in the summer of 1998. Noah's next challenge will be directing his screenplay, *Long Division for Lunatics.*

Ed Bernero was a Chicago cop for ten years before turning his hand to screenwriting. As a risk-taker, he has always followed the credo that he never wants to look back on his life with a sense of regret. After perfecting his screenwriting craft, he moved with his family to Los Angeles, where opportunities catapulted his career in television. The stories he had witnessed in Chicago led him to the stories he would script for television audiences. After completing an episode of Steven Bocho's *NYPD Blue,* Ed was hired to join the staff of another Bocho drama, *Brooklyn South.* In 1998, he continued his career as a writer and story editor for the John Wells (*ER*) drama, *Trinity.* Ed continues to experience the success he has worked hard to achieve. He is now a producer and writer for NBC's *Third Watch,* which he cocreated with John Wells and which premiered on NBC in the fall of 1999.

Carmen Brown had not always dreamed of becoming a screenwriter. What a surprise to her when, in 1992, she listened to a strong inner voice that led her to enroll in a screenwriting class in Chicago. Carmen believes that if the desire is strong enough and you're willing to work hard, then dreams can come true. Carmen's first experience with the rigors of owning her own business came in the form of a gourmet cookie business that she created and successfully developed. As her inspiration to become a screenwriter grew, she decided it was time to take a significant risk. Without knowing where the road would lead, she gave up her cookie business and immersed herself full-time in the craft of screenwriting. She is now a writer/producer, as well as operating manager of Dinner Mint Productions, LLC. Since starting her new business, she has created numerous scripts for film and television, including the screenplay, *Generosa,* which she plans to produce. She has attached numerous well-known actors to the project, including Liz Torres, and has already secured distribution.

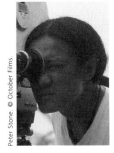

Peter Stone. © October Films.

Tony Bui's early instruction brought him into the world of filmmaking, as he fell in love with the European films that would impact his own unique vision of how he would create powerful images. Tony graduated from Loyola Marymount University with his short film *Yellow Lotus,* which screened at the 1996 Sundance Film Festival and won numerous festival awards, both nationally and internationally. At the age of nineteen, he changed his view of the world and his own place in it when he ventured to his birthplace in Vietnam for the first time since he was a young child. He returned to Vietnam many times, with each visit greatly impacting his career as a filmmaker. These experiences led to Tony's feature debut, *Three Seasons,* starring Harvey Keitel. *Three Seasons* was the first American film to be shot entirely in Vietnam. The Vietnamese-language film was produced by Open City Films and distributed by October Films in 1999. It was the winner of the Grand Jury Prize, the Audience Award, and the Best Cinematography Award at the 1999 Sundance Film Festival. It is the first film in Sundance's history to take home both the Jury Prize and Audience Award. The film also was selected for Official Competition at the 1999 Berlin International Film Festival, with Tony being the year's youngest filmmaker in competition. He was awarded the prestigious Samuel Z. Arkoff Award and the Rockefeller Nomination, and was invited to attend the Sundance Institute Screenwriting and Directing Labs, with *Three Seasons.*

Delle Chatman's mission as a screenwriter is to make certain that her stories help audiences to understand that life is to be celebrated as well as endured. Her strength as a storyteller lies in her philosophy that life is always a worthy experience. Her patience is a virtue, for after many years in development at three separate studios, her script *Free of Eden,* created by Delle and cowritten with Yule Chaise, premiered on the Showtime Network in 1999. This poignant drama, which was recognized in the Chicago International Film Festival, starred Sidney Poitier, Phylicia Rashad, Robert Hooks, and Poitier's daughter, Sydney Tamiia Poitier. Although *Free of Eden* was her first feature film to be produced, Delle's teleplays have been seen on NBC, CBS, ABC, and PBS. Earlier, she was a TV reporter for WXII-TV, the NBC affiliate in Winston-Salem, North Carolina, where she fielded hard news and covered the political beat. While at Northwestern University, she was a founding architect of the university's Center for the Writing Arts and the recipient of the university's Faculty Recognition Award for distinguished achievement. She was Director of Creative Writing for the Media Program from 1991 to 1998. Delle continues to bring her love of storytelling to the varied venues she embraces. She recently completed her first novel, *The Dove Seller,* plans to direct a feature film, and will be performing her one-woman show, *Unplugged, Unleashed, and Unknown,* on stage and on film.

Sharon Y. Cobb as been an artist since the age of four, when she began drawing pictures to become just like her uncle, whom she admired and who is a successful artist and graphic designer. Throughout her professional life, Sharon has brought pictures and words together as a publisher, editor, journalist, and graphic artist. She has always believed in her own intuition, which eventually led her down the screenwriting path. After years of dedication to her career, Sharon is now an award-winning writer with several projects in development. These include a feature for Fox 2000, starring Danny Glover (*Return of the Sweet Birds*), and a movie of the week for TBS. In addition, Sharon has sold numerous scripts to independent producers and directors and is a coproducer on many of her projects. She rewrote and polished the script for *Just Write,* starring JoBeth Williams, Sherilyn Fenn, and Jeremy Piven. Sharon also cowrote a script, *The River and the Knife* with William Kelley (Academy Award 1985, *Witness*), as well as a novelization of two episodes of *Touched by an Angel* for CBS, which have sold over 170,000 copies nationwide. Her work was presented in the 1996 Women in Film Post Oscar Showcase, and she has lectured on screenwriting at UCLA and the Directors Guild of America (DGA). She is coauthor, with UCLA screenwriting instructor Neill D. Hicks, of Secrets of Selling Your Script to Hollywood and wrote *Writing the New Noir Film* in *Film Noir Reader 2.*

Betty Hager grew up in Bayou La Batre, a small town about thirty miles from Mobile, Alabama. It was there that the seeds of her career as a writer were planted. The youngest of eight children, Betty's memories center around the sounds of shrimp boats heading out to sea, gumbo suppers, crabbing in the bay, and the beauty of the azaleas around her small home at the end of a crushed-oyster-shell road. Betty developed a keen interest in reading and writing after her mother helped to organize a library in her town. As an adult, Betty transformed many of her childhood memories into a popular children's book series called *Tales from the Bayou*. In addition to adapting several of her books into screenplays, she has written and optioned a number of other scripts for audiences of all ages. She has also cowritten eleven musicals with composer Fred Boch, which have been performed by school children all around the country as well as a few in Europe. An animation from one of the musicals is being produced by Gaither Animation in Indianapolis, Indiana.

Shane Sato

Josefina Lopez is a prolific screenwriter, playwright, and performer. Her stories carry themes that are derived from her background as a Latina woman who realized at an early age that if she wanted to be successful, she would have to use all of her inner strength and determination to fight for visibility. Josefina was born in San Luis Potosi, Mexico. She moved to Los Angeles with her family when she was five years old and, for almost thirteen years, experienced the traumatic results of living as undocumented immigrants. These memories would become the bedrock of her stories and characters. As a teenager, Josefina attended the Los Angeles County High School for the Arts, where she majored in theater. Josefina was a seventeen-year-old member of the Young Playwrights Lab at the Los Angeles Theater Center when she wrote her first play, the Emmy-winning *Simply Maria or the American Dream*. The first production in 1990 of her most produced play, *Real Women Have Curves,* earned her a six-week Playwrights Fellowship for the Izadora Aguirre Playwriting Lab. This play was also optioned as a screenplay. Josefina went on to write a number of screenplays and was on the writing staff of several television series. With a partner, she wrote and produced three television pilots for Norman Lear, ABC Productions, and UPN. Today, Josefina is busy completing a Masters Degree in Screenwriting at UCLA, while writing a new project for New Line Cinema. She also recently opened Rascuachi Rep, a theater company in Boyle Heights, Los Angeles.

Ken Mader has loved movies all of his life, especially films of the science fiction genre, which he emulated as a child with a Super 8 camera. He has been involved in the movie business for over nineteen years, having worked on such blockbusters as *The Blues Brothers, My Bodyguard, The Killing Floor,* and *The Roommate.* A self-proclaimed "mutant-hyphenate," he is an accomplished screenwriter with more than sixteen scripts to his credit. As a screenwriter, he is currently involved in two development deals, the most prominent with producer Morris Ruskin of Shoreline Pictures, the man responsible for bringing *Glengarry Glen Ross* to the screen. Ken firmly believes that isolation can be the worst contributor to creative inertia and, as a result, helped found the Chicago Screenwriters Network, which provides a supportive and caring environment for writers at all levels. Ken has optioned two of his original screenplays and was a semi-finalist in the 1995 Writer's Network Screenplay & Fiction Competition. As a consummate filmmaker, he never stops creating projects that will involve him in the totality of the process. Ken is currently in postproduction on Carnivore, an independent feature that he cowrote, produced, codirected, DP'd, and edited.

David Marconi began making movies as a child, directing his friends in Super 8 movies that he showcased to their families. He never lost his passion for making movies and eventually attended the University of Southern California (USC), where he was quickly indoctrinated to the rigors of filmmaking. David made a number of short subjects while at USC, including *Fiesta,* which has aired on HBO and Cinemax. After graduating, David worked in various phases of production on films such as *Rumble Fish* and *The Outsiders.* He was soon recognized as a talented writer and was hired for a series of studio assignments. Nevertheless, his real passion lay in directing. He seized an opportunity to write and direct a low budget film called *The Harvest,* which garnered him recognition in the action/adventure genre. His intrigue with issues of privacy, communication, secrecy, and government interference with individual rights led him to write *Enemy of the State,* starring Will Smith and Gene Hackman. David then wrote Paramount's sequel to *Mission: Impossible* and the 20th Century Fox film *wwwIII.com,* which is based on a *Wired Magazine* article by David Carlin about the potential of a World War III via a cyber attack over the Internet. David is also a coauthor of three *Agent 13* novels. Currently, he is writing an action film set in Miami for Fox 2000, to star Chris Rock.

Harold Ramis has been passionate about all aspects of the performing arts throughout his life. While a college student at Washington University in St. Louis, he became an observer of life's interesting twists and turns and began to appreciate the humor of human experiences, which led him to explore the use of laughter in his writing. In 1969, Harold began his formal training in comedy performance at Chicago's famed Second City improvisational theater troupe. In 1974, he moved to New York to help write and perform in the *National Lampoon Show*, with fellow Second City Graduates John Belushi, Gilda Radner, and Bill Murray. By 1976, Harold was the head writer and a regular performer on SCTV. His Hollywood breakthrough came in 1978, when he cowrote *National Lampoon's Animal House*. He went on to write and produce/direct a string of hits, including *Meatballs, Stripes, Ghostbusters,* and *Ghostbusters II*. He also directed and cowrote *Caddyshack, National Lampoon's Vacation,* and *Club Paradise*. Harold then directed, produced, and cowrote the comedy *Groundhog Day* and went on to direct, cowrite, and coproduce *Multiplicity*. He was the director and cowriter of *Analyze This,* a Warner Brothers comedy starring Robert DeNiro, Billy Crystal, and Lisa Kudrow. Harold prides himself in using laughter in a manner in which audiences can honor their own vulnerabilities and imperfections. His creative energy continues to flow, as he undertakes a number of new film and television ventures.

Anne Rapp's heart lies in the South where she grew up, in a small town in Texas. She remembers how sitting around the porch and swapping stories was the mode of entertainment in her small community. These were the core experiences upon which she would draw as a storyteller. Before turning her hand to writing, Anne spent sixteen years as a script supervisor. In this capacity, she worked closely with a diverse range of directors on such films as *That Thing You Do,* directed by Tom Hanks; *Tender Mercies,* directed by Bruce Beresford; *Places In the Heart,* directed by Robert Benton; *The Firm,* directed by Sydney Pollack; *Accidental Tourist,* directed by Larry Kasdan; *Spinal Tap,* directed by Rob Reiner; *The Color Purple,* directed by Steven Spielberg; and *Things Change,* directed by David Mamet. Anne determined that her next challenge was to become a screenwriter. She would use her heritage of storytelling and her attention to detail to create stories that have great significance to her. Her scripts, all directed by Robert Altman, include the humorous small-town drama, *Cookie's Fortune,* starring Glenn Close and Liv Tyler. Her other credits include a one-hour episode for the ABC-TV series, *Gun,* and a feature film titled *Dr. T.* Anne is now a visiting professor at the University of Texas in Austin, a program funded by the James Michener Foundation. There, she is able to share her thoughts regarding creative writing and what makes stories powerful with a new generation of writers. As she likes to say with a smile, her life experiences have given her enough stories to last a lifetime.

Adam Rifkin was inspired by monster movies and slapstick comedies as a child and decided early in his life that he would be a filmmaker. He attended the Academy for the Visual and Performing Arts High School of Chicago and, upon graduation, moved to Hollywood to be close to the heart of the entertainment industry. Since the move west, Adam has had a number of his screenplays produced, including the popular family movies *Mouse Hunt* and *Small Soldiers,* both for Dreamworks. His appreciation for all genres challenged him to write and direct several independent films, including *The Chase,* with Charlie Sheen; *The Dark Backward,* starring Bill Paxton, Judd Nelson, James Caan, and Lara Flynn Boyle; and *Never on Tuesday,* which featured Charlie Sheen, Nicholas Cage, and Emilio Esteves. Adam's determination and willingness to keep his dream alive make him a prolific screenwriter. Never willing to sit still for very long, Adam continues to write and create stories that appeal to large audiences. He has over ten feature films in development, including five at major studios, and with the 1999 hit *Detroit Rock City,* which he directed with stars Edward Furlong, Natashe Lyonne, and the seventies band, Kiss, he can be assured that audiences will be waiting with anticipation to witness many more of his stories.

Paul Wei was influenced by the movies he saw growing up in China and decided at a very early age that he wanted to make films. The medium became so fascinating to him that he decided to make filmmaking his career, and he was awarded a scholarship to Notre Dame University in Indiana. Paul immigrated to the United States in 1982 to attend college and to use all of his will and determination to make his dream come true. After graduating, he moved to Los Angeles, where he has written five screenplays and has made two short films, *Crazy Kids* and *Murder at Midnight.* He embraces various genres and was captivated by the documentary process, which inspired him to make two of his own, *Amazing Things in China* and *Time of Change.* Paul has worked on a number of independent films and commercials in different capacities, including production assistant, camera assistant, production coordinator, and postproduction coordinator. He recently directed and produced *Just One Touch,* an original story by Rick Persley. Paul recently scripted *The Bracelet,* a tender drama about a boy's love for his widowed mother. He will soon be producing and directing this project in California.

Resources

There are hundreds of resources available for screenwriters around the country. In this section, we are providing contact information for some of the leading and most respected guilds, organizations, groups, publications, and directories. For more information on resources in your local area, call the film commission in your nearest city or state capitol. An Internet search can also provide you with many valuable links for a variety of screenwriting resources.

Guilds

The Writers Guild of America is a labor union representing professional writers in motion pictures, television, radio, interactive technologies, and television and radio news.

- Writers Guild of America, East, 555 West 57th Street, New York, NY 10019; (212) 767-7800; *www.wgaeast.org*
- Writers Guild of America, West, 7000 West Third Street, Los Angeles, CA 90048-4329; (213) 951-4000; *www.wga.org*

Organizations and Groups

The American Film Institute (AFI) is the nation's preeminent arts organization dedicated to advancing and preserving the art of the moving image. Since 1967, AFI has served as America's voice for film, television, video, and the digital arts, with innovative programs in education, training, exhibition, preservation, and new technology. Home Web site: *www.afionline.org*

- The American Film Institute, P.O. Box 27999, 2021 North Western Avenue, Los Angeles, CA 90027; (323) 856-7600
- The American Film Institute, The John F. Kennedy Center for the Performing Arts, Washington, DC 20566; (202) 828-4000

Independent Feature Project (IFP) provides services to independent filmmakers of varying levels of experience that assist them in expressing their unique points of view. It facilitates a connection between the creative and business communities. Other goals of the organization are to expand and educate the audience for independent film, and to encourage the diversity and quality of independent production. Home Web site: *www.ifp.com*

- Independent Feature Project/West, 1964 Westwood Boulevard, Suite 205, Los Angeles, CA. 90025; (310) 475-4379; *dearifpwest@earthlink.net*
- Independent Feature Project/East, 104 West 29th Street, 12th Floor, New York, NY 10001-5310; (212) 465-8200; *ifpny@ifp.org*
- IFP/Midwest, 1803 West Byron, Suite1E, Chicago, IL 60613; (773) 281-5177
- Alliance IFP/South Collaborators, 210 2nd Street, Miami Beach, FL 33139; (305) 538-8242; *www.alliance-cinema.org; allianc1@gate.net*
- Independent Feature Project/North, 401 North 3rd Street, Suite 490, Minneapolis, MN 55401; (612) 338-0871; *info@ifpnorth.org*

The Organization of Black Screenwriters (OBS) began in 1988 to address the lack of black writers represented within the entertainment industry. Their primary function is to assist screenwriters in the creation of works for film and television and to help them present their work.

- The Organization of Black Screenwriters, P.O. Box 70160, Los Angeles, CA 90070-0160; (323) 882-4166 (OBS Hotline); *obswriter@compuserve.com*

Women in Film (WIF) is a professional organization that recognizes, develops, and actively promotes the unique visions of women in the global communications industry. Chapters are located in Atlanta, Georgia; Scottsdale, Arizona; Dallas/Houston, Texas; Denver, Colorado; Orlando, Florida; Baltimore, Maryland; New Orleans, Louisiana; New York, New York; Seattle, Washington; Beaufort, South Carolina; and Washington, D.C.

- Women in Film, 6464 Sunset Boulevard, #550, Los Angeles, CA 90036; (323) 463-6040; *www.wif.org*

Publications and Directories

- Creative Screenwriting, 6404 Hollywood Boulevard, Suite 415, Los Angeles, CA 90028; (323) 957-1405; *www.creativescreenwriting.com*
- Daily Variety; *www.variety.com*
- Los Angeles Office, 5700 Wilshire Boulevard, Suite 120, Los Angeles, CA 90036; (323) 857-6600
- New York Office, 245 West 17th Street, New York, NY 10011; (212) 645-0067
- Fade In, 289 South Robertson Boulevard, #465, Beverly Hills, CA 90211; (800) 646-3896
- The Hollywood Reporter, 5055 Wilshire Boulevard, Los Angeles, CA 90036; (323) 525-2000; *www.hollywoodreporter.com*
- Hollywood Creative Directory, 3000 Olympic Boulevard, Suite 2525, Santa Monica, CA 90404; (310) 315-4815 or (800) 815-0503; *www.hcdonline.com*
- Hollywood Scriptwriter, P.O. Box 10277, Burbank, CA 91510; (818) 845-5525; *www.hollywoodscriptwriter.com*
- The New York Screenwriter, 545 Eighth Avenue, Suite 401, New York, NY 10018-4307; (212) 967-7711 or (800) 418-5637
- Scenario: The Magazine of Screenwriting Art, 104 Fifth Avenue, New York, NY 10011; (800) 222-2654
- Script Magazine, 5638 Sweet Air Road, Baldwin MD 21013; (410) 592-3466; *www.scriptmag.com*
- Spec Screenplay Sales Directory, In Good Company Products, 2118 Wilshire Boulevard, Suite 934, Santa Monica, CA 90403; (310) 828-4946 or (800) 207-5022; *www.hollywoodlitsales.com*
- Written By (Writers Guild of America, West), 7000 West 3rd Street, Los Angeles, CA 90048; (323) 782-4522; *www.writtenby@wga.org*

●

Index

Books from Allworth Press

Selling Scripts to Hollywood
by Katherine Atwell Herbert (softcover, 6 × 9, 176 pages, $12.95)

Writing Scripts Hollywood Will Love
by Katherine Atwell Herbert (softcover, 6 × 9, 160 pages, $12.95)

The Screenwriter's Legal Guide, Second Edition
by Stephen F. Breimer (softcover, 6 × 9, 320 pages, $19.95)

Writing Television Comedy
by Jerry Rannow (softcover, 6 × 9, 224 pages, $14.95)

Writing for Interactive Media: The Complete Guide
by Jon Samsel and Darryl Wimberley (hardcover, 6 × 9, 320 pages, $19.95)

Writer's Legal Guide, Second Edition
by Tad Crawford and Tony Lyons (hardcover, 6 × 9, 320 pages, $19.95)

Technical Theater for Nontechnical People
by Drew Campbell (softcover, 6 × 9, 256 pages, $18.95)

Creating Your Own Monologue
by Glenn Alterman (softcover, 6 × 9, 192 pages, $14.95)

Promoting Your Acting Career
by Glen Alterman (softcover, 6 × 9, 224 pages, $18.95)

An Actor's Guide—Your First Year in Hollywood, Revised Edition
by Michael Saint Nicholas (softcover, 6 × 9, 272 pages, $18.95)

Writing.com: Creative Internet Strategies to Advance Your Writing Career
by Moira Anderson Allen (softcover, 6 × 9, 288 pages, $19.95)

Marketing Strategies for Writers
by Michael Sedge (softcover, 6 × 9, 224 pages, $16.95)

Money Secrets of the Rich and Famous
by Michael Reynard (hardcover, 6¾ × 9½, 256 pages, $24.95)

Please write to request our free catalog. To order by credit card, call 1-800-491-2808 or send a check or money order to Allworth Press, 10 East 23rd Street, Suite 510, New York, NY 10010. Include $5 for shipping and handling for the first book ordered and $1 for each additional book. Ten dollars plus $1 for each additional book if ordering from Canada. New York State residents must add sales tax.

To see our complete catalog on the World Wide Web, or to order online, you can find us at *www.allworth.com*.